Peace, Democracy & Development in Africa

Adonis & Abbey Publishers Ltd

St James House
13 Kensington Square,
London, W8 5HD
United Kingdom

Website: http://www.adonis-abbey.com
E-mail Address: editor@adonis-abbey.com

Nigeria:
Suites C4 – C6 J-Plus Plaza
Asokoro, Abuja, Nigeria
Tel: +234 (0) 7058078841/08052035034

British Library Cataloguing-in-Publication Data
A catalogue record for this book is available from the British Library

ISBN: 9781909112711

Peace, Democracy and Development in Africa

Edited by

David J. Francis, Arthur Bainomugisha and Sabastiano Rwengabo

ADONIS & ABBEY
PUBLISHERS LTD

Acknowledgement

The Editors are grateful for the assistance from different authors, individuls, and institutons, which has made this volume possible. We are grateful for support from development partners who supported the research that produced the book chapters. In a special way, we are thankful to the Hewlett Foundation whose support to ACODE enabled much of the research carried out by the authors. ACODE is also grateful to the Democratic Governance Facility (DGF) contributing partners: The Netherlands, Norway, Sweden, United Kingdom (UK), and the European Union (EU). The DFID through Practical Action (Lima) also supported research on local content which is the focus of one of the book chapters.

The Think Tank Imitative (TTI) provides core funding to ACODE that made it possible to explore a wide range of issues on governance within Uganda while at the same time making the staff and research associates committed to scholarship.

Special thanks go to Professor David Francis and Professor Kenneth Omeje who, until recently, were based at the Bradford University John and Elnora Ferguson Centre for African Studies (JEFCAS), for their technical and professional assistance in preparing this volume for publication. Profound debt is owed to the ACODE technical team who worked in concert with the Bradford team to prepare and transform this volume into publishable form.

Table of Contents

Chapter One: Peace, Democracy and Development in Africa:
Introduction to Core Issues
Arthur Bainomugisha and Sabastiano Rwengabo ......…......................................17

Chapter Two: Limits of Liberal Peace in Africa
David J. Francis ....…...............................47

Chapter Three: SIERRA LEONE and Subversion of SOCIAL
CONTRACT
David J. Francis
....65

Chapter Four: Breaking the Conflict Trap In Uganda: Constitutional
and Legal Reforms
Nicholas Opiyo, Arthur Bainomugisha and Barbara Ntambirweki
....…..............................93

Chapter Five: Democracy and Enhancing Sustainable Livelihoods in
Uganda: Lessons from Performance of Special Interest Groups in the
Sixth and Seventh Parliament
Arthur Bainomugisha and Elijah Dickens Mushemeza
....…..............................121

Chapter Six: Monitoring Legislative Representation: Environmental
Issues in Uganda's 7th Parliament
Arthur Bainomugisha, Elijah D. Mushemeza & Sabastiano Rwengabo
....…..............................147

Chapter Seven: The Dilemma of Natural Resource-Dependent Pastoral
Communities in Africa: The Case of Teso- Karamoja Border Conflict
Arthur Bainomugisha, John Bosco Ngoya and Wilson Winstons Muhwezi
...................................…...177

Chapter Eight: The Legislature and Politics of Budget Oversight: A
Comparative Study of Selected Countries in the East African Community
Elijah Dickens Mushemeza
....….............................203

Chapter Nine: East African Customs Union Protocol: Stakeholders' Participation In The Negotiation Process
Onesmus Mugyenyi, Flavian Zeija and Sabastiano Rwengabo
....229

Chapter Ten: From Concept to Action: The Protection and Promotion of Farmers' Rights in East Africa
Ronald Naluwairo
....259

Chapter Eleven: Community-Based Property Rights in East Africa
Godber W. Tumushabe and Sabastiano Rwengabo
....279

Chapter Twelve: Policy Options and Conclusion
Sabastiano Rwengabo and Arthur Bainomugisha
....309

Index..323

Notes on Contributors

David J. Francis is a Sierra Leonean 'technocratic politician', academic and author, currently serving as the Chief Minister of the Government of Sierra Leone. Professor Francis has been a distinguished international academic and served as Professorial Chair of African Peace & Conflict Studies, Head of Department of Peace Studies, Director of the John & Elnora Ferguson Centre for African Studies (JECAS) and UNESCO Chair at the University of Bradford in United Kingdom.

Arthur Bainomugisha is the Executive Director of ACODE; a leading public policy research think-tank in Eastern and Southern Africa. He was a Technical Advisor for Uganda Peace Support Team on South Sudan and was involved in brokering a peace agreement between SPLA (IO) and Government of Uganda, after war broke out in December 2013. He lectures Peace and Conflict Studies in the Department of Religion and Peace Studies at Makerere University College of Humanities and Social Sciences. He was a Civil Society Fellow at the International Peace Institute (IPI), a New York-based public policy think-tank. He has authored several publications, book chapters and articles on Peace, Security, Natural Resources and Governance. A holder of PhD and Master's degrees in Peace and Conflict Studies from the University of Bradford (UK), Bainomugisha has a Diploma in National Security from Galilee Institute (Israel) and a Bachelor of Mass Communication degree from Makerere University, Uganda.

Sabastiano Rwengabo is a Political Scientist and Independent Consultant on Fragility and Resilience Assessments, Political Economy Analysis, and governance. He holds a Doctor of Philosophy (PhD) from the National University of Singapore (NUS), where he was a Research Scholar, President's Graduate Fellow, and Graduate Teacher (2010–2014). He has research interests in international politics and security, regionalism, nationalism and nation building and civil-military relations. Dr. Rwengabo is the author of *Security Cooperation in the East African Community* (Trenton NJ: Africa World Press, 2018).

Wilson Winstons Muhwezi is Director of Research at ACODE and Associate Professor of Behavioural Sciences and Mental Health at Makerere University College of Health Sciences. He was jointly awarded a PhD by Karolisnka Institutet and Makerere University in 2007. He is a social worker with expertise in community-based work, public policy, advocacy, evaluation and mentorship. His competencies straddle design of curricula, managing vulnerability, building resilience; and research in mental health, psychosocial functioning, natural resource use and local governance. He has run workshops and trainings in research approaches, data management and analysis, scientific writing and public policy analysis. He has taught and examined students in several global universities. What sets him apart from professionals in his field is his niche associated with involvement in matters straddling social and health sciences. His publications include text book chapters and numerous scholarly articles published in international peer-reviewed journals.

Onesmus Mugyenyi is a Research Fellow and Deputy Executive Director at ACODE. He is a researcher and legal practitioner. He has previously served as Acting Secretary of Tropical Africa Bank, Lecturer at the National College of Business Studies, Nakawa; and has taught Commercial and International Business Law at Makerere University Business School and Faculty of Economics and Management, Makerere University, Kampala. He holds a Master of Laws majoring in international economic law and environmental policy from Makerere University. He also holds a post-Graduate Diploma in Legal Practice from Law Development Centre, and is enrolled as an Advocate of the High Court of Uganda. He has extensive research experience, has provided consultancy services, and published onissues of international trade and natural resources governance.

Ronald Naluwairo was formerly a Senior Research Fellow at ACODE and is a Senior Lecturer at the School of Law, Makerere University. He holds a PhD from the University of London, LL.M from the University of Cambridge, LL.B (Hons) from Makerere University and a Diploma in Legal Practice from Law Development Centre. He has extensive experience on natural resource governance and human rights issues. He is a published scholar on issues of natural resource governance and human rights.

Elijah Dickens Mushemeza is an academic, and author. He is a Professor of Political Science and Development Studies at Ankole Western University and a Senior Consultant at ACODE. Previously he worked as Dean Faculty of Business and Development Studies at Bishop Stuart University. He holds a BA degree in Social Sciences, an MA degree in Development Studies and a PhD degree in Political Science from Makerere University. He is also a consultant on Education, Governance, Poverty, Politics, Conflict, Forced Migration, Security, Oil and Gas, and Development issues generally in Africa. He has also previously worked as a Coordinator of the MA programme in International Relations and Diplomatic Studies in the Department of Political Science and Public Administration, Makerere University. He has taught at Mbarara University of Science and Technology. Professor Mushemeza is a past alternate Executive Committee member of the Council for the Development of Social Science Research in Africa.

Godber Tumushabe is the former Executive Director of ACODE. He is a member of the Bar in Uganda and an Assistant Lecturer at the Faculty of Law at Makerere University where he teaches international law, environmental law and jurisprudence. Godber received his first degree in law (LLB) from Makerere University, Kampala in1993. He attended a postgraduate Bar Course at Uganda's Law Development Centre and later joined the Faculty of Law at Makerere University where he obtained a Master's Degree in Law (LLM) in 1996. In 1997, Godber joined a Nairobi- based public policy think tank – the African Centre for Technology Studies (ACTS) as a Visiting Fellow and rose through the ranks to become a Senior Research Fellow in 1999. At ACTS, Godber directed Africa-wide policy research projects on environmental governance and conservation of natural resources.

Barbara Ntambirweki is a Research Fellow at ACODE under the Trade, Innovations and Biotechnology Policy Programme. She is also a Lecturer at the Uganda Pentecostal University where she teaches Introduction to law, International law and Contract law at their Kampala campus. Barbara previously worked with Women and Law in Southern Africa Research Trust Swaziland (WLSA) as an Assistant Research Officer. Barbara holds a Bachelor degree in law (LLB) from Makerere University Kampala. She attended the post graduate bar course at Law Development Centre in 2006. In 2009 she obtained a Masters degree in

Law (LLM) from the University of Cape Town in South Africa. Barbara provides both research and administrative support to the various projects under the Programme.

Flavian Zeija was a Research Associate at ACODE. He also served at Senior Lecturer in Makerere University Business School (MUBS). He has excellent skills in analytics, lecturing, public speaking, management, and contract negotiation. He has strong education professionalism and is a holder of a Doctor of Philosophy (Ph.D.) focused in Law and Corporate Governance from University of Dar es Salaam, School of Law. Currently he is the Principal Judge of the High Court of Uganda with proven competencies in adjudication and administration of Justice.

John Bosco Ngoya is Head of Moroto Regional Office, Saferworld, a leading international organization in the fields of conflict and gender sensitive programming. Working as a Technical Advisor for Civil Peace Service of the GIZ and thereafter as freelance consultant, he has extensively engaged in facilitating participatory land and resource-based conflict resolution and peace building processes in the Karamoja and Teso Sub-regions. He lectured at the School of Management and Entrepreneurship – Kyambogo University and has over fifteen (15) years experience in teaching and development work. He holds a Master of Arts in Peace and conflict studies (MUK), a Master of Management Science - Financial Management (UMI), Graduate Certificate in Civil Society Initiatives (SIT – USA) and a Bachelor's Degree in Education. He is a passionate Karimojong pastoralist and a hardened believer in a people's ability to re-engineer their own transformation. He has variedly worked in the Karamoja and the neighboring regions in the fields of research and programmatic work and does possess a practical touch to community driven initiatives.

Nicholas Opiyo is a human rights lawyer, founder and Executive Director of Chapter Four Uganda, a human rights organization. He has worked on a broad range of critical human rights issues in Uganda, and was a key leader in drafting and advocating for Uganda's law criminalizing torture. With Chapter Four, he defends anti-corruption and pro-democracy activists. He has acted as Secretary of the Uganda Law Society. In 2017, he received the German Africa Prize and in 2015 he was the Recipient of the Alison Des Forges Award for Extraordinary

Activism from Human Rights Watch. He studied Law at Uganda Christian University Mukono.

List of Abbreviations

ACODE	-	Advocates Coalition for Development and Environment
ACTS	-	African Centre for Technology Studies
ADF	-	Allied Democratic Forces
AFISMA	-	African-led International Support Mission in Mali
AIDS	-	Acquired Immunity Deficiency Syndrome
AMISOM	-	African Union Mission in Somalia
APC	-	All Peoples Congress Party
AU	-	African Union
AWEPA	-	Association of European Parliamentarians with Africa
CA	-	Constituent Assembly
CAG	-	Controller and Auditor General
CAMPFIRE	-	The Communal Areas Management Programme for Indigenous Resources
CAR	-	Central Africa Republic
CBD	-	Convention on Biological Diversity
CBEG	-	Centre for Budget and Economic Governance
CBNRM	-	Community Based Natural Resources Management
CBO	-	Convention on Biodiversity
CBOs	-	Community Based Organisations
CBPRS	-	Community-Based Property Rights
CCM	-	Chaama Cha Mapinduzi
CESCR	-	Covenant on Economic, Social and Cultural Rights
ICESCRs	-	International Covenant on Economic, Social and Cultural Rights
CET	-	Common External Tariff
CFM	-	Collaborative Forestry Management
CFM	-	Community Forestry Management
CHOGM	-	Commonwealth Heads of Government Meeting
CI	-	Conservation International
COMESA	-	Common Market for Eastern and Southern Africa
COMINAK	-	Compagnie minière d'Akokan

CPR	-	Common Pool Resources
CRC	-	Constitutional Review Commission
CSOs	-	Civil Society Organisations
DENIVA	-	Development Network of Indigenous Voluntary Organisation
DFID	-	Department for International Development
DGF	-	Democratic Governance Facility
DP	-	Democratic Party
DPP	-	Director of Public Prosecutions
DRC	-	Democratic Republic of Congo
EABC	-	East African Business Council
EAC	-	East African Community
EACSO	-	East Africa Community Services Organisation
EAHC	-	East African High Commission
EALA	-	East African Legislative Assembly
ECCAS	-	Economic Community of Central Africa
ECF	-	Equatorial Gueane Civic Fund
ECOMOG	-	Economic Community of West African States Monitoring Group
ECOWAS	-	Economic Community of Western African States
EDF	-	Electricite de France
ENR	-	Environment and Natural Resources
EU	-	European Commission
FAO	-	Food and Agriculture Organisation
FEDEMU	-	Federal Democratic Movement
FGDs	-	Focus Group Discussions
GATT	-	General Agreement on Tariffs and Trade
GDP	-	Gross Domestic Product
HIV	-	Humane Immune Deficiency Virus
HLTF	-	High Level Task Force
HRC	-	Human Rights Commission
HRCSL	-	Human Rights Commission of Sierra Leone
HSM	-	Holy Spirit Movement
ICC	-	International Criminal Court
ICCPR	-	The International Covenant on Civil and Political Rights
ICCPR	-	The International Covenant on Civil and Political Rights

ICDP	-	Integrated Conservation and Development Projects
ICDPS	-	Integrated Conservation and Development Projects
ICGLR	-	International Conference on the Great Lakes Region
ICT	-	Information Communication and Technology
IDPS	-	Internally Displaced Persons
IGARD	-	Intergovernmental Authority on Development
IGG	-	Inspector General of Government
IITC	-	Inter Institutional Trade Committee
ILO	-	International Labour Organisations
IMF	-	International Monetary Fund
IUCIN	-	International Union for the Conservation of Nature
JEFCAS	-	The John & Elnora Ferguson Centre for African Studies
KANU	-	Kenya African National Union
KAR	-	King's African Rifles
KIs	-	Key Informants
KNA	-	Kenya National Assembly
KY	-	Kabaka Yekka
LAPSET	-	Lamu Port Couth Sudan Ethiopia Transport
LARRP	-	Land Acquisition, Resettlement and Rehabilitation Policy
LCs	-	Local Councils
LEGCO	-	Legislative Council
LRA	-	Lords Resistance Army
MDGs	-	Millennium Development Goals
MINUSMA	-	United Nations Multidimensional Integrated Stabilization Mission
MNLA	-	National Movement of the liberation of Azawad
MoFPED	-	Ministry of Finance, Planning and Economic Development
MPs	-	Members of Parliament
MPs	-	Members of Parliament
MRC	-	Mombasa Republican Council
MUJAO	-	Movement for Unity and Jihad in West Africa
MWLE	-	Ministry of Water, Lands and Environment

NASSIT	-	National Social Security and Insurance Trust
NFA	-	National Forest Authority
NGO	-	Non-Governmental Organisation
NGOs	-	Non-Governmental Organisations
NN	-	United Nations
NPRC	-	National Provisional Ruling Council
NRA/M	-	National Resistance Movement/Army
OAU	-	Organization of African Unity
ONS	-	Office of National Security
PAC	-	Public Accounts Committee
PBO	-	Parliamentary Budget Office
PBOs	-	Parliamentary Budget Office
PEAP	-	Poverty Eradication Action Plan
PGRFA	-	Plant Genetic Resources for Food and Agriculture
PIC	-	Prior Informed Consent
PNOWB	-	Parliamentary Network on the World Bank
PSF	-	Private Sector Foundation
RC	-	Resistance Councils
RECs	-	Regional Economic Communities
RUF	-	Revolutionary United Front
SADC	-	Southern African Development Community
SAPs	-	Structural Adjustment Programs
SDGs	-	UN Social Development Goals
SIGS	-	Special Interest Groups
SLDF	-	Saboat Land Defence Force
SLPP	-	Sierra Leone Peoples Party
SMDL	-	Saboat Movement for the Defence of Land
SOMAIR	-	Société des Mines de l'Air
SPLA	-	Sudanese Peoples Liberation Army
SPLM/A	-	Sudanese Peoples Liberation Movement/Army
TANU	-	Tanganyika African National Union
TK	-	Traditional Knowledge
TRC	-	Truth and Reconciliation Commission
TRIPPS	-	Trade-Related Aspects of Intellectual Property Rights
TRIPS	-	Trade Related Aspects of Intellectual Property Rights
TTI	-	Think Tank Initiative

UEDCL	-	Uganda Electricity Distribution Company Limited
UFFA	-	Uganda Freight Forwarders Association
UFM	-	Uganda Freedom Movement
UMA	-	Uganda Manufacturers Association
UN	-	United Nations
UNAMSIL	-	United Nations Mission in Sierra Leone
UNCED	-	United Nations Conference on Environment and Development
UNCHR	-	United Nations High Commissioner for Human Rights
UNESCO	-	United Nations Educational, Scientific and Cultural Organization
UNLF	-	Uganda National Liberation Army
UPC	-	Uganda Peoples' Congress
UPDA/M	-	Uganda People's Democratic Army
UPDF	-	Uganda People's Defence Forces
USAID	-	United States Agency for International Development
UTWG	-	Uganda Technical Working Group
UWA	-	Uganda Wildlife Authority
UWS	-	Uganda Wild Life Society
WCED	-	World Commission on Environment and Development
WIPO	-	World Intellectual Property Organisation
WTO	-	World Trade Organisation
WWF	-	World Wildlife Foundation

CHAPTER ONE

Peace, Democracy and Development in Africa: Introduction to Core Issues

Arthur Bainomugisha and Sabastiano Rwengabo

Introduction

Africa has come a long way. Its economic growth has been faster than the global average since 2000, registering an average growth rate of 5% and showing relative buoyance during a recessive period. Eight out of the world's top 10 performing countries are in Africa. ICT advancements that could have bypassed the continent are serving to show how Africa can leapfrog its development through technology. Mobile penetration rose from 1% in 2000 to 54% in 2012 surpassing the number of mobile users in the US, India or Europe … contrary to common perceptions of conflict, the vast majority of Africans live in countries that are democratic (democratizing), peaceful…. Economic performance is at its best since independence. Africa's GDP of $2.2 trillion in 2013 represented a more than threefold increase from $600 billion registered in 2000, one of the fastest growth rates in history. It took China 12 years to double GDP per capita, India 17 years and the US and Germany between 30 and 60 years' It is time for Africa

Dr Carols Lopes, Executive Secretary,
UN Nations Economic Commission for Africa,
NewAfrican Magazine, October, 2015.

Peace, security and democracy are pre-requisites for sustainable development. Development in turn leads to the consolidation of peace and democracy. This in no way implies that developed democratic societies are free of conflicts and insecurity, but that they tend to have effective mechanisms and economic wherewithal to prevent the escalation of these issues. The mutually reinforcing relationship between these conditions is indisputable. By all means, Africa aspires to attain them preferably simultaneously. Against this realization, the African Union (AU) has developed a comprehensive strategy for supporting democracy in its member states and peace building initiatives in conflict-affected countries. Africa has progressively overcome some of the many obstacles that make it difficult for the continent to achieve the socio-economic and political development aspirations of its people.

Nevertheless, development is a function of leadership, for it consists the application of human capabilities onto natural resources to generate transformative outcomes. In much of the developing world however; confident, committed, visionary and accountable leadership is in short supply. Thus, current hurdles of peace, democracy, and development remain elusive and stifle the transformation (Aseka, 2005) of a continent that was bedevilled by slavery, colonialism, post-independence state fragility complicated by Cold War rivalries, structural adjustments programmes imposed by the IMF [International Monetary Fund] and the World Bank, and protracted violent conflicts. Africa currently faces the challenge of raising to the occasion and proving its potential by fulfilling its responsibility and obligation as a key player in international affairs. No wonder the 2019 Oxfod-Africa Conference was held under the theme "Asserting Africa's [Global] Relevance", as though Africa was ever irrelevant or had lost its relevance in gobal affairs. This reflects not just Afro-pessimism that tends to resurfance in conversatons about the nature and future of global peace, democracy, and development, but also interest in Africa's strategic future.

For Africa to capture the moment and achieve socio-economic and political transformation of its people, the leadership must deal with one stark paradox: despite the continent's resource endowment, Africa still lags behind the world in many development aspects. Africa is not poor; it is underdeveloped. Africa is not irrelevant nor has it lost its relevance; its strategic potentialities have not been tapped and/or appropriated. The continent's excessive but ineffective foreign aid dependence (Moyo, 2008), traumas of fluctuations and vagaries of global market prices and international financial systems, democratic deficits, and endemic conflicts, limit Africa's abundant potentials and capacities to lend itself a long term basis for sustainable peace and development (Francis, 2005).

Violent conflicts remain a common feature of Africa's political landscape. Their consequences have been devastating: deaths of millions of people, internal displacement and generation of refugees within and outside the continent, capital flight, environmental degradation, and democratic reversals in some countries that had made progress politically (Chingono, 2016). These conflicts slowdown the pace of Africa's development. Africa also remains disunited as a continent with some many small and unviable states that were randomly divided as part of colonial subterfuge. In response to these challenges, the AU, the African research and intellectual community, and the international community have advocated the promotion of democracy and peace building as affirmative interventions that can transform the continent into a viable and respected player in international affairs (Francis, 2005). Continental and sub-continental (regional) organisation has also been part of this broad-based, multifaceted undertaking to achieve these related developmental outcomes: peace, democracy, and development.

Conceptualizing Peace, Democracy and Development

A deep understanding of the subject matter being explored in this book requires conceptual simplification of the rather multi-meaning concepts of peace, democracy, and development. These concepts, though related and interlinked, attract multiple definitions that sometimes render it difficult to conceptually operationalise them. For brevity's sake we avoid complicated conceptualisations and provide simpler definitions as much as we are able to share with our readers.

What is Peace?

The definition of peace varies with religion, culture or subject of study. However, most people define peace as mere absence of war or violence within and between groups, communities, societies and polities. Yet this seems too narrow. While peace and security are interchangeable, peace is broader than security. Peace is more complex than simply mere absence of violence (Davies-Vengoechea, 2004). Peace can be at small social scale, say at village level, community level, and even personal levels. It obtains in the realms of the political, socioeconomic, psychological and beyond, straddling all respects of human existence. Peace can also entail calmness from ecological pressures, what is implied by "ecological peace" in Chapter Four of this volume.

Peace takes place within and between individuals, groups, communities, and polities–hence such notions as inter-community peace (such as between the Iteso and Karamojong in Chapter 6) and inter-state peace, or "amity", as is understood in international relations. At continental, such as African, level; or global level, we can talk of regional, continental or global peace to imply: (i) absence of intra-regional and inter-regional violence or disastrous devastations, (ii) absence of international violence, such as world war; as well as (iii) absence of regional or global economic turmoil and disasters. It follows that one kind of peace leads to other aspects of peace: for instance, absence of political peace, that is, insecurity, threatens peaceful economic transactions which afflicts societal wellbeing and thus stymies psychosocial peace. Complex public health emergencies (CPHEs), such as the 2013-2016 Ebola Virus Disease (EVD) outbreak in the Mano River Union (MRU) of West Africa, threaten peace and security–and tend to have devastating consequences for economic developemt and societal wellbeing.

While states claim the desirability of peace, there is little agreement about its meaning and how to realise it (McCandless and Karbo, 2011). On the other hand, Gultang introduces notions of positive and negative peace. He defines "negative peace" as the absence of direct violence, especially violent conflict or war; and "positive peace" as the absence of structural violence and presence of social justice (Galtung, 1964). On the other hand, Mahatma Mohandis Gandhi suggested that if an oppressive society lacks violence the society is nonetheless not peaceful, because of injustice and oppression. The end of violence may mark the beginning, not the maturity of, peace, hence peace entails attainable social goals beyond nonviolence (Galtung, 1969).

The foregoing conceptualisation indicates that semblances of peace and experiences of peace differ: semblances are non-violent situations; experiences involve social justice and respect for human dignity that can only obtain in a mature, integrated, and consensual democracy (like, perhaps, Switzerland and Norway). Another view, the Kantian hypothesis, avers that democratic societies have inbuilt mechanisms for peaceful conflict resolution. This democratic peace theory has acquired liberal hype with the view that intra-democratic and inter-democratic peace is law-like (Rosato, 2003). But this approach stresses negative peace and not positive peace that entails social justice, equity, and respect for human dignity. Hence, Africa requires positive peace which is, in many respects, a function of democratic maturity.

What is Democracy?

Democracy is about the state, the way its government is constituted, the mandate it holds, and how it executes that mandate. It is about political institutions and political practice, and the logics of competition for power. Democracy mainly entails "the plurality of opinions, freedom of expression, multi-party political system, political competition, free and universal multiparty elections, respect for fundamental and human rights, rule of law and accountability of the rulers" (Stan, 2004). Equality before the law and structural equity are important, though not perquisites, for defining a polity as a democracy. Some of today's democracies, especially in Western Europe and North America, are afflicted by structural inequalities, structural violence, and oppression even as they hold seemingly regular free and fair elections. India's Caste system and the USA's racial inequalities and prejudices speak volumes about this idea.

While there is no universally-acknowledged definition of democracy, a number of tenets underpin all democracies. For example, democracy rests upon the principle of majority rule, coupled with respect for individual and minority rights. While respecting the will of the majority, democracy must protect the rights of individuals and minority groups. Democracies guard against all-powerful central governments and create checks and balances to ensure that leaders are accessible and responsive to people's needs. Democracies also understand as one of their primary functions the protection of human rights, such as freedom of speech and association, the right of equal protection under the law, the opportunity to organize and participate fully in the political and cultural life of society, and provision of equal opportunities for the realisation of one's potential. There is a recognition that democracies are diverse, reflecting each nation's unique political, socio-economic and cultural metamorphosis.

Citizens in a democracy have rights and freedoms. They also have responsibility to participate in the political system. The system, in turn, protects their rights and freedoms. Democratic societies are committed to the values of tolerance, cooperation and compromise. Democracies recognize that reaching consensus requires compromise which may not always be attainable under conditions of institutional immaturity. Though most underdeveloped societies are under pressure to democratize, some analysts warn that a minimum level of institutional development underpinned by economic capacity to provide political goods is necessary for the attainment of democracy. Without functioning political institutions, the democratization process can create disorder, chaos, and disrupt socioeconomic development of a given society (Huntington, 1968). In this view, therefore, democracy and development are bedfellows.

What is Development?

Development as a peace and security imperative typically refers to the process and strategies through which societies and states seek to achieve more prosperous and equitable standards of living. Development activities have usually been confined to socio-economic growth, provision of health and education services, and improvements in infrastructure–to the Pettian "growth of numbers and incomes", and the concern with "the exact content of standards of living" (Sen, 1988, page 10). This is narrow too. Development entails not just improvements in the economic, infrastructural, and techno-scientific realms; it encompasses ideational, intellectual, sociocultural, and perceptional transformation of society, which affects relations within and between societies (Sen, 1988).

From the foregoing, development is both a process and an attainment. As a process, it implies progressive change in the socioeconomic and techno-scientific conditions of a given society. This entails progression toward high-end levels of human existence. The process of development never ends: hence, so-called "developed" societies are in fact developing. As an attainment or end result, development involves the acquirement of specific indicators of positive change, such as reaching levels of sociopolitical, economic, technological and scientific, as well as ideational improvement. For instance, the attainment of national integration, and correspondingly erasure of socio-cultural identity fault-lines in a country through nation building (Rwengabo, 2016b), is considered development inasmuch as the attainment of levels of wealth and technological sophistication is. Africa's challenge, then, has been the attainment of the desired levels of positive change in all respects.

Peace, democracy and Development Nexus in Africa

This section focuses on peace, democracy and development nexus, challenges and possibilities for Africa to navigate the 21st century more successfully than it did the 20th, a century that was marked by depredations of colonialism and costly conflicts (Nehma and Zeleza, 2008). Democracy and peace are both prerequisites for sustainable human development (IDEA, 2016). The explanation of Africa's predicament has been underdevelopment that underpins the limitations in democracy, constitutionalism and rule of law, and as a conflict management framework that would buttress the continent against external shocks and internal self-destruction. Faced with costly conflicts, the AU has set itself aspirational goals to support democracy and sustainable peace in African countries. The AU's goal, for example, states that by 2020 all guns will be silent. A culture of peace and tolerance will be nurtured in Africa's children and youth through peace education (African Union, 2015).

In order to promote democracy and peace building, the AU has built an expansive and robust normative framework, coupled with structural mechanisms for implementing the framework. The normative framework is part of the AU's efforts to promote democratic governance and rule of law, both of which are critical for people-centred socio-economic development. The AU has also been pragmatic in promoting peace and security on the continent. For example, unlike the Organization of African Unity (OAU) Charter of 1963, which embraced the doctrine of non-interference in the internal affairs of member states, the AU Constitutive Act (2000) embraces a new doctrine of non-indifference to human rights abuses within the territory of AU member States. The shift has emboldened the AU in its democracy-promotion and peace-building mandate, especially in fragile and conflict-affected states.

The combination of the Constitutive Act (2000), the 2000 Lome Declaration, and the African Charter on Democracy, Elections and Governance, 2007, forms an institutional building block for the AU framework for promoting democracy across Africa. In order to fulfil its mandate of promoting and democracy, the AU has developed a specific institutional set up, the Peace and Security Council to deal with conflict prevention and unconstitutional changes of government. The Peace and Security Council has a broad mandate that includes promoting peace, security and stability in Africa and the creation of an enabling environment for sustainable development. Another crucial mechanism is the African Peace and Security Architecture (APSA) whose mandate is early warning, conflict prevention, peace support operations, peace-building and post-conflict reconstruction and development (Vines, 2013). While the rhetoric is still different from practice, the establishment of the above-mentioned frameworks demonstrates a continent that is determined to overcome underdevelopment, war proneness and governance failures in order to achieve socio-economic and political transformation.

The recent intervention in Somalia under the AU Mission in Somalia (AMISOM) is but a case in point where Africa has stood its ground, amidst costs, to rescue toe troubled Somali state and restore sanity in a chaotic political landscape (Rwengabo, 2015). The AU has also given mandate to regional entities, called Regional Economic Communities (RECs), to address peace and security challenges arising within regions while also undertaking regional development initiatives. The ECOWAS interventions in Liberia and Sierra Leone during the 1990s and in Gambia in 2017 are but few of the many examples of regional peace-building and humanitarian initiatives (Rwengabo, 2018).

Transformations in East Africa: Cases of Africa's Peace, Democracy and Development Trajectory

This section outlines transformations in East African countries to demonstrate the region's peace, democracy, and development trajectory since the post-colonial times of Uganda, Kenya, and Tanzania. While East Africa is broader than these three countries, they constitute a unique geopolitical landscape around which the future of East Africa and the Nile Valley revolves, hence impacting a greater African landscape in many ways. For one, these countries were the original members of the vibrant EAC, which indicates years of interstate cooperation. Second, these countries share Lake Victoria, the source of the River Nile, making them key to the strategic transformation of the Nile Valley. Third, these countries were under the same colonial control after 1919, and faced similar challenges regarding the socioeconomic and political destiny of the region (Buell, 1928).

Finally, apart from membership to the EAC, these countries are also members of other sub-regional cooperation arrangements under SADC,

IGAD, and the International Conference for the Great Lakes Region (ICGLR) (Rwengabo, 2016a), as well as tripartite arrangements encapsulating the EAC, SADC, and the Common Market of Eastern and Southern Africa (COMESA). Therefore, this section is intended to depict the socio-economic and political challenges that have persistently confronted Africa for most of the post-independence period. More attention is paid to Uganda than Kenya and Tanzania because unlike them Uganda has experienced costly civil wars, coups, purges, and other afflictions that represent the African experience more than the seemingly outlier experience of Tanzania.

Transformation in Uganda: Peace, Democracy, and Development

Uganda became a single polity in 1894 after colonial Britain declared it a British Protectorate. The constituent parts of what became Uganda were in existence long before 1894, and had undergone periods of state formation and destruction, empire building and imperial decline, as well as nation building and state consolidation in an otherwise heterogeneous socio-political landscape (Kanyeihamba, 2002). These pre-colonial states, and different ethnic groups at different stages of state formation, were forcefully brought under one colonial rule. Like elsewhere in Africa, Uganda was carved out primarily to serve the political, economic, and strategic interests of the colonial power and at independence she was granted the 'legal fiction' of sovereign statehood (Francis, 2006).

Consequently, Uganda has demonstrated increasing vulnerability to internal and regional insecurity, which has compounded the challenges of building viable mechanisms for dealing with peace and security issues: because British colonialists forcefully brought together different state and non-state polities and groups. These groups were at different levels of political development. Their consent to become one nation was not sought. As a result, the challenge of state formation and nation building continues to threaten Uganda's political stability under conditions of ethno-political self-assertiveness (The Independent, 2010).

Uganda became independent on 9 October 1962. Milton Obote, who headed a young political party, the Uganda People's Congress (UPC), became the Prime Minister with executive powers, while Freddie Mutesa II, the monarch of Buganda kingdom to whom were aligned the royalist KabakaYekka (KY–King Only) party, became Uganda's first President.

The UPC and a conservative traditional Movement pushed for the allegiance with KY, a political alliance which defeated Benedicto Kiwanuka of the Democratic Party (DP), a party formed to champion the interests of non-Protestants, Muslims, and minority groups, who felt marginalized by Uganda's monarchy. As such, the political leadership after 1962 was determined to neutralize the DP (Kabwegyere, 1995). The period 1962-1966 was a drama-filled transitional epoch. The independence constitution went on trial, created a hotchpotch form of government that was both federal and unitary, and was vague on federalism (Kanyeihamba, 2002).

By 1965 the UPC-KY alliance had collapsed. The KY had been dropped from the coalition. Yet traditional, conservative elements had penetrated UPC and acquired its active supporters. This bred infighting, which gave rise to factions with capitalist and socialist leanings within the party. Soon in-fighting erupted, which forced Obote to drag the army into politics in order to strengthen his positions. He reshuffled the army, and Idi Amin, who had been a deputy to Brigadier Shaban Opolot, was made Army Chief of Staff and overall Army Commander (Kanyeihamba, 2002). In civil-military relations lingo, this amounted to interference in internal affairs and institutional autonomy of armed forces, and threatened the Obote regime's stability (Rwengabo, 2013).

The deepening constitutional standoff culminated in the abrogation of the independence constitution on 22 February 1966. Obote abolished the post of President and Vice President. He assumed all the powers of government. The Lukiiko, Buganda Kingdom's Parliament, tried to resist these moves by calling upon the Central Government to remove itself from Bugandan soil. This provided an opportunity to Obote for a final showdown with the president and King of Buganda. On 24 May 1966, the army, now led Idi Amin, attacked the King's palace and forced him to flee into exile where he died a poor and heartbroken man three years later.

The Constituent Assembly later discussed and adopted a new unitary republican constitution for Uganda in 1967. This constitution combined the presidential and parliamentary forms of government, retained multipartyism even as opposition parties remained very weak, experiencing desertions and lacking organizational capacity, the UPC continued to undermine the opposition: by 1969 Obote declared Uganda a one-party state, which ignited chaos as UPC's internal contradictions intensified and the party degenerated into factionalism which culminated in the military coup of 1971 that brought Idi Amin to power. Amin suspended the constitution and established a reign of terror characterised by purges, murders, and suppression (Rwengabo, 2013). Peace was no more. Democracy was no more. Development was at a standstill. The country was sliding backward.

The overthrow of Amin's dictatorship in 1979 paved way for the Uganda National Liberation Front (UNLF), formed during the Moshi Conference in Tanzania in 1979, and led by Obote, to come to power. Instead of creating a new political order, the UNLF faced serious political and security challenges. While conference delegates elected Professor Yusuf Lule as chairman of a new, broad-based movement, who consequently, formed the first UNLF Government after Amin, under the watchful eye of Lule Uganda degenerated into factionalism and political intrigues that led to his sudden downfall. Lule was subsequently replaced by Godfrey Binaisa, who also failed to improve the political situation. Corruption, suspicion, intrigue and rumour-mongering became rampant in a country that needed committed leadership to champion the reconstruction process. Soon the removal of Binaisa from power marked the demise of the UNLF and the ascendance to power of the Military Commission led by Paul Muwanga and deputised by Yoweri Museveni.

The Commission organised elections in 1980, which were controversially won by Obote's UPC, hence giving Obote a second shot at presidential office. Most political groups accused the UPC of rigging the 1980 elections. Museveni and other political groups launched s guerrilla war against the Obote government mainly from central Uganda, which led to destructive counterinsurgency operations in which many civilians in Luwero Triangle lost lives. Peace remained elusive. Democracy was under test. Development was slowed down by the war. Soon Obote fell to a coup staged by Generals Bazilio Okello and Tito Okello in 1985, who tried unsuccessfully to hold peace talks with Museveni's National Resistance Army/Movement (NRA/M) in vain. They soon fell to the NRA in January 1986. Museveni became president.

To most Ugandans, especially those living in Buganda sub-region who suffered greatly under the second Obote government, the NRM victory brought hope and optimism (Mutibwa, 2008). For the first time, soldiers serving in the Uganda Army were perceived as belonging to the population they were protecting. Yet the victorious NRA was being perceived differently in northern Uganda, the base of previous governments, as foreigners or Banyarwanda, which is partly responsible for the LRA rebellion. But the NRM inherited a nearly collapsed state. The economy was in a state of ruin. Infrastructure was in a state of disrepair. People lacked basic goods like soap, sugar and salt. Ironically, compared to other African countries, at independence Uganda's economy was one of the strongest in Black Africa (Kanyeihamba, 2002). Economic mismanagement was one of the reasons Amin cited for overthrowing. After Amin, Obote failed to restore economic and political sanity. To win international recognition and the badly-needed foreign exchange, the Obote II Government accepted conditionalities imposed by the International Monetary Fund (IMF), but like Moyo has revealed about donor aid such money did not benefit the common people. This was the state of affairs inherited by the NRM.

As part of transformation agenda, the NRM had crafted a "Ten Point Program" as a basis for social, economic and political reconstruction of the country, a vehicle to deliver the NRM's promised "fundamental change" that was intended to set it apart from the past rapacious governments that had ruled Uganda. The NRM/A revolution in Uganda was apparently aimed at carrying all the people or at least a great majority, through purposive and positive mobilization programs, to do good for Uganda by demonstrating true nationalism. The NRM mainly because it lacked enough members with requisite political experience, built a broad-based coalition comprised of representatives from former political formations, strengthened the army and intelligence services, and restored disciplined in the armed forces. The Resistance Council (RC) system of governance started from the national to village level and allowed people to make decisions that directly affected their lives. The rebel-movement-turned-government also embarked on a constitution-making process that culminated in the Constituent Assembly (CA) elections of 1993. By 1995, when the constitution was promulgated, popular participation in elections had shown some positive results, and the 1996 and 2001 elections were tested under the 1995 constitution.

Since 1986, Uganda has an impressive annual economic growth rate of 6.4%, largely because of improvement in the policy environment; restoration of peace and stability in most parts of the country; and rehabilitation of infrastructure and increased capacity utilization (Tripp, 2010). The picture, though is different in northern Uganda where the LRA rebellion took government, until 2006 to contain. It was almost impossible to rehabilitate the infrastructure and implement meaningful development programs in the region. Equally, donors supported Museveni, and, like Ghana, heralded Uganda as "a pioneer of macroeconomic stabilization and structural adjustment in sub-Saharan Africa" (Moncrieffe, 2006, page 17). Critics and supporters alike acknowledge that the NRM deserves credit for improving and sustaining peace and security in most parts of the country, introducing universal primary and secondary education, allowing for a fairly free press, and encouraging citizen's participation through an elected government (Moncrieffe, 2006, page 18).

In spite of these achievements, Uganda still faces serious challenges. Northern Uganda still lags behind due to the armed conflict. Thirty years of political monopoly has witnessed the NRM government face increasing internal and external pressure to free political parties which it grudgingly did in 2005 without allowing the opposition sufficient space and freedom to organsie and mobilise (Khisa and Rwengabo, 2017). The 2006 general elections suffered irregularities and malpractices: the opposition claims rigging in favor of the ruling NRM, indicating limited trust in political and state institutions (Kiiza et al., 2008). The return to a multiparty system had not solved Uganda's democratic challenges: the ruling party influenced parliament to change the constitution and remove term presidential term limits, which ensured that incumbent Museveni, who had ruled for 24 years, continued to stand for re-election indefinitely, hence threatening Uganda's future stability and potentially costing the country its democratic dividends (Kategaya, 2006). Eriya Kategaya, who was widely considered as Number Two to President Museveni in the NRM hierarchy, noted that he was shocked by the constitutional change:

> In my naïve thinking, I believed that President Museveni will live up to the stature of a statesman and be the first President of Uganda to retire as per the Constitution and thereby set a constitutional precedent. I strongly believe that this should be done for the sake of the future stability of this country. I have spent most of my youth running up and down and even went into exile because of bad politics and I don't wish my children to experience the same problems (Kategaya, 2006).

The foregoing demonstrates the political–and potentially economic and security–uncertainty Uganda now faces. The current state of the 1995

Constitution is being contested. One of the key democratic reforms that civil society and opposition parties are demanding is the re-instating of the two presidential term limits and non-temperance with the presidential age-limit in the constitution. Since independence Uganda's army has remained a dominant player in politics: coups, counter-coups, civil wars, and purges have defined the country's political landscape, stifling the development and consolidation of peace, state institutions, and the economic base. Consequently, the army in Uganda invokes sad memories among the citizens who, since colonial times, have suffered at the hands of armed groups. Loyalty of the Uganda People's Defence Forces (UPDF) today seems to lie with the Head of State and not the State and society itself despite ongoing civil-military cooperation initiatives in the UPDF. Unlike Kenya whose armed forces have stayed out of direct political interference, and Tanzania where the society was demilitarized after 1964, Uganda retains uncertainty regarding its civil-military future as well as its evolution into post-Museveni peace, democracy, and development.

Transformation in Kenya: Peace, Democracy, and Development

Kenya's post-independence period witnessed political stability but a fragile peace. Democracy also suffered a fractured ethno-political landscape that prevented the development of political parties that are free from ethnic undertones. Unlike Uganda, however, Kenya has avoided serious civil wars, coups and purges while at the same time suffering authoritarian tendencies during the 1980s-2000s that culminated in the post-2007 elections violence with devastating consequences for the country and the region. Exceptions to the country's avoidance of civil wars consist in the experience of the Saboat Movement for the Defence of Land (SMDL) during the 2000s, threat from the Mombasa Republican Council (MRC), which has secessionist tendencies, and challenges of terrorism (Rwengabo, 2017). These realities indicate that the country has failed not only in building lasting peace but also in achieving democracy. At the same time the levels of socioeconomic development, equity, social justice, and national integration that would help it build and consolidate peace and democracy remain elusive.

Kenya got independence in 1961 after the Mau Mau rebellion of the 1950s, led by, among others, Jomo Kenyatta, had rendered colonial control difficult. The conflict was rooted in land expropriation and alienation of the indigenous peoples in the fertile Kenya highlands as colonial settlers from Europe had displaced Africans from their lands rendering them squatters in their homeland (Kanogo, 1987). Soon it expanded and appealed to other grievances like socioeconomic marginalization and political oppression of the colonial regime. While there had been other anti-colonial rebellions, such as the Nandi rebellion, the Mau Mau was most important for it is the one that ushered in independence for the country under Kenyatta. It was also dominated by the Kikuyu ethnic group, which made it an ethno-political conflict in many respects, though it also created cleavages that later informed local politics that still affect Kenyan politics (Branch, 2009).

The first challenge that Kenyatta's Kenya National African Union (KANU) faced was the integration of the heterogeneous geopolitical space into a nation. Though Swahili language had taken root following years of Afro-Asian interactions on the East African Coast, Kenyatta seems not to have prioritized nation building as Nyerere did. Kenyatta dominated the Kenya political landscape until 1978 when he died. Using personal magnetism and charisma, he became a political magnet that easily punished opponents or rewarded loyalists and cronies. This created a clique of few individuals who surrounded the president and dispensed benefits to the Kikuyu especially from Kiambu, Kenyatta's home area, where many powerful ministers also hailed: James Gichuru, Moiyu Koinange, Njoroge Mungai (Muriuki, 1979), as well as Charles Mugane Njonjo, a person believed to have worked with Bruce MacKensie, a Caucasian member of the Kenyatta Cabinet, and convinced the Kenyan establishment to abandon the EAC in 1970s (Ogot, 2006).

Without a civil war against the Kenyatta regime, Kenya enjoyed negative peace. But during the Kenyatta era there was a steady centralisation of power in the Office of the President. The government passed a Preservation of Public Security Act which permitted detention without trial, trampling against civil and other human rights. Democracy also suffered as the opposition was weakened: Kenya People's Union was banned. Its leader, Oginga Odinga, was detained. Allegations of assassinations of Kenyatta's potential rivals escalated. Kenya became a de facto one party system (Stewart and O'Sullivan, 1998). As ethnic Kikuyu from central Kenya benefited from Kenyatta's patronage system under a capitalist approach to development, other ethnic groups, save perhaps for Oginga Odinga's Luo, benefited too. Capitalism endeared Kenya to

Western Europe and North America during the Cold War. With such support formal education expanded, foreign investment came in, and the economy grew under the domination of 'White Settlers.' Many observers attributed pre-Moi stability to Kenyatta's leadership and charisma and dominant position that balanced political forces in the country, but it seems the regime was built around some structural, institutional, and social configurations that ensured a balance within the military infrastructure, centralisation of power within the central state, "and neutralisation of potential foci of organised opposition." This should explain why when Kenyatta died in 1978 and was replaced with Moi, stability remained and a non-Kikuyu faced no coup d'état (Tamarkin, 1979).

Daniel Arap Moi's ascendency to the presidency was an unusual peaceful, non-conflictual, non-haphazard succession. This experience was remarkable. It represented peaceful leadership succession after the death of a president, partly because the government suppressed public discussion of the succession issue, dealt with political dissent harshly (Khapoya, 1979), and Moi used his political tenacity to reign high for almost 3 decades. He inherited a steady professionalization of the armed forces which were originally dominated by the Nandi and other minority groups. Through coup-proofing techniques not worth elaborating here, Moi was also able to secure his position and consolidate his rule contrary to coup-afflicted countries like Uganda.

Soon Moi knew he needed to do something to endear himself to a broad spectrum of Kenyans and consolidate his rule: appear to right the apparent wrong of the Kenyatta era. Moi "released all twenty six political detainees across the ethnic spectrum, most of whom had been languishing in jails for years", and promised Kenyans that his administration would not condone drunkenness, "tribalism", corruption, and smuggling, problems already deeply entrenched in Kenya" (Korwa and Munyae, 2001) But soon crony capitalism, political corruption, and repression were intermixed with elections to keep the Moi regime going. Most elections witnessed violence in isolated areas. But negative peace inherited under Kenyatta continued. The economy had grown under Kenyatta: coffee and tea production had expanded, the tourism industry grew, and investments in infrastructure continued to facilitate economic activity. But this had been dominated by the Kikuyu.

And now the Kalenjin [and other disadvantaged 'tribes' in the Rift Valley) had come in. Moi set to address this imbalance in exchange for absolute loyalty to his rule. Elections were held but rigged. An alliance was forged between the Kikuyu and the Kalenjin to ensure continuity. Corruption increased as Moi built a kleptocracy around himself. Poverty levels increased, development slowed. The struggle for democracy, between 1980s and early 2000s, was a bitter one pursued by disaffected elites, local citizens, and international agitators. But these efforts were smoothed by post-Cold War US concerns with economic mismanagement, corruption and human rights violations. Moi kept hold on to power throughout the 1992, 1997, and 2002 elections, and in a turn of events Mwai Kibaki won against Moi's preferred candidate, Uhuru Kenyatta, in 2002 (Balkan, 2004). The west was also concerned about potential threats to its bastion of interests in eastern Africa following violence in elections between 1992 and 2002. Thus, Kibaki inherited a country riddled with corruption and mismanagement, but which had had the benefit of a professional army that desisted from interfering in politics.

Though Mwai Kibaki inherited a stable polity at the central state level, he faced two threats to negative peace: a civil war in the Elgon Mountain, the Saboat Movement for the Defence of Land (SMDL) broke out in the early 2000s, and by 2005 had caused mayhem and attracted international attention. Counterinsurgency operations were also brutal and violated human rights unlike before. Second, the operations of the Mombasa Republican Council (MRC), which is accused of using terrorist tactics, almost spoke to Islamic radicalization in the country that fed in regional terrorism. Thus, while the country also suffered armed cattle rustling in the northwest these groups, coupled with terrorism and extremist militia groups like the Mungiki, were the strongest threats to national peace and security on a large scale (Rwengabo, 2017).

The climax of Kenya's failed peace, democracy, and development trajectory was the post-2007 election violence. The presidential election was hotly contested. The incumbent, Mwai Kibaki, a Kikuyu, faced off with Raila Odinga, a Luo, in a country suffering ethno-political divisions. Both contenders claimed victory. Ethnic violence erupted as the Luo, Odinga's co-ethnics combined with other disaffected groups and attacked Kibaki's co-ethnic Kikuyu and their supposed allies. Hundreds of thousands of were displaced; some forced into internally displaced people's (IDPs) camps, others fleeing to neighbouring countries as refugees. An estimated more than 1,200 people were killed (Republic of

Kenya, 2008). Regional and international interventions forced a rethinking of the Kenyan political landscape and promulgation of a new constitution in 2010.

The international dimension of justice came in following the 2007-2008 crisis: the International Criminal Court (ICC) indicted Uhuru Muigai Kenyatta and William Samurai Ruto, leaving out Kibaki and Odinga in a strange international-judicial process not free from accusations of selective application of justice in international law (ICC, 2011). It is unclear whether western powers, mainly Britain and the USA, targeted Kenyatta to prevent his ascendance to the presidency. Strangely he and his co-accused, Ruto, was elected to the presidency in 2013 (Gabe, 2013). The ICC process did not end impunity in Kenya as it failed to successfully hold anyone accountable for the 2007-8 crisis. Kenyatta is one of the leaders that have pushed Kenya back to a record economic performance. By 2016, Kenya's economy was apace with the fastest growing economies in the world. Infrastructure developments started under Kibaki were completed and others started. The Standard Gauge Railway and highways are some of these developments that have been added to the ambitious Lamu Port-South Sudan-Ethiopia-Transport (LAPSSET) Corridor project.

In 2013 Uhuru Kenyatta won the elections and set the country to the pace of development by embracing regional integration initiatives and pushing for aggressive domestic economic pursuits, and got promising results of explorations in the oil and gas sector. He also struggled with terrorism and extremism from especially the Somalia-based al-Shabaab and domestic criminal elements. Together with the AMISOM forces Kenya is struggling against terrorism in the region centred in the struggling Somali polity. Kenya will hold its second election under the new constitution in August 2017. East Africa and the world wait to see if Kenya will revert to violence that characterised the 1992, 1997, 2002, and climaxed in the 2007 elections, or demonstrate political maturity and transcendence of the previous structural and institutional deficiencies that had trampled upon peace, democracy, and development in one of Africa's most promising politico-economic landscape.

Transformation in Tanzania: Peace, Democracy, and Development

Tanzania may not be a liberal democracy but is politically stable. It may not be socioeconomically as strong as Kenya but is the most ethnopolitically united country in Africa. The country may not be ranked amongst the Middle Income countries but enjoys more social amity than similarly-heterogeneous countries in the world. Tanzania's defining characteristic is not just political stability and domestic security characterised by absence of a coup culture and absence of civil war experiences. The defining feature is the paradox of nation building in East Africa's most heterogeneous country.

The country suffers comparable ethnic heterogeneity and complexity with most African societies. Despite the country's ethnic, linguistic, religious, regional, and racial heterogeneity, Tanzania remains an outlier compared to most other heterogeneous African countries including Kenya and Uganda. The government undertook a triple process of depoliticisation of ethnicity to reduce the propensity for political groups to rely on ethnicity for political contestations. The language policy, the forced Swahilisation of the entire country, ensured that everyone learnt and spoke Kiswahili, which eased communication across ethno-linguistic groups. The leadership also encouraged people to intermarry across ethnic, racial, and regional groups in order to promote national unity. Progressively, ethnic, religious, and regional prejudices that afflict Uganda died out (Rwengabo, 2016b).

On the politico-military front, Tanzania inherited a colonial security infrastructure, and the Tanzania People's Defence Forces (TPDF) is a successor to the colonial Kings African Riffles (KAR). While in countries like Uganda and Nigeria military interventions in politics became a normalcy and the armed forces acquired an unwelcome but permanent presence in politics, Tanzania evolved differently. The ruling Tanzania Africa National Union (TANU), later Chaama Cha Mapenduzi (CCM), under the leadership of the politically astute and philosophically sophisticated Julius K. Nyerere, de-politicised the military by infusing in it nationalist and Pan-African ideals. The colonial armed forces in Tanzania had been drawn from "seven ethnic groups dispersed countrywide", constituting five per cent of Tanzania's ethnic groups (Omari, 2002).

Following the 1964 army munity, which was regional and widespread throughout East Africa (Mazrui and Rothchild, 1967), Nyerere disbanded the mutinying army and planned to construct a new army. TANU youth were recruited to replace the military, from across the country's ethnic and status groups, as Nyerere called upon members of the TANU Youth

League, "wherever they are, to go to the local TANU office and enrol themselves. From this group we shall try to build a nucleus of a new army for the Republic of Tanganyika"(Omari, 2002, page 94). This created a new army that would depend upon membership to the socialist party, while the party neutralised possible challenges to its authority from the armed forces. This fusion of political ideology into the military went concurrent with appointment of political commissars in the military to ideologically orient the armed forces. As a result, the military's this recruitment, the new military ethos, and emerging civil-military relations ensured a concordance between the ruling party and armed forces while also ensuring civilian control over the military. Hence, Tanzania avoided coups, civil conflicts, and ethnopolitical rivalries.

While on the political front Tanzania is under a dominant party, the CCM, there is less political repression than Kenya's Moi or Uganda's post-colonial political uncertainties and repressions. What is unique about Tanzania is that despite socioeconomic underdevelopment the country did not suffer sufficient grievances to cause political unrest. Nyerere's Ujamaa was a kind of African socialism. Under Nyerere, "the central objective of Ujamaa was the attainment of a self-reliant socialist nation", though with resource limitations "Implementation was a major challenge" that afflicted Ujamaa (Ibhawoh and Dibua, 2003). The policy was aimed at coalescing peasant producers into villages of co-operative production, initially through voluntaristic emphasis that peasants should initiate control and run their villages themselves, a kind of local-level democracy, and later administrative coercion and compulsory villagization that practically suffered the slow transformation of the economy. As a result, "the increasingly bureaucratic implementation of the policy has acted as a barrier to political mobilisation and to the release of productive forces" (Raikes, 1975). As a result, Ujamaa was abandoned not because it was a bad policy strategy but because it required capacity and resources to operationalise it.

Soon Tanzania towed the path of capitalism and embraced Structural Adjustment Programs (SAPs) during the 1990s. Liberalised development replaced villagised development, through mechanisation and privatisation, the state withdrew from economic controls, mining rights were privatised and land reforms undertaken (Gibbon, 1995). When Jakaya Kikwete became president in the December 2005 presidential election, he continued with liberalisation programs, but was re-elected for a second term with 61% of the votes in October 2010. Under Kikwete,

Tanzania steadily grew at an estimated rate of 7% (Dagne, 2010). Challenges also erupted as growth was not equitable. In urban areas, petty street traders, the Machinga, responded to the political and socio-economic transformation by creating unique credit transactions that Ogawa has called "Mali Kauli", which are conducted by middlemen and microscale retailers, sustain urban credit transactions while also profiteering from these dealings through norms of reciprocity and mutual trust (Ogawa, 2006). Soon Tanzania suffered afflictions like land grabbing due to surging interests in agriculture, biofuels, tourism, hunting, forestry (Nelson et al., 2012), and the gas sector. Corruption is also on the rise and costing the country hugely in terms of resources, lost time, and distorted investments (Madaha, 2012).

In November 2015, John Pombe Magufuli was elected to replace Kikwete, as the CCM acquired another turn after more than 50 years in power. It remains to be seen whether the rapidly-developing mining and oil and gas industry will keep the pace of development consistent with the country's socio-political stability. President Magufuli has demonstrated enthusiasm for swift action to reforms the state's institutional infrastructure, fight corruption, cut down public expenditure and waste, prioritize infrastructure development, renegotiate deals, and undertake efficient governance to a level that borders on autocratic tendencies (Mwalupinde, 2017). Magufuli recently signed a deal with Uganda's Museveni to construct the East African Crude Oil Pipeline which will transport crude oil from western Uganda to the Tanzanian port of Tanga. It remains to be seen whether Magufuli will consolidate peace and security, resolve conflicts between mainland Tanzania and the island of Zanzibar, and undertake rapid development.

Book Structure and Contributors' Perspectives

The chapters in this book mainly used qualitative research methodology, relying on both primary and secondary data sources. Primary data was collected using in-depth interviews with key informants especially policy makers, development partners and academics. Observations and focus group discussionsmethods were also used. The secondary data collection methods included literature review of key documents such as academic publications, government and organisational reports, newspaper and magazine articles, and Internet sources. These were supplemented with in-depth and periodic peer review under the institutional framework of ACODE. The research process for this book took more than a decade, and it should not surprise the reader to find some of the content 'aged'.

This book volume is organized under twelve Chapters. The introduction provides an overview of the nexus between peace, democracy and development in Africa before underlining the East African experience of conflicts, democratic deficit, and socioeconomic underdevelopment that need urgent attention. It also discusses the steps taken by the AU to ensure that the continent is freed from protracted violent conflicts by silencing the guns by 2020.

Chapter two focuses on the civil war in Mali and the perception of threat posed by Islamist Jihadists and Al-Qaeda-linked terrorists to international peace and security. Based on extensive research field visits across West Africa in the past decade and more recently in Mali and using focus group discussions and semi-structured interviewees of key national and regional actors and civil society organisations, the author provides a critical understanding of the security problems posed by this complex and dynamic region in the post-Cold War period and the challenges its presents to the donor-driven peacebuilding. The chapter ends by concluding that despite the donor-driven Liberal peacebuilding-oriented French military intervention, Mali is a threat to international peace and security and it is set to shape the patterns of new conflicts, wars and security threats emanating from the Sahel and Maghreb regions in the coming decades. Mali clearly shows that military action and donor funding alone are not enough to end civil wars, win the long-term peace and address the fundamental problems associated with wars, terrorism, Islamist extremist and Jihadi economic opportunism in the Sahel region and West Africa, nor will they immediately lead to post-war peacebuild-ing and state reconstruction, especially when the French have indicated that the intervention in Mali is not about post-war nation building. The fundamental grievances of the Tuaregs and other northern groups still remain unresolved, whilst the majority of the Malian population live in extreme poverty. Mali and West Africa, like Afghanistan, Iraq and Libya, demonstrates the limits of donor-driven peacebuilding and brings into sharp focus the unintended consequences of Liberal peacebuilding.

Chapter three draws the reader's attention to Sierra Leone and the subvention of the social contract. While Sierra Leone is presented as having made significant progress in consolidating post-war peacebuilding and state reconstruction by organising three relatively free and fair democratic elections and the peaceful transfer of power, the author argues that a lot still remains to be done. Notwithstanding the putative success, post-war Sierra Leone is described as staring at fundamental grievances instigated by the decade-long civil war as well as subversion of the social contract which continue to create depressing socio-development indicators. The chapter concludes by drawing from a Constitutional Review Commission that was put in place and its recommendations which illustrate that all is not lost in post-war Sierra Leone. The argument is that the real challenge is what the ruling and governing elites will do to the revised progressive social contract constitution. That will be the litmus test as to whether Sierra Leone will emerge in the coming decade as a developed, effectively governed, inclusive middle income country.

Chapter four looks at the Conflict trap in north-eastern Uganda, a border region shared between Uganda and Kenya. The authors propose constitutional and legal reforms that would be necessary to break this legacy of armed and unarmed conflicts in the country that have gnawed at the marrow of peace, security, democracy, and development in the country. They propose constitutional reforms that can pave way for national reform processes that can feed into and influence constitutional amendments, such as on land acquisition, presidential age limit, and the President's proposals to deny bail for murder, rape, treason, defilement and riot suspects. These issues, if debated and consensual, can address the country's democracy deficits, resolve political conflicts, widen the democratic space, and continue Uganda's constitutional development.

In chapter five, the authors assess the relationship between parliamentary representation and livelihoods, focusing on representatives of Special Interest Groups (SIGs) in Uganda's parliament. Whether or not these forms of representation translate in actual livelihood improvements is a serious question for rethinking the choices and practices of parliamentary ring-fencing in democratising Africa. In chapter six, the authors assess the logic of participatory environmental decision making. Looking at the context of legislative representation of issues related to environment and natural resources in Uganda's 7th parliament (2001-2006). They reveal that the 7th Parliament, which operated under No-Party Movement System, ended a decade of constitutional rule under that democratic experiment that, while unique to Uganda in some respects at the time, provides useful lessons for thinking about parliamentary representation in Uganda under the post-2005 multiparty system. They reveal that high levels of members' absenteeism undermined parliament's performance on ENR and possibly other issues; that the strong influence of the executive undermined members' performance on ENR legislation; and politico-constitutional transitional process dominated the 7th parliament's time and energy. Consequently, only seven Bills were passed pertaining to ENR, and that none of the tabled Private Members Bills directly related to ENR. Participation and debates of members demonstrates MPs' sensitivity to ENR issues that directly affected their constituents, not broad national ENR future.

In chapter seven, the author examines the degree to which manifestos of political parties reflected environmental concerns, and reveals that at major political turning points, environmental issues are always relegated to the bottom line of the political agenda. Moreover, a young, inexperienced, poorly resourced opposition that focuses its energy on expanding its political space and unsitting the ruling National Resistance Movement (NRM), which diverts their attention from ENR issues. Chapter eight builds on the issues raised in chapter two. The authors examine the border conflict between neighbouring communities: the Karimojong and the Iteso, both of whom straddle the Uganda-Kenya border. Marginalisation of these communities often results in conflicts that are rooted inand reflect environmental scarcity, colonial legacy of marginalising the Karamoja region, unclear border demarcation along Katakwi and Moroto districts, and the transhuman lifestyle of the Karimojong. Politicization of border issues by political elites during elections; general political instability uncertainty; inadequacies in land governance all work to exacerbate these conflicts. Solving such disputes, therefore, requires depoliticisation, improvements in land governance, and a holistic approach to the Karamoja question in the Uganda-Kenya border region.

Chapter nine examines the budget process as a political process, underlining the political imperatives of resource allocation. Legislative budget oversight is critical for democratic governance in East Africa, since: (i) government accountability is successful when public officials are answerable for their actions and/or inactions; (ii) government efficiency and effectiveness in parliamentary oversight committees and the national audit institutions, both working independently but complementary, to ensure value for money; and (iii) equitable distribution of scarce resources at national level facilitates peace and stability in society. Therefore, positive outcomes on democratic governance are achievable if the administration of the legislature focuses on continuous training and other capacity-building initiatives necessary for individual legislators and the institution of Parliament to analyse budget documents and audit reports; provide the necessary IT infrastructure for quick access to information; fight corruption; and ensure timely checks upon the executive to prevent it from crossing its legally-constituted boundaries.

Chapter ten takes on another regional perspective like Chapter seven and assesses the participation of non-state stakeholders in the negotiations leading to the EAC customs union. The authors reveal that strong partnerships between governments, the private sector, and civil society were missing during negotiations contrary to the provisions of the Treaty on people-centred integration. This has implications for understanding regionalism: (i) the need to learn from the customs union to inform latter process like the common market and monetary union; (ii) examining the relationship between stakeholder participation in negotiations and implementation of resulting protocols; and (iii) comparative analysis of the nexus between stakeholder engagement and peaceable development initiatives in which prevention of disruptions, legitimacy, and conflict management measures are inbuilt in the negotiations and resulting protocols. To that extent, the EAC customs union was less a form of conflicts management measure unlike the European integration.

Chapter eleven examines the protection and promotion of farmers' rights in East Africa. The author explores and analyses the concept of farmers' rights and makes a case for countries in East Africa to recognise and adequately protect farmers' rights. This leads him to an exploration of the different policy options for the protection and promotion of farmers' rights in East Africa. He also makes a case a for why countries in East Africa should recognise and protect farmers' rights not just in the interest of food security but also in accordance with the provisions of the EAC Treaty and thus the East African basis of such protections.

Chapter twelve undertakes a philosophical examination of Community-Based Property Rights (CBPR), and dismisses the putative concepts with which it has been conflated. Tumushabe and Rwengabo then undertake a theoretical analysis that specifies the concept of property as it relates to other putative concepts, examine the legal basis of CBPR in international, regional, and national laws, and then examine the relevance of CBPR for peaceful development in East Africa. Chapter 12 integrates these ideas by linking Peace, Democracy and Development in Africa, and outlines the Challenges and Opportunities available in East Africa to transition the region to stability and progress.

References

African Union (2015) *Agenda 2063: The Africa We Want*. Addis Ababa: AU Commission.

Aseka, E. M. (2005) *Transformational Leadership in East Africa: Politics, Ideology and Community*. Kampala: Fountain Publishers.

Balkan, F. D. (2004) 'Kenya After Moi', *Foreign Affairs*, 83(1), pp. 87–100.

Branch, D. (2009) 'Defeating Mau Mau, Creating Kenya: Counterinsurgency, Civil War, and Decolonization', *African studies Series*. Cambridge: Cambridge University Press, (111).

Buell, R. L. (1928) 'The Destiny of East Africa', *Foreign Affairs*, 6(3), pp. 408–426.

Chingono, M. (2016) 'Violent Conflicts in Africa: Towards a Holistic Understanding', *A Journal of Social Science Research*, 3(2), pp. 199–218.

Dagne, T. (2010) 'Tanzania. Background and Current Conditions'. Washington DC: Congressional Research Service.

Davies-Vengoechea, X. (2004) 'A Positive Concept of Peace', in Kemp, G. and Fry, D. P. (eds) *Keeping the Peace: Conflict Resolution and Peaceful Societies around the World*. New York and London: Routledge.

Francis, D. J. (2005) *Uniting Africa, Building Regional Peace and Security Systems*. New Hampshire: Ashgate Plushing Company.

Francis, J. D. (2006) *Uniting Africa: Building Regional Peace and Security Systems*. Aldershot: Ashgate.

Gabe, J. (2013) 'US Official Says Kenya's Elections Have Consequences', *Voice of America*. New York. Available at: http://www.voanews.com/.

Galtung, J. (1964) 'An Editorial', *Journal of Peace Research*, 1(1), pp. 1–4. Available at: https://www.jstor.org/stable/422802.

Galtung, J. (1969) 'Violence, Peace, and Peace Research', , *Journal of Peace Research*, 6(3), pp. 167–191.

Gibbon, P. (ed.) (1995) *Liberalised Development in Tanzania: Studies on Accumulation Processes and Local Institutions*. Uppsala: Karolinska Institute.

Huntington, S. P. (1968) *Political Order in Changing Societies*. New Haven, London: Yale University Press.

Ibhawoh, B. and Dibua, J. I. (2003) 'Deconstructing Ujamaa: The Legacy of Julius Nyerere in the Quest for Social and Economic Development in Africa', *African Journal of Political Science*, 8(1), pp. 59–83.

ICC (2011) 'The Prosecutor v. William Samoei Ruto and Joshua Arap Sang'. Hague: ICC.

IDEA (2016) 'Promoting Democracy and Peace in Africa. The Role of the African Union', *Policy Brief*. Available at: www.idea.int/democracydialog (Accessed: 30 August 2017).

Kabwegyere, B. T. (1995) *The Politics of State Formation and Destruction in Uganda*. Kampala: Fountain Publishers Ltd.

Kanogo, T. (1987) *Squatters and the Roots of Mau Mau, 1905-63*. Baskerville: Oxford Publishing Services.

Kanyeihamba, G. W. (2002) *Constitutional and Political History of Uganda: From 1894 to the Present*. Kampala: Fountain Publishers Ltd.

Kategaya, E. T. (2006) *Impassioned for Freedom, Uganda, Struggle against Idi Amin*. Kampala: Wavah Books Ltd.

Khapoya, V. B. (1979) 'The Politics of Succession in Africa: Kenya after Kenyatta', *Africa Today*, 26(3), pp. 7–20.

Khisa, M. and Rwengabo, S. (2017) 'Beyond Legal Reforms in Understanding Opposition Underperformance', in Oloka-Onyango, J. and Ahikire, J. (eds) *Controlling Consent: Uganda's 2016 Elections*. Trento: NJ: Africa World Press.

Kiiza, J., Sabiti-Makara and Rakner, L. (2008) *Electoral Democracy in Uganda: Understanding the Institutional Processes and Outcomes of the 2006 Multiparty Elections*. Kampala: Fountain.

Korwa, A. G. and Munyae, I. M. (2001) 'Human Rights Abuse in Kenya Under Daniel Arap Moi, 1978- 2001', *African Studies Quarterly*, 5(1), pp. 1–16.

Lopes, C. (2015) 'Africa's Time', *New African Magazine*. An IC publication, (554). Available at: https://www.questia.com/magazine/1G1-432679465/it-is-africa-s-time.

Madaha, R. M. (2012) 'The Corruption Noose. Will Tanzania Ever Develop?', *Africa Review*, 4(1), pp. 48–64.

Mazrui, A. A. and Rothchild, D. (1967) 'The Soldier and the State in East

Africa. Some Theoretical Conclusions on the Army Mutinies of 1964', *The Western Political Quarterly*, 20(1), pp. 82–96.

McCandless, E. and Karbo, T. (eds) (2011) *Peace, Conflict and Development in Africa*. Costa Rica: University for Peace. Available at: http://www.upeace.org/pdf%5CREADER_webpages.pdf.

Moncrieffe, J. M. (2006) *Beyond Categories: Power, Recognition and the Conditions for Equity*. Background Paper for the World Development Report.

Moyo, D. (2008) *Dead Aid: Why Aid Makes Things Worse and How there is A Better Way for Africa*. New York: Farrar, Straus and Giroux.

Muriuki, G. (1979) 'Central Kenya in the Nyayo Era', *Africa Today*, 26(3), pp. 39–42.

Mutibwa, P. (2008) *The Buganda Factor in Uganda Politics*. Kampala: Fountain Publishers.

Mwalupinde, O. (2017) 'Magufuli's dilemma: corruption and the pursuit of democracy', *St Andrews Africa Summit Review*, 1, pp. 1–3. Available at: https://ojs.standrews.ac.uk/index.php/SAASUM/article/view/1 402/1071.

Nehma, A. and Zeleza, P. T. (eds) (2008) *The Roots of conflicts in Africa. The Causes & Costs*. London: James Curry.

Nelson, F., Sulle, E. and Lekaita, E. (2012) 'Land Grabbing and Political Transformation in Tanzania', in *Paper presented at the International Conference on Global Land Grabbing Cornell University*. Ithaca, NY. Available at: http://www.maliasili.org/wp content/uploads/2012/03 /LandGrabbinginTZ.pdf.

Ogawa, S. (2006) 'Earning among Friends" Business Practices and Creed among Petty Traders in Tanzania', *African Studies Quarterly*, 9(1–2), pp. 23–38.

Ogot, B. (2006) *My Footprints on the Sands of Time: An Autobiography*. Kisumu: Anyange Press Limited.

Omari, A. H. (2002) 'Ourselves To Know. Civil-military relations in Tanzania'. Pretoria: Institute for Security Studies. Available at: https://www.issafrica.org/uploads/OURSELVESOMARI.PDF (Accessed: 22 June 2016).

Raikes, P. L. (1975) 'Ujamaa and rural socialism', *Review of African Political Economy*, 2(3), pp. 33–52.

Republic of Kenya (2008) *Report of Commission of Inquiry into Post-Election Violence*. Nairobi: Justice Philip Waki Commission Report.

Rosato, S. (2003) 'The Flawed Logic of Democratic Peace Theory',

American Political Science Review, 97(4), pp. 585–602.

Rwengabo, S. (2013) 'Regime Stability in Post-1986 Uganda: Counting the Benefits of Coup-Proofing', *Armed Forces and Society*, 39(3), pp. 531–559.

Rwengabo, S. (2015) 'AMISOM and African-Centred Solutions to Peace and Security Challenges', *AfSol Journal*, 1(1), pp. 91–138.

Rwengabo, S. (2016a) 'Institutional Design and the Implementation of the APSA', *Africa Development*, XLI(4), pp. 107–138.

Rwengabo, S. (2016b) *Nation Building in Africa: Lessons from Tanzania for South Sudan, MINDS Discussion Paper.* Dar es Salaam.

Rwengabo, S. (2017) *Security Cooperation in the East African Community.* Trento NJ: Africa World Press.

Sen, A. (1988) 'The Concept of Development', in Chenery, H. and Srinivasan, T. N. (eds) *Handbook of Development Economics.* Harvard: Havard University, pp. 10–24.

Stan, F. (2004) *The Security-Development Nexus: Conflict, Peace and Development in the 21st Century.* New York. Available at: https://www.ipinst.org/wp-content/uploads/publications/security_dev_nexus.pdf (Accessed: 30 August 2017).

Stewart, F. and O'Sullivan, M. (1998) *Democracy, Conflict and Development - Three Cases.* 15. Oxford. Available at: https://www.google.com/url?sa=t&rct=j&q=&esrc=s&source=web&cd=2&cad=rja&uact=8&ved=2ahUKEwjZwr-WnMXgAhWhSxUIHe-qAdgQFjABegQICRAC&url=http%3A%2F%2Fwww3.qeh.ox.ac.uk%2Fpdf%2Fqehwp%2Fqehwps15.pdf&usg=AOvVaw1lu7fEr2RjeV2JgXM-HBQH.

Tamarkin, M. (1979) 'From Kenyatta to Moi: The Anatomy of a Peaceful Transition of Power', *Africa Today*, 26(3), pp. 21–37.

The Independent (2010) 'Mao's Election and Secession of the Nile State', 11 September. Available at: http://www.independent.co.ug/index.php/column/guest-column/68-guest-column/2590-maos-election-and-secession-of-the-nile-state. (Accessed: 11 September 2010).

Tripp, A. M. (2010) *Museveni's Uganda: Paradoxes of Power in Hybrid Regime.* London: Lynne Rienner.

Vines, A. (2013) 'A decade of the African Peace And Security Architecture', *International Affairs*, 89(1), pp. 89–109.

CHAPTER TWO

Limits of Liberal Peace in Africa

David J. Francis[1]

Introduction

The civil war in Mali and the perception of threat posed by Islamist Jihadists and Al-Qaeda-linked terrorists to international peace and security led to the French military intervention in January 2013 to end the terrorist take-over of Mali, prevent the collapse of the state and spread of insecurity and instability in the conflict-prone and fragile regions of West Africa and the Sahel as well as protect France's strategic national interests. But what were the real reasons for France's pre-emptive military intervention in Mali and what do the French and their allied UN, ECOWAS, and African Union (AU) conflict stabilisation interventions say about donor-driven peacebuilding in Africa, often framed as Liberal peacebuilding intervention?

According to the Afro-pessimist literature and international media coverage, the West Africa region has emerged as the new threat to international peace and security at the beginning of the 21st century (Kaplan, 1994; *The Economist*, 2000). Liberal peacebuilding in all its diverse manifestations has been offered as the panacea to manage and resolve the 'chaos' in this resource-rich but troubled region. It is therefore not surprising that the sub-region has seen a myriad of forcible and non-forcible interventions by multiple actors and agencies including key Western governments; global governance institutions such as the United Nations; the leading sub-regional organisation -the Economic Community of West African States (ECOWAS) and its military-security wing -ECOMOG; private military companies and mercenaries. It is important to stress that far from being the 'Afro-pessimist's paradise'

---

[1] This chapter was written in 2014 when the Professor served as Head of Department of Peace Studies at the University of Bradford, UK

(Buzan and Waever, 2003), the West African region, despite its challenges, has emerged as one of the fastest growing economies with the capacity to manage and resolve some of its violent civil wars through assertive regional peacekeeping thereby creating the conducive environment for fragile peace, security for ordinary peoples, democratic consolidation and socio-economic progress. In simple terms, West Africa is not a 'Hopeless' region. Notwithstanding, the problems and challenges faced by West Africa have been used to justify the donor-driven peacebuilding intervention, framed as Liberal Peacebuilding.

But West Africa demonstrates the limits of donor-driven peacebuilding and its underlying liberal peacebuilding intervention in Africa. Based on extensive research field visits across West Africa in the past decade and more recently in Mali, using focused-group discussions and semi-structured interviewees of key national and regional actors and civil society organisations, the author provides a critical understanding of the security problems posed by this complex and dynamic region in the post-Cold War period and the challenges its presents to the donor-driven peacebuilding.

What does Liberal Peace say about West Africa?

The failed and collapsed states in West Africa reflects all the basic assumptions of liberal peacebuilding. The sub-region has been the largest 'recipient' of international peacekeeping, peacebuilding and state reconstruction intervention programmes in countries such as Liberia, Sierra Leone, Mali, Cote d'Ivoire andGuinea Bissau. The prominence of external interventions to end violent wars, build peace and reconstruct failed and collapsed states has generated a controversial debate amongst policy practitioners and academics, questioning the efficacy, underlying assumptions and motivations driving these interventions. To be clear, Liberal Peacebuilding is premised on the Liberal Peace thesis derived from the Kantian principles that posit that economic interdependence, democracy and the rule of law create the durable foundations for world peace (Kant, 1917; Willett, 2005; Richmond, 2014). But what are the basic assumptions of liberal peacebuilding? Since the 1990s, Liberal peacebuilding has led to four basic assumptions used to explain the imposition of liberal peacebuilding agenda not only in West Africa but in other parts of the world. Firstly, that unstable, poverty-ridden, fragile/ failed and collapsed states pose a threat to international peace and security, often perceived as the 'coming anarchy', the 'new threat' in the post-Cold War and post-9/11 eras because they serve as breeding ground and safe havens for terrorist networks and transnational criminal groups.

The much-quoted example, is the failed state of Somalia and how it poses a threat to international piracy and maritime commerce (Kaplan, 1994). According to Fukuyama, 'weak and failing states have arguably become the single most important problem for international order' (Fukuyama, 2004). The West African sub-region reflects this basic liberal peacebuilding assumption. The region has been the home of some of the worst forms of state failure and collapse as well as bloody civil wars instigated by fundamental grievances and violent competition amongst the corrupt ruling and governing elites over strategic mineral resources and access to state power and its patrimonial resources. From extreme poverty to the Ebola epidemic and to perennial violent wars and armed conflicts and terrorist attacks such as the abduction of more than 200 girls by the Nigerian terrorist group, Boko Haram, in April 2014, clearly illustrates that the sub-region is not only a threat to Africa but to international peace and security.

The second assumption is that, this perception of threat posed by West Africa justifies the imposition of donor-driven peacebuilding intervention projects based on the introduction of: democratisation (i.e., periodic elections), rule of law, marketisation (free market economy based on neo-liberal economic policies), and public institution building. The violent wars and terrorist attacks as well as non-military sources of threat to security such as drug trafficking, arms smuggling and the Ebola pandemic have created opportunities for externally-driven diverse forms of military and non-forcible 'humanitarian' interventions to stabilise the so-called disorder in West Africa. The military-security interventions have led to peacekeeping and conflict stabilisation deployments by ECOWAS-ECOMOG and the UN, mercenaries and private military companies. The socio-economic and political interventions have led to donor-driven democratisation, economic liberalisation and state reconstruction interventions in the war-torn and post-conflict countries such as Liberia, Sierra Leone, Cote d'Ivoire, Mali and Guinea Bissau. The underlying principle of this assumption is that it links state (re)building as a key aspect of post-war peacebuilding because without viable and functioning state authority and institutions, conflict and instability will continue to threaten international peace and security (Francis, 2012).

The third liberal peacebuilding assumption, according to Willett, is that it has led to an international consensus on peacebuilding and policy convergence between the 'Security' and 'Development' community with the increasing 'securitisation of development', and the 'developmentalisat ion of security', what Cramer describes as 'a new kind of development in reverse'(Willett, 2005). West Africa has been the largest recipient of post-war peacebuilding and state reconstruction projects funded by the donor community in an attempt to 'buy peace' in this mineral-rich but badly governed region. This is a manifestation of the donor-driven peacebuilding. The fourth basic assumption is that peacebuilding in transition societies in West Africa now casts peacebuilding assistance as apolitical, technical and a practical challenge (G8 Africa Action Plan, 2005; Willett, 2005; Cramer, 2006; Buur et al., 2007; Chandler, 2007; Newman and Paris, 2009; Paris, 2010). This assumption is not backed by credible evidence and if anything, Liberal peacebuilding interventions have emerged as highly political activities.

In general, Liberal peacebuilding in Africa has been much criticised because the neo-liberal political and economic interventions only end up creating 'phantom states', lacking in local ownership and legitimacy and the interventions fail to address the root causes and fundamental grievances of the conflict. In fact, the donor-driven Liberal peacebuilding interventions are often embedded in Western-centric political and economic assumptions about the state and state-society relations, often smacking of neo-colonialism. They are not only framed as short-term, quick-fix and exit strategy oriented interventions, but they are often motivated by the pursuit and protection of strategic Western and donor interests as well as Western business interests (Willett, 2005; Chandler, 2006; Francis, 2012). Even though Kant had earlier warned about the unpleasant aspects and limitations of Liberal peace, the global experiment with Liberal peacebuilding and its corollary, donor-driven peacebuilding continues unabated with massive investment of finance, economic, military and diplomatic capital to enforce liberal democracy and open market economies in regions such as West Africa. The on-going Mediterranean migrant crisis that has claimed the lives of more than 3,000 desperate migrants attempting to cross from Libya and Syria to Europe is an example of the unpleasant aspect of the Liberal peace intervention by President Sarkozy and Prime Minister Cameroon in 2011 to end the dictatorship of Col. Gaddaffi and make Libya conducive to Western business. It is against this background that the conflict in Mali took place and the inevitable French military intervention, underpinned by liberal peacebuilding imperatives and pursuit of French strategic interests.

Mali: a New Kind of Civil War

The current civil war in Mali is a complex mix of long-term fundamental grievances by diverse actors and groups. To understand this, we have to look at the context that produced this current armed conflict, the most serious since political independence from France in 1960. Mali is a landlocked state surrounded by seven neighbouring countries. With a population of 15.8 million, Mali is one of the poorest countries in the world and has suffered decades of drought, persistent food shortage, locust infestations, civil wars and recurrent political instability, with 64% of the population living below the poverty line (UNDP, 2015). The depressing socio-economic and development indicators are compounded by the fact that the country is highly dependent on gold and Uranium mining (the 3rd and 4th largest producer) and agricultural exports for revenue. Mali is constantly threatened by spill-over of violent conflicts from neighbouring countries and with large swaths of porous borders, the country has been affected by cross-border banditry, kidnapping and terrorism.

The immediate post-colonial political history, 1960 – 1991, was blighted by one-party rule and military dictatorships. This unstable post-independence period led to the informalisation of the state governing institutions by the corrupt ruling and governing elites to serve their vested neo-patrimonial interests. The ensuing personalised rule and bad governance led not only to the politicisation of the army and security agencies but also to the fragility of the state. By the time democratic politics was re-introduced in Mali in 1992, with the election of the first democratic president, Alpha Konare, Mali had no credible foundation for democratic politics and functioning democratic institutions and practices. Between 1992 – 2012, Mali was touted by the international community as the beacon of democratic example in a West African region torn by civil wars and authoritarian regimes. In fact, during this period, Mali was show-cased as a 'success' story of donor-driven/Liberal peace-driven democracy building experiment. The reality was that Mali was nothing more than a façade democracy and a fragile state unable to address its fundamental political, governance, security and socio-development challenges (Lacher, 2008; Gettleman, 2010; Fearon and Laitin, 2011; Straus, 2012).

The recent Tuareg rebellion against the government of Mali was because of their marginalisation and exclusion from the state governing socio-economic and political processes. Historically, the Tuaregs are nomadic Berber people who lived in the Sahel and Saharan regions of Mali, Niger, Algeria, Burkina Faso and Libya. They called the Tuareg homeland Azawad. The fundamental grievance of the Tuaregs is based on their claim of decades of discrimination and exclusion from the political and economic processes by successive Bamako-based governments. The Tuaregs have therefore taken up arms against the Malian government, fighting for a separate state and rights of the Tuareg minority. Between 1985 and 2009, the government signed several peace deals and ceasefires agreements after a very violent Tuareg rebellion, without addressing, on a long-term basis, the fundamental problems of marginalisation and exclusion of the Tuareg minority. The promise by successive governments for greater political autonomy and devolved rule for the Tuaregs in the north never materialised because successive governments only ended up co-opting high-profile Tuareg leaders into the neo-patrimonial governance of the state. After the collapse of the Gaddaffi regime in Libya in 2011, heavily-armed Tuaregs and non-Tuaregs, who had been part of Gaddaffi's army, returned to northern Mali with sophisticated weaponry (NOREF, 2012). Together with previous Tuareg rebel groups, they formed MNLA in 2011 as the political – military platform to continue the fight for self-rule. It was this group of heavily armed and well-trained MNLA-led fighters that routed the government forces in March 2012 and declared northern Mali the independent state of Azawad. It is important to stress that the Tuaregs are only one of several ethnic groups in the north of the country with armed elements and particular grievances.

But the Tuareg rebellions in the north have always been complicated by the link with and involvement of Islamist Jihadist groups and the threat they pose to Mali, its neighbours, especially the wider regions of North Africa, the Sahel and West Africa. These security and terror threats led to the signing of bilateral military and security agreements and the formation of a Joint Counter-Terrorism Command between 2009 – 2010 with Niger, Algeria and Mauritania to tackle Islamist extremism and terrorism in the region. As the crisis unfolded in Mali, Ansar Al Dine and the Movement for Unity & Jihad in West Africa (MUJAO) expanded the Islamist Jihadist rebellion beyond the Tuaregs by incorporating other ethnic groups historically opposed to the Tuareg rebellion such as the Songhai and Bella groups. Even before the outbreak of the Malian crisis, northern Mali had become a breeding ground and safe haven for diverse groups of Jihadists and militants led by AQIM (Keenan, 2009). These groups not only exploited the fundamental grievances of the local population against the government of Mali and its repressive military and security forces but also organised a sophisticated criminal enterprise that involved drug and human trafficking, arms and cigarette smuggling and kidnapping of western nationals for ransom. This criminal enterprise became a valuable source of funding and was profitable for all stakeholders including corrupt government of Mali officers, state security agencies who were supposed to be fighting them, local leaders, separatist rebels and Islamist extremists. The Sahelian criminal enterprise and its profitable economic and financial opportunities made Jihadi insurgency a lucrative economic activity. As such, economic opportunism became a motivation for the growing number of Jihadi groups in the region (Marchal, 2012).

In effect, poverty, bad governance, marginalisation and exclusion of large sections of the Malian populace from the political and economic processes and failure to address fundamental grievances by the ruling and governing elites and their French backers in Mali created the breeding ground for Islamist extremists to gain a foothold and organise a profitable criminal enterprise that became mutually beneficial to all stakeholders. At the outbreak of the new civil war, the country was already on the verge of implosion because of the fragile nature of the state, the effect of decades of bad governance and the ineffective political and economic management of the state and the corrosive effects of the neo-liberal Structural Adjustment economic policies imposed by the IMF and World Bank. Both Tuaregs and the diverse Islamist groups are united in their fight against the common enemy, the government of Mali.

The current armed conflict is a product of three distinct but interrelated types of conflicts that have coalesced to produce the civil war. First, it is a secessionist rebellion by Tuareg ethnic groups in northern Mali fighting for a separate independent state. Second, the crisis in Mali is a political and constitutional crisis occasioned by the military overthrow of the democratically elected government. Third, the conflict is also an attempt by Islamist Jihadists to militarily takeover Mali and establish a terrorist state based on Sharia Islamic law.

The trigger for the political crisis was sparked off in March 2012 when Tuareg rebels attacked towns in northern Mali, signalling the start of a new armed rebellion. The government of President Amadou Toumane Toure (ATT) and the armed forces of Mali demonstrated their lack of capacity and ability to deal with the new Tuareg rebellion. Malian soldiers felt under-resourced to respond to the new Tuareg insurgency. As such, disgruntled soldiers turned a mutiny against President Toure for his ineffective response to the Tuareg rebellion, into a military coup on 22 March 2012 that deposed the president and suspended constitutional rule, ahead of planned democratic elections in April 2012. The military junta led by Capt. Amadou Sanogo, promised to end the Tuareg rebellion in the north. As expected, the West African regional group, ECOWAS, and the African Union mobilised the international community not to recognise the junta and expelled the military regime from the regional and continental organisations.

The military coup provided the strategic opportunity for the Tuareg rebels who had now formed an alliance with the Islamist Jihadist group, Ansar Al Dine, to tighten their military control over large parts of northern Mali, beyond the control of both government and armed forces of Mali. In April 2012, Tuareg separatist rebels, now formally constituted as the National Movement of the Liberation of Azawad (MNLA) and in alliance with Ansar Al Dine, seized control of the whole of northern Mali and declared an independent Tuareg state of Azawad. This declaration only worsened the political crisis and showed the inability of the military junta to deal with the deepening conflict. Concerted international pressure forced the junta to hand over political power to a civilian interim government led by President DioncoundaTraore in April 2015.

Despite the installation of civilian political authority, the junta leaders were still the key players and effectively, the de facto leaders of Mali. In addition, the strategic military alliance between the Tuareg MNLA rebels and its Ansar Al Dine and Al Qaeda allies, led to rapid military advances that saw the capture of the main northern cities of Timbuktu, Gao and Kidal. But Ansar Al Dine and its Jihadist allies soon emerged as the main power in the alliance with the MNLA rebels and hijacked the Tuareg separatist rebellion to serve their Jihadi and economic opportunism cause. The declaration of northern Mali as an independent Islamic state - Islamic State of Azawad- ruled by Islamic Sharia Law, was endorsed by

Al Qaeda in the Islamic Maghreb (AQIM) and other Jihadist groups in North Africa and the Sahel.

The unstable political and military situation led to the formation of a Transitional Government of National Unity headed by Prime Minister Cheick Modibo Diarra in August 2012 and it included five close allies of the Junta leader, Capt. Sanogo. But the eminent advance on the seat of government in Bamako by the militarily strong and co-ordinated Islamist extremists and their MNLA allies forced the international community into action. In November 2012, ECOWAS, with the support of the African Union and UN, agreed on a co-ordinated military intervention force to recapture northern Mali, but was scheduled for deployment in September 2013. As the political crisis unravelled, the Islamist Jihadists and their allies attacked and captured the central city of Konna on 10January 2013 and planned to advance on Bamako.

This military attack on Konna changed the direction of the crisis because events on the ground now dictated the nature and urgency of the response to the Malian crisis, shifting the focus from political dialogue to military action. The eminent attack and possible capture of Bamako and the potential consequences on Mali, its neighbours and the volatile West Africa region as well as French strategic interests, led to the decisive French military intervention in Mali on 11 January 2013. Based on extensive interviews in Bamako, it is instructive to note that there was no verifiable evidence to confirm that there was eminent rebel/Jihadists attack on Bamako, but the French interpreted that the military successes of the Jihadists as a credible threat to justify pre-emptive military intervention. The preponderant French military intervention, supported by Malian troops, the ECOWAS-led AFISMA forces and other western countries, in less than three weeks, ended the Tuareg separatist rebellion, recaptured all major cities in northern Mali, dispersed the Islamist rebels, most of whom melted into the civilian population and tactically retreated into the mountain ranges, caves and the inhospitable desert terrain that they are familiar with.

The French-led ECOWAS and donor-driven military, political, diplomatic and financial interventions were designed to end the disorder in Mali because of the perception that the civil war threatened France's national security and strategic interests. The French intervention achieved its immediate and short-term objective, preventing the takeover of Bamako by Islamist extremists and the emergence of a terrorist state, ending the secessionist rebellion in northern Mali and helping the government of Mali re-establish its control and sovereignty over its territories. The French military intervention led to the deployment of AFISMA (African-led International Support Mission to Mali) and the UN peacekeeping force, MINUSMA. As part of the donor-driven peacebuilding logic based on short-term, quick fix and exit strategy oriented interventions, France immediately handed security responsibility over to MINUSMA (UNSC, 2013) in May 2013 and organised an international donor conference for peacebuilding and post-war state reconstruction in Mali that pledged US $4 billion. With the support of the international community and MINUSMA, France imposed liberal democracy in Mali even before all the guns were silent, with the holding of presidential and general elections between July-August 2013. The 'Phantom state' and new government propped up by France has not been able to address the fundamental grievances of the Tuareg separatists, opposition parties and militant Islamist groups. Between September 2013 – August 2015, there have been a series of violent attacks by Tuareg separatists and the Al Qaeda-linked Jihadists and ISIS terrorists against the Malian forces, UN bases and troops as well as Western nationals. By all indications, the French-led Liberal peacebuilding intervention has not created peace and security in Mali and seems incapable of winning the peace in the long-term because the fundamental grievances and root causes of the civil war are still left largely unresolved.

French Military Intervention in Mali and the Pursuit of Strategic Interests

The civil war led to a range of external and regional military, political and diplomatic interventions to resolve the conflict. The interventions can be broadly categorised as external including France and other key western states and intergovernmental organisations including ECOWAS, AU, EU and UN. All of these intervening actors are promoters, sponsors and agencies of the donor-driven Liberal peacebuilding agenda. France was the dominant player and its preponderant military intervention was the most significant in bringing about a rapid and decisive military end to the war. In justifying the reasons for French military intervention, President Hollande stated that France had no alternative but to intervene and prevent the emergence of a terrorist state that will have serious national security repercussions for France and the West. The collapse of the state of Mali and the inability of the armed forces to defend the country and stop the military advances of the separatist rebels and their Islamist allies, coupled with the failure of deployment of troops from African countries, France was therefore forced to act unilaterally, but with the approval of the international community including the UN Security Council Permanent Members and African regional actors. The legality of the French military invention was never in doubt because France has an historic colonial obligation to respond to a request from the Interim President of Mali for French support and intervention to end the crisis, even though the interim president had no democratic mandate.

In addition, the UN Security Council Resolution 2085 which was facilitated by France, had authorised the deployment of an ECOWAS-led AFISMA intervention force. By all indications, the French intervention was a pre-emptive military strike against Islamist rebels in Mali. Worthy of note is that President Hollande had earlier refused to intervene in support of beleaguered President Bozize of Central Africa Republic (CAR) in December 2012 (Martin, 1985; The Ticklish, 2011; Kinshasa, 2011; Melly, 2013). The apparent U-turn on Mali was because of the threat posed by Mali and how this resonates with the domestic audience, i.e., the emergence of a terrorist state and its impact on France – very much using the mantra of the Liberal peacebuilding basic assumption that disorder exists in Mali and it is the responsibility of France to restore order.

In justifying the intervention, the French Defence Minister, Jean-Yves Le Drian, stated that: *'The threat is that a terrorist state will be created near Europe and France . . . we had to react before it was too late'* (Daneshkhu, 2013). France had maintained a consistent position on the civil war in Mali and used its political influence and leadership at the UN Security Council, the EU, AU and ECOWAS to mobilise international support to resolve the armed conflict. Throughout the crisis, France staunchly supported military intervention to prevent rebels and Islamists takeover of the whole of Mali, but preferred African forces to do the fighting. Based interviews in Paris, Bamako and Abuja (ECOWAS HQs) the failure to deploy African troops, in the face of eminent rebel and Islamist advance on Bamako, forced France into action.

President Hollande on his visit to Mali, three weeks after French military intervention, was given a rapturous welcome by the Government and people of Mali and treated like a hero, in scenes reminiscence of President Sarkozy's visit to Benghazi in Libya after the fall of Gaddaffi's regime in 2011 or President Bush's *'Mission Accomplished'* statement on Afghanistan in May 2003 on board the USS Abraham Lincoln aircraft carrier. President Hollande and the majority of French citizens saw the link between the threat posed by Islamist militants in Mali and the threats from its own domestic Islamist extremism and terrorism. The logic of the French intervention is that failure to act in Mali will inevitably spiral out of control with direct impact within France.

The decision by President Hollande to decisively intervene in Mali has had a positive impact on his political fortunes and the image of France. For most of his first year in office, President Hollande was criticised as too soft, overly consensual and not capable of decisive actions. As one media analyst puts it, the president has suddenly *'become a new kind of leader'* (Schofield, 2013). Once again, foreign military intervention helped to bolster the image of a president whose domestic political rating was in decline (Le Parisien, 2013). In addition, France's international image was enhanced by its leadership to militarily take on and *'defeat'* the separatist and Islamist rebels in Mali. In effect, Mali became a crucial test for the largely untested foreign policy approach of President Hollande, whose first year in office was embroiled in domestic issues. The intervention in Mali shows that France is not about to end its long history of military interventions in Africa, often dictated by imperatives of national security and strategic interest, and largely framed by the opaque France Afrique tradition (Chafer, 1992, 2002; Gregory, 2000; Taylor and Williams, 2004; Charbonneau, 2008).

President Hollande's claim that France has *'no interest other than the goal of fighting against terrorism'* was one that should have been treated with scepticism. I argue that the French military intervention in Mali was to protect its vast economic interests and energy security in neighbouring Niger, in pursuit of achieving core objectives of the donor-driven peacebuilding (Chafer, 2002). The spillover of the conflict in Niger and the potential implosion of that country will continue to have a devastating impact on French economic interests and energy security. The pre-emptive military intervention in Mali was, in effect, a strategy to protect French economic and energy security interests in Niger. France has significant economic and Uranium mining interests in Niger. The civil war in neighbouring Mali was perceived as a serious threat to Niger considering the fact that employees of the French Nuclear Company,

Areva operating in Niger and French engineers had been kidnapped and smuggled across the border to Mali for ransom. To put this in perspective, France depends on Uranium imports from Niger for its energy security. Nuclear power is the primary source of electricity in France and it is described as a *'success story'* for producing cheap and CO2-free energy. In 2004 alone, France produced 425.8 TWh out of the total product of 540.6 TWh of electricity, i.e., 78.8% from nuclear power, the highest in the world.

In economic and financial terms, France is the largest exporter of electricity in the world, with an estimated €3 billion annually in sales. The two main electricity generation companies, Areva and EDF (Electricite de France) operate the 59 nuclear plants in France. French nuclear power industry depend heavily on the Uranium from its two uranium mines in Niger, namely, SOMAIR (open pit mine) and COMINAK (underground mine). These mines are owned by a French-led consortium and operated by French interests. Therefore, the security and stability of Niger is of vital national security interest to France.

When Islamist militants launched two co-ordinated attacks on the towns of Agadez and Arlit in May 2013 on the French military base and the largest Areva Uranium mine, killing 23 soldiers and civilians, France did not hesitate to send in Special Forces to destroy the terrorist groups responsible for the suicide attack. Based on this, it is reasonable to conjecture that the pre-emptive military intervention in Mali, was in effect, a foreign economic policy strategy to protect and secure French Nuclear industry and its energy security, especially against the backdrop of the current economic recession and austerity in France. In effect, the France Afrique policy is far from being a thing of the past. Under Hollande, it was not only alive but expanding rapidly whereby France was set to replace the US military dominance in Africa. With the taste of 'success' in Mali, French military bases and networks are now present across sub-Saharan Africa whereby *'Operation Burkhane'* saw the deployment of 3,000 troops in five African countries to fight terrorism and Jihadism and to protect France's strategic interests, often distinguished as Liberal Peacebuilding intervention.

Conclusion

Despite the donor-driven Liberal peacebuilding-oriented French military intervention, Mali is a threat to international peace and security and it is set to shape the patterns of new conflicts, wars and security threats emanating from the Sahel and Maghreb regions in the coming decades (Karen and Sherman, 2003; Duyvesteyn and Angstrom, 2005; Francis, 2005). The main security concern in Western capitals is that the Al Qaeda Franchise and more recently, ISIS, should not be given the opportunity to establish themselves in Mali. What is more, Mali is situated in a volatile, unstable and conflict-prone West Africa region. The neighbouring countries have had their own share of civil wars, Islamist Jihadists and terrorist activities. The last thing any neighbouring state wants is a failed state on its doorstep, exporting violent extremism and terrorism for which they are ill-prepared to deal with.

Since the French intervention, there have been increasing attacks against French citizens, with 15 hostages taken by Islamist extremists in the region and described as retaliatory attacks. French nationals have become the most targeted and prized hostages taken by terrorist groups in the region. Despite domestic support for French military intervention, there have been fears of the possible security risks and terrorist reprisal against French nationals, cities and forces in Mali as well as targeted kidnappings of French citizens. Even before the outbreak of the Malian crisis between 2010 – 2012; there have been increasing targeted kidnappings of French citizens by Islamist extremists in the region for ransom payment. The French intervention has heightened the security threats against the 30,000 French citizens in West Africa. There is increasing concern that some militant extremists amongst France's five million Muslim population, the majority of whom are from North Africa and West Africa, may use this intervention in Mali to seek 'revenge' on French soil. These fears are based on the fact that France has had a long battle in the 1990s with Islamist extremists in France. The intervention in Mali led to a rise in domestic terror threat level, with President Hollande promising to increase protection at public building and transport networks. But this did not prevent the November 2015 ISIS terrorist attack in Paris that killed 130 people, the *'Charlie Hebdo'* newspaper, killing 17 people and the Paris Jewish Supermarket attack in 2014, in which one of the terrorists described the attack as *'totally legitimate'* and a revenge attack for France's intervention in Mali and other Muslim countries.

What is more, Mali's domestic political, governance and security problems are far from over with the intervention of French forces to impose Liberal peacebuilding that benefits France and the West. The Tuareg rebellion is only contained but not resolved, the political and military situation is chaotic with the army exerting a powerful, but destructive influence in the governance of this fragile state. This prevailing domestic situation, in the face of extreme poverty, marginalisation and absence of essential social services, creates the breeding ground for recruitment to extremist ideas and the conducive environment for the continuation of insurgency warfare against French forces. Islamist extremists in Mali and the region feed on local grievances and they do take advantage of the state weakness and lack of control over large swaths of ungovernable territory in northern Mali. In addition, the corrupt ruling and governing elites in the region exploit the Al Qaeda terrorist and Jihadi brand for criminal enterprise and profit by not doing enough to end kidnaping of foreign nationals for profit.

This complex domestic situation and conflict environment will inevitably draw France into a *'war of occupation'* by the former colonial master and thus become an effective propaganda tool for recruitment to the Jihadist cause in Mali. Mali clearly shows that military action and donor funding alone are not enough to end civil wars, win the long-term peace and address the fundamental problems associated with wars, terrorism, Islamist extremist and Jihadi economic opportunism in the Sahel region and West Africa, nor will they immediately lead to post-war peacebuilding and state reconstruction, especially when the French have indicated that the intervention in Mali is not about post-war nation building. Simply put, the French-led Liberal peacebuilding in Mali was primarily about ending violence and war and not about long-term peacebuilding. The fundamental grievances of the Tuaregs and other northern groups still remain unresolved, whilst the majority of the Malian population live in extreme poverty. Mali and West Africa, like Afghanistan, Iraq and Libya, demonstrates the limits of donor-driven peacebuilding and brings into sharp focus the unintended consequences of Liberal peacebuilding.

References

Buur, L., Jensen, S. and Stepputat, F. (eds) (2007) *The Security-Development Nexus: expressions of sovereignty and securitisation in Southern Africa.* Cape Town: HSRC Press.

Buzan, B. and Waever, O. (2003) *Regions and Powers: the structure of International Security.* CUP.

Chafer, T. (1992) 'French African Policy: Towards Change', *African Affairs*, 91(362), pp. 37–51.

Chafer, T. (2002) 'Franco-African Relations: No Longer So Exceptional', *African Affairs*, 101(404), pp. 343–363.

Chandler, D. (2006) *Empire in Denial: The Politics of State-Building.* London: Pluto Press.

Chandler, D. (2007) 'The Security-Development nexus and the rise of "anti-foreign policy", *Journal of International Relations and Development*, 10, p. 362.

Charbonneau, B. (2008) *France and the New Imperialism: Security policy in sub-Saharan Africa.* Aldershot: Ashgate.

Cramer, C. (2006) *Civil War is not a Stupid Thing: accounting for violence in developing countries.* Hurst Publishers Ltd.

Daneshkhu, S. (2013) 'Mali puts pressure on French Foreign Policy', *The Financial Times*, 13 January.

Duyvesteyn, I. and Angstrom, J. (eds) (2005) *Rethinking the Nature of War.* Abingdon: Franck Cass.

Fearon, J. and Laitin, D. (2011) 'Sons of the soil, migrants, and civil war', *World Development*, 39(2), pp. 199–211.

Francis, D. (2012) *When War Ends.* Ashgate.

Francis, D. J. (2005) *Uniting Africa, Building Regional Peace and Security Systems.* New Hampshire: Ashgate Plushing Company.

Fukuyama, F. (2004) *Statebuilding: Governance and World Order in the Twenty First Century.* London: Profile Books.

G8 Africa Action Plan (2005) *Progress Report by the G8: African Personal Representatives on the implementation of the African Action Plan.* London: G8.

Gettleman, J. (2010) 'Africa's endless wars: why the continent's wars never end', *Foreign Policy 178*, pp. 73–75.

Gregory, S. (2000) 'The French Military in Africa: Past and Present', *African Affairs*, 99(396), pp. 435–448.

Kant, I. (1917) *Perpetual Peace.* London: Allen & Unwin.

Kaplan, R. (1994) 'The Coming Anarchy', *Atlantic Monthly*, February.

Karen, B. and Sherman, J. (eds) (2003) *The Political Economy of Armed Conflict. Beyond Greed and Grievance*. London: Lynne Rienner Publishers, Inc.

Keenan, J. (2009) *The Dark Sahara: America's War on Terror in Africa*. London: Pluto.

Kinshasa, L. (2011) 'Neocolonial crisis in Ivory Coast is a part of imperialism's crisis!', *African Socialist International*.

Lacher, W. (2008) 'Actually Existing Security: The Political Economy of the Saharan Threat', *Security Dialogue*, 39(4), pp. 383–405.

Le Parisien (2013) 'BVA Polls', January.

Marchal, R. (2012) *The coup in Mali: the result of a long-term crisis or spillover from the Libyan civil war.*

Martin, C. (1985) 'The Historical, Economic and Political basis for France's African Policy', *Journal of Modern African Studies*, 23, pp. 189 – 208.

Melly, P. (2013) 'Central African Republic crisis: another French intervention', *BBC African News*, 2 December. Available at: www.bbc.co.uk-world-africa-25183377.

Newman, R. and Paris (eds) (2009) *New Thinking on Liberal Peacebuilding*. UNU Press.

NOREF (2012) *Is a military intervention in Mali unavoidable?*

Paris, R. (2010) 'Saving Liberal Peacebuilding', *Review of International Studies*, 36, pp. 337–365.

Richmond, O. (2014) *Peace: A Very Short Introduction*. Oxford: Oxford University Press.

Schofield, H. (2013) 'France's Mali Intervention a risk of 'new Hollande', *BBC News*. Available at: www.bbc.co.uk/news/magazine 14/01/2013.

Straus, S. (2012) 'Wars do end! Changing patterns of political violence in sub-Saharan Africa', *African Affairs*, 111(443), pp. 179–201.

Taylor, I. and Williams, P. (2004) *Africa in International Politics: External involvement on the continent*. New York: Routledge.

The Economist Magazine (2000) 'Hopeless Continent', May, pp. 13–19.

The Ticklish (2011) 'France robbing Africa through the Colonial Pact", 9 March. Available at: www.theticklish.blogspot.com/2011/03/france-robbing-africa-through-colonial.html.

UNDP (2015) *Human Development Report: Work for Development*. New York.

UNSC (2013) *Resolution 2100 Adopted by the UN Security Council at its 6952nd Meeting on 25th April 2013.*

Willett, S. (2005) 'New Barbarians at the Gate: losing the Liberal Peace in Africa', *Review of African Political Economy*, (106), p. 569.

CHAPTER THREE

SIERRA LEONE and Subversion of SOCIAL CONTRACT
David J. Francis[2]

Introduction

T he West African state of Sierra Leone has come to represent two distinct iconic images of Post-Cold War Africa. First, the bloody civil wars in the 1990s presented Sierra Leone as the very manifestation of the *'Hopeless Continent'*. Within a decade, post-war Sierra Leone has been portrayed as one of the emerging *'Lion Economies'* and the so-called *'Africa Rising'* phenomenon because of its spectacular economic growth rates of between 8% - 20% before the outbreak of the Ebola epidemic. Second, the international community and, in particular, the global governance institutions such as the United Nations and World Bank have presented Sierra Leone as a successful example and working model of liberal peacebuilding that designed and implemented how to end bloody civil wars, build the peace and reconstruct failed and collapsed states. The UN Secretary General, Ban Ki moon, triumphantly stated in 2010,

> Sierra Leone has been a successful story of maintaining peace after a decade of bloody civil conflict and has impressed the rest of the world … the country is seen as an example of post-conflict recovery (Francis, 2012, page 14).

There is clear evidence to justify the optimism of the international community in that with the end of the civil war, the country has made significant progress in consolidating post-war peacebuilding and state reconstruction by organising three relatively free and fair democratic elections and the peaceful transfer of power by the ruling Sierra Leone Peoples Party (SLPP) to the opposition All Peoples Congress (APC)

---

[2] This chapter was written in 2016, before Professor David Francis was appointed as Chief Minister of the Government of Sierra Leone in April 2018.

party, a rarity in the capricious and violence-prone electoral politics in Africa.

Notwithstanding this putative success, post-war Sierra Leone is still wracked by fundamental grievances that caused and/or instigated the decade-long civil war as well as the subversion of the Social Contract constitutions which continue to create depressing socio-development indicators whereby widespread poverty and marginalisation remains endemic with 60% of the population living on less than US $1.25 a day; 60% youth unemployment or underemployment and 59% adult illiteracy of the 6 million population. This resource-rich but poorly governed state of Sierra Leone is one of the poorest countries in the world and ranked 181 out of 187 countries (UNDP, 2016). By all indications, the post-war depressing socio-economic and development indicators and the continuation of pre-war fundamental grievances and the subversion of Social Contract certainly pose a serious threat to peacebuilding, security, stability, state re-construction and democratic consolidation.

To understand the subversion of social contract and how this contributed to the descent into civil war and state collapse, this chapter examines the political economy context of Sierra Leone and critically examines two fundamental conflict drivers namely: i. structural factors created by the entrenched British colonial rule and its legacies and, ii. The predatory neo-patrimonial nature of domestic politics and political culture. The common feature of these conflict drivers is that both the British autocratic colonial rule and the kleptocratic political governance in post-independent Sierra Leone designed and implemented successive social contracts in the form of constitutions that were, to all intents and purposes, extractive, predatory and developed to maintain the status quo that ensured the dominance and exploitation by the political elites and governing class, be they British colonial rulers or Sierra Leoneans now in charge of the state. In fact, these extractive colonial and post-colonial social contract constitutions contributed to creating the fundamental grievances that led to war and state collapse. The fundamental question that this case study raises is what happens when the political elites (colonial and post-colonial) fail to fulfil their own part of the social contract? Do we expect the people and society to fulfil or even respect their own side of the social contract, especially when the social contract had been extractive and predatory?

The Sierra Leone case study raises the fundamental question of the relevance of extractive and predatory social contract and whether it can guarantee long-term peace, security, stability, socio-economic development, democratic consolidation and the efficient political and economic management of the state. Rather than simply apply to the context of Sierra Leone the Weberian construction and western-centric assumptions of the *'state'* and *'society'*, this case study examines the type and nature of the *'state'* and *'society'* in the particular context of Sierra Leone. The case study of Sierra Leone argues that designing an excellent social contract is simply not enough. What is importantly needed to support the success of a resilient social contract is effective leadership, viable and inclusive institutions and a political culture that prioritises the general good rather than the narrow, individual, sectional and patrimonial interests. The imperative to build and sustain a resilient social contract should be at the heart of post-war peacebuilding and state reconstruction in Sierra Leone. To provide a critical understanding of the central argument advanced in this chapter, I conducted two research field visits to Sierra Leone between October 2016 and January 2017. I interviewed 34 relevant stakeholders, representing the diversity of the country around gender, education, regions, ethnicity, religion and political affiliation. The core findings have helped to construct a new interpretation of the civil war and state collapse in Sierra Leone.

Context: Crises of State Formation and Nation-Building

Political independence from British colonial rule in April 1961 bequeathed an extractive and predatory state system whereby the new independent leaders, now divided along ethnic and political party lines of the SLPP and the APC, struggled to forge a state out of the disparate 17 ethnic nations and to build national identity that transcends ethnic and regional interests. The SLPP governments of Prime Minister Milton Margai and Albert Margai between 1961 and 1967 faced all the political, socio-economic and development challenges of a newly independent state, though with a relatively strong extractive-based economy with Gross Domestic Product (GDP) growth at 32% in the 1960s and peaked at 107% in the 1970s. The military interventions in 1967/68, instigated by the divisive political ethnicity between the SLPP and APC, undermined the nascent multi-party democratic dispensation. The restoration of constitutional rule and the APC government of Prime Minister and later President Siaka Stevens led to the introduction a Republican Constitution in 1971 and the declaration of one-party system of governance in 1978. The APC one-party dictatorships of president Stevens and President Joseph Momoh ended after 24 years, with another military coup in 1992 led by Capt. Valentine Strasser and later, Brigadier Julius Maada Bio, of the National Provisional Ruling Council (NPRC) military junta.

Due to international pressures and the inability of the NPRC junta to end the civil war that broke out in March 1991, led by Corp. Foday Sankoh, of the Revolutionary United Front (RUF), Brig. Bio organised democratic elections and handed power over to the democratically elected government of the SLPP-led government of President Ahmad Tejan Kabbah in 1996. The overthrow of President Kabbah's government in 1997 by a coalition of rebel and military faction led by Major Johnny Paul Koroma precipitated the intervention of the Economic Community of Western African States (ECOWAS) peacekeeping force (ECOMOG) to restore the democratic government of President Kabbah in 1998. The 1999 Lome Peace Agreement finally ended the decade-long civil war that provided for a power-sharing arrangement, amnesty for those involved in the civil war and the deployment of UN peacekeeping force (UNAMSIL). Since the end of the civil war, Sierra Leone has seen the democratic transfer of power from the SLPP to the APC-led government of President Ernst Koroma in 2007. Post-war Sierra Leone has made significant progress in post-war recovery, peacebuilding and state reconstruction, given the scale and enormity of the challenge of post-war peacebuilding.

Historically, given the externally dependent nature of its extractive-based and subsistence agricultural-based economy, Sierra Leone's GDP amounts to US $8.4 billion (World Bank, 2016), with spectacular economic growth which peaked at 20.1% in 2013. The Ebola outbreak in 2014 adversely affected several sectors of the economy. Sierra Leone's main exports are to the following key destinations including, China, UK, USA, Belgium-Luxembourg, The Netherlands, United Arab Emirate, India, South Africa and Cote d'Ivoire. The main exports are Diamonds (US $127 million); Iron Ore (US $122 million); Titanium Ore (US $105 million); Aluminium Ore (US $54.2 million); and Cocoa Beans (US $22.4

million; coffee and fish. Mining accounts for nearly 20% of GDP and makes up an estimated 80% of the total export revenue. The main imports are refined petroleum; rice, cars, telephones, coconuts, Brazil nuts, building materials, electrical and medical equipment. The Economic Complexity Index ranks Sierra Leone as the 160th largest economy in the world. Subsistence agriculture forms the main stay of the economy comprising 54% of the GDP with two-thirds of the population, mainly rural areas of the country, involved in subsistence and un-mechanised farming for their livelihood. The GDP per capita is US $1,400 and the public debt make up 34.6% of GDP (World Bank Group, 2015). The Ebola outbreak, the drastic fall in global commodity prices especially iron ore and the strength of the value of the US dollar have exposed the economy of Sierra Leone to serious risk including significant reduction in government revenue and the increase in debt repayment obligations.

The brief political, economic and development history of post-colonial Sierra Leone illustrates that the resource-rich country is categorised by the UNDP Human Development Index as one of the poorest countries in the world. The perennial depressing socio-economic and development indicators demonstrate the failure of governance and the inability of the post-independent leadership to effectively manage the political and economic processes of the country, with the country still excessively dependent on external development assistance aid, mounting to 50% of public investment programmes financed and underwritten by external development co-operation partners and agencies. The externally dependent nature of the extractive economy still remains unchanged and the undiversified economic and agricultural-based continue to exhibit the same colonial inherited economic structures that have consigned the country to the traditional and marginalised role as mere producer of raw materials (cash crops and mineral resources). The combination of leadership failure and the nature of domestic politics based on neo-patrimonialism have led to the politics of decline and underdevelopment in post-independent Sierra Leone.

In the run up to the 2007 general elections, local communities and people that had not benefited from the peace dividend in post-war Sierra Leone developed a popular anti-SLPP government mantra *'We can't eat peace'*. A similar anti-austerity/anti-APC government popular slogan has now emerged in the run up to the March 2018 general elections: *'We can't eat roads'.* Those who have not benefited from President Koroma's *'Agenda for Change'* and *'Agenda for Prosperity',* despite the large scale roads infrastructural development mainly in the capital city, Freetown, question the relevance of government investment in roads construction when the majority of the population do not have access to basic necessities of life. Successive governments in post-independent Sierra Leone have not been able to demonstrate the performance legitimacy of statehood and despite the fact that the post-colonial state has emerged as the dominant player in public life and state-society relations, it has not been able to deliver on its welfare and security functions for the majority of Sierra Leoneans.

Subversion of Social Contract: conflict drivers for civil war and state collapse

Why is modern Sierra Leone poor, underdeveloped, ravaged by war and badly governed since independence from British colonial rule? The crisis of state formation and nation building in Sierra Leone is a combination of complex and interrelated domestic and external factors, ranging from structural conditions created by colonial rule and its legacies to leadership failure, unprogressive political culture, bad governance that involves the worse forms of neo-patrimonialism, political ethnicity and clientelism.

But what is social contract? To be clear, a social contract is a political philosophy that emerged in the 17th and 18th century propounded by the enlightenment philosophers such as Thomas Hobbes, John Locke and Jean-Jacques Rosseau. In its simplist form, the political understanding of social contract is a voluntary agreement for mutual benefit between the state and society or the community as a whole. It requires the surrender of some liberties in the interest of the common good and crucially, the consent of the people or governed is important as it forms the basis of government. The underlying principle of social contract states that since it is a voluntary agreement between two parties, it assumes that when one part violates the terms of the agreement then the contract is deemed invalid. In a democratic context, it assumes that the people have the right to vote out of office the government that has failed to deliver its side of the bargain or to fulfil the purpose for which it was elected to office.

The basic understanding is that societies are organised and controlled by governments and that societies/people mutually benefit from living and interacting together. But this relationship between government oversight and societies/people living together requires laws and rules. Social contract provides this framework for state-society relations, i.e., how people and government interact based on clear demarcation of roles, duties and responsibilities to make the social contract framework work. As such, social contract implicitly interrogates the traditional political, moral and normative sources of power and privileges the imperative for governments (rulers/governors) and the people/society (governed/ruled over) to work together in partnership for the common good. The understanding is that the social contract will counter the 'state of nature' where people live without rules and laws (Hobbes, 1999). John Locke aptly captures this notion of partnership in that 'people had to willingly do things like pay taxes and serve in the military, but in return the government had to listen to their desires and provide for their need' (Locke, 1690). In effect, social contract implicitly means that people are forced to respect each other and their differences as the only way to leave in peace.

This means giving up some of our freedoms and obey a higher authority, i.e., government, so that everyone in the society has right and entitlement to life, liberty and property. In fact, Locke and Rosseau argue that if the government does not fulfil its side of the bargain of the social contract then the people have a right to overthrow the government if it fails to fulfil its purpose, i.e., protect and guarantee life, liberty and property. This background raises the question as to whether it is possible to apply 17th and 18th century conceptions of social contract to the context of Africa's weak and failed states, in particular, the post-war fragile state of Sierra Leone?

Based on the above analysis, how do we explain the two major conflict drivers in the context of Sierra Leone? First, the structural condition created by the British colonial rule and colonial legacies were only made possible because of the colonial extractive social contract constitutions designed and implemented to exploit colonial Sierra Leone and ensure the dominance and perpetuation of the colonial rule, power and privileges. Second, the nature of domestic politics based on neo-patrimonial governance by the ruling and governing elites in post-independent Sierra Leone who equally designed and implemented extractive and predatory social contract constitutions to ensure the dominance of the political elites and access to state power and its patrimonial resources that led to the exclusion and marginalisation of vast sections of the population.

Colonial rule and colonial legacies created long-term structural conditions that contributed to war and state collapse in Sierra Leone. In 1808, Sierra Leone was made a British Crown Colony, a possession of the British Empire and in 1896, the hinterland/interior was declared a British protectorate, effectively subjecting the whole country to British imperial autocratic colonial rule. After nearly 160 years of British colonial rule, Sierra Leone gained political independence in April 1961. During this period, the colonial rule designed and imposed extractive and predatory social contract constitutions. To govern and exploit this new imperial acquisition, the British colonial government promulgated several social contract constitutions. The 1808 Crown Colony 'constitution' combined the powers of the executive, legislature and judiciary in the Governor-in Council colonial governors (all white men) who were responsible not to the people they governed but to the British monarch and parliament. This was unsurprising because the Crown Colony was established as a settlement for freed slaves who had become social misfits (Black Poor) in London and other cities after the abolition of the slave trade 1772. The establishment of the Crown Colony made it possible for the settlement to serve as a British colonial legal outpost for the trial of captured slaves and owners. Under the Crown, settlers lost all rights to participate and be represented. In effect, this 'experiment in social engineering' cast in humanitarian and Christian religious terms, was primarily an effort to get rid of the social and economic problems created in UK cities by the Black Poor. Despite the humanitarian and anti-slavery motivations that led to the settlement of the Black Poor in Sierra Leone, the underlying considerations were political, economic and commercial, i.e, another lucrative coastal trading and economic and output for the British empire.

The 1863 social contract constitution (Blackhall Constitution) was not fundamentally different because it continued and guaranteed the extractive and predatory colonial exploitation of Sierra Leone. The 1863 Constitution ended the Governor's Council administration of the colony; provided for a separate executive and legislative council, though made up of largely appointees of the colonial governor serving as Governor and Commander-in-Chief; only two representatives were chosen from amongst the local population and often pro-colonial government supporters; and the governor served as president of both the executive and legislative councils with sweeping discretionary powers. In effect, the colonial social contracts were designed to be extractive, predatory and to perpetuate the dominance of colonial rule in Sierra Leone. To put this into context, Sierra Leone was nothing more than a valuable and lucrative piece of real estate for the British Empire and the extractive social contracts were designed and imposed to achieved this fundamental motivation.

As such, British colonial rule in Sierra Leone was part of the wider European colonisation project and the scramble for the partition of African into European economic, commercial, political, military-security spheres of interests and influence, underpinned primarily by extraction and mercantilist exploitation. As the British Prime Minister, Lord Salisbury, sarcastically commented, 'We have been giving away mountains and rivers and lakes to each other, only hindered by the small impediment that we never knew exactly where they were' (Meredith, 2005). The colonial extractive social contract constitutions that emerged from the Berlin Conference of 1884-85 ended up creating fundamental structural problems and grievances that served as drivers of conflict and war in post-independent Sierra Leone.

It is important to highlight that colonial rule did not go unchallenged in colonial Sierra Leone, and to use Locke and Rosseau's interpretation of social contract, the people/societies took every opportunity to resist, challenge and overthrow by violent means British colonial domination. Between 1884 – 1956, there were riots, strikes, violent insurrections and wars against British colonial rule. The most prominent was the House Tax war in 1898 led by the Temne Chief BaiBureh in the North and the Mende war in the East. The House Tax war was a reaction of the people and chiefs against the imposition of an annual 'House Tax' in the protectorate and the erosion of the customary powers of the chiefs. The British colonial administration brutally crushed the House Tax war and rebellion in the north and east of the country, summarily executing some of the leaders and exiled to the Gold Coast (now Ghana) the main chiefs that led the war including BaiBureh, Nyagua and BaiSherbro.

The anti-democratic and authoritarian colonial rule subjected Sierra Leoneans to taxation with representation, with the societies and people not having a say in the decisions that directly affected their lives. The small mercantilist elites and colonial administrators formed the ruling and governing class, monopolising political and economic powers that supported the extractive and predatory interests of the British Empire.

With the wind of change that led to the end of colonial rule and empire across the world in the post-Second World War period, Sierra Leone was granted independence in 1961. In preparation for the transfer of political power and decolonisation in Sierra Leone, the 1961 independence constitution was agreed at Lancaster House in London. The 1961 constitution was designed to perpetuate neo-colonial dominance and the exploitation of post-independent Sierra Leone. Based on an interview with the former Vice President of Sierra Leone, Solomon Berewa stated that 'The British gave us a constitution at independence with our hands and feet tied and told us to run. But we have not been able to run and they have the audacity to blame us'.

Colonial rule had significant consequences and created fundamental structural grievances and in some cases, eroded or destroyed the rich traditional socio-cultural and political institutions, indigenous societal agencies and cultural resources used to govern pre-colonial Sierra Leone. The colonial intension was deliberate and purposive, to replace, subvert and destroy Sierra Leone's socio-cultural, economic and political institutions and way of life with a new dominant and all pervasive foreign British socio-development and political institutions and norms. The view of Lord Macaulay in his address to the British Parliament in 1835 is instructive:

> I have travelled across the length and breadth of Africa and I have not seen one person who is a beggar, who is a thief. Such wealth I have seen in this country, such high moral values, people of such calibre, that I do not think we would ever conquer this country, unless we break the very backbone of this nation, which is her spiritual and cultural heritage and therefore, I propose that we replace her old and ancient education system, her culture. For if the Africans think that all that is foreign and English is good and greater than their own, they will lose their self esteem, their native culture and they will become what we want them, a truly dominated nation" (Macaulay, 1835).

Sierra Leone and the rest of Africa became a *'truly dominated nation'*. Siaka Stevens, the first Executive President of Sierra Leone emphatically stated, *'Britain is the country on which we tried to model ourselves after independence'*. Some of these structural grievances include laying the foundation of the crisis of state formation and nation building by imposing an Indirect Rule of governance which created two types of state: a civic colonial state and a customary state controlled by traditional leaders/Paramount Chiefs often amendable to British colonialism. The divide and rule colonial policy created divisions between the North and rest of country as well as between the Colony/capital city and 'up-country' protectorate; between the Krios and protectorate peoples; and between the educated and privileged Krios and Protectorate elites against the large rural poor population. Politics during colonial rule was based on nepotism, patron-clientelism and often smacking of outright racism, and the autocratic control of the subjected peoples of Sierra Leone. Education was left in the hands of Christian missionaries –the foot soldiers of colonial rule- rather than any serious investment in national education planning to empower Sierra Leoneans to take over governance of the state. Even where the colonial administration was involved in educational development it was primarily to promote an elitist education to ensure the dominance and perpetuation of colonial rule and influence, such as the establishment of Bo School in 1906 to educate the sons of Paramount Chiefs. Those regions that resisted British colonial rule such as Bai Bureh's Northern Sierra Leone, where neglected access to Western educational development and training.

According to Herbert Morrison, a senior UK Labour politician, granting independence to unprepared and untrained Africans, including Sierra Leoneans was 'like giving a child a latch-key, a bank account and a shot-gun' (Meredith, 2005, page 11). The extractive and exploitative nature of colonial rule coveted Sierra Leone into an externally dependent economy that prioritised mining of strategic mineral resources and the production of cash crops for export. Based on research field visits in Sierra Leone, out of 34 interviewees, 22 categorically stated that colonial rule and its legacies in SL created fundamental structural grievances that contributed to the outbreak of war and state collapse in post-independent Sierra Leone.

The second main cause of war and state collapse has to do with the predatory neo-patrimonial governance and prebendal political culture in the nearly 60 years of independence designed and controlled by the Kleptocratic ruling and governing elites that managed the nature of domestic politics and how this created fundamental grievances in the country. Governance and politics in post-independent Sierra Leone have not followed the rational Weberian conception of the state and state-society relations. In Sierra Leone, politics and access to public office has been about access to state power and its patrimonial resources. This led to the privatisation, informalisation and subversion of the state governing institutions to serve the strategic and vested sectional interests of the ruling and governing elites. Prebendal politics in Sierra Leone, as organised and managed by the small ruling and governing elites in control of the *'Shadow State'* (Reno, 1995), effectively converted the 'Official State' into a laisse faire market place for patrimonial accumulation with no distinction between the public and private realm of the state (Francis, 2001).

To coerce the consent of the people and societies, the political elites in control of the state designed and implemented new extractive and predatory social contract constitutions including the 1971 Republican constitution, the 1978 One-Party Constitution under President Siaka Stevens and the 1991 multi-party constitution. The 1971 constitution was a politically driven social contract motivated by the strategic and sectional interests of the APC government of Siaka Stevens to consolidate his power and control over the state. Learning from the fallout of the political ethnicity (South-East SLPP vs. Northern-based APC) that led to the military coup after the hotly contested 1967 general elections, Stevens as the new Prime Ministers, mobilised the adoption of a new constitution in 1971. The 1971 constitution transformed Sierra Leone into a republic with a presidential system (executive president) of governance with a parliament based on multi-party politics. To further consolidate and concentrate political and economic power in the APC and its president, President Stevens introduced the worse form of extractive social contract constitution that replaced the multi-party presidential system into a one-party APC dictatorship.

The 1978 constitution replaced the 1971 constitution and co-opted the opposition SLPP into the governing APC party and recognised the APC as the only legal and legitimate political party. The 1978 constitution increased the term limit of the president from five to seven and conferred sweeping executive powers on the president to appoint the head of the judiciary (Chief Justice) and Electoral Commissioners. In effect, the legislature and the judiciary became answerable to President Stevens. The 1978 constitution was the worse form of personalisation of political power similar to the colonial social contract constitutions. As the former Foreign Affairs Minister, Abdul Karim Koroma, in the corrupt and weak government of President Momoh stated, 'In the politics of the time there was a distinct disregard for democratic methods and procedures. Victory (one-party elections) was determined by the amount of money, propaganda and violence mobilised and dispensed' (Koroma, 1996).

To all intents and purposes, the 1978 extractive and predatory social contract constitution converted President Stevens into a British colonial governor in sole control of this resource-rich country. In effect, the post-independent leaders, like their former colonial masters, crafted and implemented extractive and predatory social contract constitutions that served particular, sectional, ethic interests to maintain the dominance and exploitation of the small ruling and governing class. Based on my research field visits and interviews, all 34 respondents categorically stated that poor governance and the subversion of social contract were the primary reasons for the war and state collapse. The politics of decline and underdevelopment in post-independent Sierra Leone created fundamental grievances. Some of these include the privatisation and subversion of state governing institutions that led to the politicisation of the armed forces and the police whereby these institutions where used to commit gross violations of human rights, the violent intimidation and brutalisation of the population.

Any government that came to power (democratic or military coup) generally catered for its regional, ethnic and sectional political power-base and supporters to the exclusion of the majority of the population in the political and economic management of the state. The decades of poor governance and bad leadership led to economic crisis, increasing poverty, underdevelopment and depressing socio-development indicators. The economy continued to operate along the lines of the colonial extractive-based and subsistence agricultural-based economy whereby the country because a net importer of its staple food, rice. The education system continue to promote the colonial education system that privileged the creation of so-called *'White Collar jobs'*, with the majority of university graduates not able to find jobs, are unemployed or under-employed and not able to integrate themselves into the labour market. With high unemployment levels, fewer opportunities for social and economic empowerment of the youth and increasingly depressing socio-development indicators created political tensions and violence that the small ruling and privileged class could no longer contain or clamp down on.

Re-interpretation of Civil War and State Collapse

The dominant interpretations of the civil war and state collapse in Sierra Leone have mainly focused on three debates. First, that 'greed' and the resource curse theories explain the war in Sierra Leone (Collier, 2000; Cramer, 2006; Keen, 2006) Second, that the civil war is a manifestation of the new barbarism and 'mindless violence' linked to the marginalisation and dispossession of the youth bulge without economic, social, educational, employment and self-actualisation opportunities (Kaplan, 1994; Luttwak, 1995; Bradshaw, 1996). Third, that the political economy of violence and neo-patrimonial decline explains the bloody civil war and state collapse (Reno, 1995; Richards, 1996; Francis, 2001). In all these interpretations of the conflict drivers and causes of the civil war and state collapse, no one has interrogated the role and contribution of the subversion of social contract as a significant factor responsible for war and state collapse in Sierra Leone.

The case study of Sierra Leone argues that the civil war and state collapse is a product of the subversion of the social contract which made it possible for the vast majority of Sierra Leoneans to be disposed and denied access and entitlement to existential necessities as well as liberty (oppressive and repressive constitutions and government policies), life (politically-motivated treason charges and executions) and property. To use Locke and Rosseau's interpretation of what a social contract between the state/government and society/people is supposed to be, the poor, disposed and marginalised people and societies in Sierra Leone therefore had the right to 'overthrow' (violent or democratic electoral politics) governments 'of, by and for' a small extractive and predatory political elites that failed to fulfil the purpose for which they were elected to govern.

The two key conflict drivers in the context of Sierra Leone are inextricably linked and intersect at sectional, local, societal, national and international levels. The fundamental causes of the civil war and state collapse in Sierra Leone have shown that no society/people cannot respect or trust the state/government/rulers if they do not fulfil their part of the social contract bargain or the purpose for which they exists. In fact, the history of mistrust and unpeaceful relations between the state/government and society/people in colonial and post-colonial Sierra Leone have largely being the product of perception of the people and society that the government/state/rulers have often breached the terms of the social contracts. To be clear, both the colonial and post-independent constitutions created opportunities for the dominant political class to assume power, take control and craft social contracts in particular ways that served, protected and perpetuated the interests, privileges and advantages of the exclusive political club of ruling and governing elites. Both the colonial and post-colonial social contracts where never designed to create a society of equals, despite the pretentions of the 1961, 1971 and 1991 post-independent constitutions in Sierra Leone.

Building Resilient Social Contract for Peacebuilding & State Re-construction

The post-war depressing socio-economic and development challenges as well as the problems of peacebuilding and state reconstruction illustrates that to build, maintainand sustain peace, the Sierra Leone needs more than mere absence of war and violence, i.e., negative peace. To build and sustain peace in post-war Sierra Leone, the country needs a resilient social contract that is not driven by the extractive interests of the ruling and governing elites. A resilient social contract in the context of Sierra Leone means a dynamic, proactive and voluntary agreement between the state and society/between the governed and governors on how to live and interact together to achieve common and inclusive interests relating to progressive socio-economic and political development. Social contract as represented by institutions, governance processes and constitutional mechanisms serve as the framework or central hub to peacefully mediate diverse and often competing interests and demands from and by different and disparate sections of society overtime.

What role can a resilient social contract play to transform the country from poverty to prosperity? The decade-long brutal civil war and its devastating consequences provided harsh lessons for the small ruling and governing elites that the business of governance has to fundamentally change with a primary focus on inclusive institutions, inclusive economic growth and inclusive political participation and representation. The 1999 Lome Peace Agreement and the Truth and Reconciliation Commission (TRC) in 2004 recommended a review of the 1991 national constitution, as the supreme social contract law for all Sierra Leoneans, to make it more inclusive, representative and to depart from its extractive and predatory provisions. The TRC, in particular, recommended that the revision of the 1991 constitution should make justiciable important aspects of the social contract between the state and society relating to the protection of human rights and rule of law; promotion of good governance; fight against corruption and the effective management and governance of mineral resources of the country for the benefit of all; protection and empowerment of women, children and youth; and reparations for war victims.

With the end of war, the post-war SLPP government of President Tejan Kabbah (1996-2007) and the APC-led government of President Ernst Koroma (2007–2018) have made significant efforts to develop and implement institutions and policies as a credible basis for post-war social contract that will build, maintain and sustain long-term peace, security, stability, justice, development and democratic consolidation. Some of the political, economic and development institutions, structures and policies introduced and implemented by both governments include the creation of the Office of National Security (ONS); National Social Security and Insurance Trust (NASSIT); Human Rights Commission of Sierra Leone (HRCSL); Anti-Corruption Commission; National Youth Commission Act (2009) establishing the National Youth Commission with a dedicated government Ministry of Youth Affairs; political governance and development reforms including Decentralisation and Local Government, Civil Service reform, Judicial and legislative reforms, Political Parties Registration Commission, Media reform, Agriculture and Food Self Sufficiency reform, Healthcare reform; Agenda for Change (Second

Poverty Reduction Strategy Paper : 2008 - 2012) and Agenda for Prosperity (Third Generation PRSP: 2012-2018)

Perhaps the most significant post-war development to design and implement an inclusive and resilient social contract is the review of 1991 constitution as recommended by the Lome Peace Agreement and the TRC. A Constitutional Review Commission (CRC) was launched by President Koroma in 2013 and headed by a retired Chief Justice, Edmond Cowan, with a committee comprising 80 members drawn from across the country including relevant and diverse stakeholders in the society, political parties, democratic institutions, NGOs, civil society organisations, traditional rules/Paramount Chiefs, Disabled Groups, Women organisations, academic institutions and students bodies, youth organisations, donor and development co-operation partners, the media and key independent organisations. The CRC mandate was to review the 1991 Constitution and the 2008 Peter Tucker Constitutional Review Commission Report. After extensive nation-wide consultation, the Commission presented its final report in March 2016 and the key recommendations are to be approved in a national referendum in September 2017.The CRC made significant recommendations that will change the nature of governance and develop a new resilient social contract for post-war Sierra Leone. The CRC states that 'the main goal of the revised constitution is to strengthen the existing multi-party democracy and to create an open and transparent society' (CRC Final Report, Feb. 2017).

But to understand and appreciate the relevance of the CRC recommendations as a new post-war social contract for Sierra Leone, it is important to provide the context that led to the promulgation of the 1991 constitution. The 1991 constitution was a product of and largely influenced by the popular domestic opposition to the APC one-party dictatorship in the 1970s and 1980s and the devastating economic development and political crises it created in the country. The 1991 constitution was also influenced by the changed international political environment with the end of the Cold War and the East-West Communist/Socialist versus Capitalist ideological hostilities, marking the end of support for puppet regimes and the support for pluralistic political dispensation and re-introduction of multi-party democracy. Faced with a changed international environment and the outbreak of civil war in eastern Sierra Leone, the 1991 constitution was rapidly promulgated after a rather hasty 'nation-wide' consultation. Importantly, the new constitution re-introduced multi-party democracy, recognised the separation of powers between the three branches of government i.e., executive, legislative and judiciary, with oversight and institutional accountability powers. But the devastating consequences of the APC one-party rule and the popular opposition it generated led to the overthrow of the APC government by the Capt. Strasser-led NPRC junta in 1992, effectively suspending the new 1991 constitution.

With this background to the 1991 constitution, the CRC recommendations have been described as the most liberal, progressive, equality-focused and inclusive social contract in clarifying the relationships, duties and responsibilities between the governed and governors in post-war Sierra Leone. The CRC proposed four new Chapters for inclusion into the revised 1991 constitution including, local government and decentralisation; citizenship; land, natural resources and the environment; and, information, communication and the media. Importantly, it made specific recommendations pertinent to the executive, legislature and the judiciary, to address the perennial governance failures and the extractive nature of the social contract constitutions that only protected the interests of the ruling and governing elites. For the first time in the history of the modern Sierra Leone, the proposal is made to enshrine long-term national development planning into the constitution with the creation of a National Development Planning Commission. To ensure inclusivity, transparency, accountability, and to avoid discrimination of all Sierra Leoneans, the CRC recommended that violations of political, civil, economic and social rights of the citizens should be justiciable and enshrined in the constitution, rather than simply 'discouraging' or 'prohibiting' violations by the state or government. Three illustrative examples to emphasis the significance of the CRC recommendations include:

The Executive

Learning from the experience of the constitutional crisis created by President Koroma in March 2015 when he unilaterally sacked his Vice President, Alhaji Sam Sumana, in contravention of Sections 50 and 51 of the 1991 constitution, the CRC recommended that the President, mandated as 'guardian of the Constitution of Sierra Leone' should never again be given the opportunity to manipulate the constitution or act in an unconstitutional manner in pursuit of strategic political interests. To this end, the CRC recommended that the term, 'Supreme Executive Authority' (section 40 (1) be changed to 'Chief Executive' and the President and Vice President can only be removed according to the provisions of sections 50 and 51 of the 1991 constitution. To further avoid potential political crisis and the desire of seating presidents to change the constitution to secure a Third Term or continue to hold onto power, the CRC recommendation enshrined the principle of only two terms of office for the president and fixed date for holding national elections and inauguration of the President. CRC recommended the separation of the position of Minister of Justice and the Attorney General (section 64 (1) whereby the Attorney General, as the principal legal adviser to the government shall not seat in cabinet as this should be the role and responsibility of the Minister of Justice.

The Legislative

To guarantee the separation of power, the CRC recommended the removal of the President from Parliament and that Paramount Chiefs should not be members of the parliamentary system whereby, previous constitutions have given 12 parliamentary seats to Paramount Chiefs. The parliamentary Paramount Chiefs have always been pro-government and have been described in the TRC report as part of the crisis of state formation and nation building in post-independent Sierra Leone. The Chiefs were now to have their own established House of Chiefs.

The Judiciary

To guarantee the independence of the judiciary, the CRC recommended that the financial autonomy of the judiciary be enshrined in the constitution and the separation of powers between the executive and judiciary. Importantly, the CRC recommended that the president should no longer appoint the Chief Justice, but that the Judicial and Legal Service Commission should assume this responsibility to ensure an independent, impartial and transparent appointment of the Chief Justice, subject to parliamentary approval.

The CRC recommendations mark the start for building a resilient social contract that will be at the centre of post-war peacebuilding and state reconstruction. But Sierra Leone needs more than designing a liberal and progressive inclusive social contract constitution that protects all. The key drivers for a resilient social contract in the particular context of Sierra Leone include the end of subversion and manipulation of the constitution, the supreme social contract law of the land, by the small ruling and governing elites in pursuit of vested political and economic interests. Important key drivers to build, and sustain resilient social contract includes inclusive, viable and accountable governance institutions; effective, transparent and strong leadership committed to democratic developmental state model; and a fundamental positive change in the political culture that consistently and predictably privileges national interests and the common good over and above the sectional, parochial and self interests.

An important development to underscore the of efforts to build and sustain resilient post-war social contract include the progress made by the government of Sierra Leone to implement two global social contracts in the context of Sierra Leone. They include, the UN Social Development Goals (SDGs) 2030 relating to peace and security and New Deal for fragile states. Sierra Leone has signed up to and is one of the eight pilot countries for the New Deal for Engagement in Fragile States (International Dialogue for Peacebuilding and Statebuilding) that was established in 2011 (Busan Agreement) and led by the G7 and G20 countries with the support of the global governance institutions such as UN, World Bank, IMF, OECD, EU. The primary aim is to support war-torn, post-war, conflict-prone and fragile states to set their our development priorities for international engagement in line with the basic principles of aid effectiveness, peacebuilding and statebuilding goals. The New Deal global social contract that post-war Sierra Leone has signed up to is based on three core pillars.

First, it has five peacebuilding and statebuilding goals which stress that politics, security, peace, justice, institutions and economics are the foundation for long-term development. Second, the FOCUS principles identify the political causes of fragility, support nationally owned and led plans, and achieve mutual accountability for results through compacts.

Third, TRUST principles that commit partners to aid effectiveness and national capacity building. The government of Sierra Leone has used the New Deal global social contract process to design and implement the national development priority programme called 'Agenda for Prosperity' (2012-2018). Much has been made by the government of President Koroma about the potential impact of the New Deal and the 'Agenda for Prosperity' development priority. Suffice to say that the New Deal is yet another top-down, elitist, state-centred prescription that claims to put countries such Sierra Leone in the 'driving seat', even when they do not have the resources to implement their own development plans.

Speaking to focused groups of unemployed and marginalised youth at Kru Bay and market women in Congo Town about their perception of the government's 'Agenda for Change' and 'Agenda for Prosperity', they all described the government's development agenda as a 'scam'; 'APC 419 to enrich themselves'; and that, the 'Agenda for Change' is simply an 'Agenda for Corruption' and the 'Agenda for Prosperity' is yet another 'Agenda for Poverty'. But a caveat to add here is that the interviews were conducted during the period of the hardship faced by ordinary people because of the austerity measures implemented by President Koroma's government as part of the 'Agenda for Prosperity', so one would expect these unemployed youth and poor market women to give very negative comments about the New Deal-supported development plan in Sierra Leone. Notwithstanding, there is very little evidence of the impact of the New Deal social contract in Sierra Leone and the majority of the populace are not even aware of it existence as a global social contract framework to support Sierra Leone.

Another global social contract that has been promoted by the government of Sierra Leone is the UN Sustainable Development Goals (SDGs) 2015-2030 that replaced the Millennium Development Goals (MDGs) 2001. The 17 SDGs and, in particular, the SDG 16 on Peace, Security, Justice and inclusive institutions, is critical to forging resilient social contract in post-war Sierra Leone. What is the potential impact of the new SDGs on Sierra Leone when the country did not achieve any of the eight targets relating to the MDGs relating to eradication of poverty and hunger; universal primary education; gender equality and women empowerment; child mortality; maternal health; HIV/AIDS, Malaria and other diseases; environmental sustainability and global partnership for development?

In fairness, the decade-long brutal civil war made it impossible for Sierra Leone to achieve any of the MDGs. However, some progress was made in achieving the MDGs relating to HIV/AIDs, but the outbreak of the Ebola epidemic crudely exposed the dysfunctional healthcare delivery system in the country. With the end of the war and the relatively successful progress in post-war recovery, Sierra Leone is now well placed to implement the SDGs global social contract to improve the lives of the poor people, with verifiable targets that governments in Sierra Leone will be held accountable for. The greatest challenge is where will the funds come from to support the long-term implementation of the global social contract SDGs in Sierra Leone? In effect, for poor and badly managed post-war countries such as Sierra Leone, the global social contract SDGs are mere aspirational goals.

Conclusion

Acemoglu and Robinsons (2012), in *"Why Nations Fail"* argue that inclusive institutions are critical or explain why some countries prosper and are developed and why others remain poor and underdeveloped. Acemoglu and Robinson's central claim when applied to the context of Sierra Leone partly explains the failure of social contract and the descent into civil war and state collapse in the post-independence era. As the key conflict drivers in the context of Sierra Leone have shown, the colonial and post-colonial social contract constitutions and the political and economic institutions developed were extractive and not inclusive, primarily serving and protecting the political and economic powers of the authoritarian, bureaucratic and anti-democratic British colonial rule as well as the small ruling and governing elites in post-independent Sierra Leone. Notwithstanding, it is important to stress that institutions are not the only important drivers that determine whether countries prosper or fail. From another perspective, Yew (2000) in *"From Third World to First: Singapore and the Asian Economic Boom"* emphasises the fact that leadership, the prevailing Cold War context and the domestic security threats were the key factors that determined the remarkable and successful transformation of Singapore from a poor Third World 'fishing village' and a decrepit British colonial trading post in South East Asia to a prosperous First World country.

But Yew's benign authoritarian leadership to promote a Developmental State model in Singapore could hardly be applicable to the context of post-independent Sierra Leone. This is not to discount the importance of the key role that effective and strategic leadership played in the transformation of Singapore, a critical factor that has been missing in the post-independent political development of Sierra Leone. Based on the 'inclusive institutions' argument advanced by Acemoglu and Robinson and the 'effective leadership' imperative put forward by Yew, it is reasonable to assume that these important factors determine the success and sustainability of social contracts. In the context of post-independent Sierra Leone, the leadership failure and lack of inclusive institutions and, crucially, the implementation of extractive and predatory social contract constitutions have determined why this resource-rich country has not prospered and the state has failed, collapsed and remains one of the world's poorest countries.

The extractive and predatory nature of the social contract constitutions and the failure of and lack of inclusive political and economic institutions in post-independent Sierra Leone largely explains why the constitutions, as the most important representation of a social contract in modern Sierra Leone, are not able to moderate and limit the power of those elected or appointed to public offices because they are forever using political power, influence and connections to secure economic and financial opportunities as well as neo-patrimonial largess for themselves, political supporters, ethnic groups and sectional interests. In the absence of and failure to develop inclusive political institutions that are mutually supportive and reinforcing in terms of governance and accountability, the political class have systematically subverted, privatised and informalised the post-independent social contract constitutions and state governing institutions to serve their extractive prebendal interests. As such, politics or more precisely, holding public office, irrespective of political party affiliation and ideological persuasion (often, the majority of the political elites do not even have or believe any politico-development ideology), is simply about the rule and dominance of the rather small ruling and governing political and economic elites who have become guarantors and gatekeepers of this neo-patrimonial state based on extractive and predatory social contract.

For the kleptocratic elites, their first basic instinct (prebendal) when elected or appointed to any public office is to steal and amass wealth. Wealth, political power and socio-economic and development opport-unities and privileges are only opened to and re-cycled amongst the small political elites, thereby increasing elite wealth and power as well as perpetuating the grip of the political elites on state power in Sierra Leone. It really does not matter which political party is in power, either APC or SLPP, the story is the same. In effect, the extractive and predatory social contract in Sierra Leone partly explains the persistent poverty, underdevelopment and violent competition amongst the ruling and governing elites for access and control over state power as manifested by the successive military coups and civil war.

Post-war Sierra Leone is a divided society along wealth, power, access and entitlement to basic services and existential necessities of life (food, shelter, education, healthcare, employment). The majority of the population and, in particular, the rural poor, are permanently red-lined into poverty and deprivation, with generations entrapped in a vicious cycle of poverty trap. The political elites have incentive to maintain the extractive and predatory social contracts because the status quos benefits them. A recent illustrative example is that the Governor of the Central Bank of Sierra Leone, Dr. Kaifala Marah, in his attempt to secure the presidential nomination of the ruling APC party for the March 2018 elections, acted in complete contravention of the Sierra Leone Banking Regulations Act 2011. The Bank Governor in March 2017 financed a 700 million Leones skills development scheme for mainly the APC youth as a populist vote-winning political project to enable him to secure the APC presidential nomination.

The Bank Governor and the President that appointed him are fully cognisance of the fact that the Central Bank's mandate is restricted to monetary policy, exchange rate management, financial sector regulation and inflation. Both President Koroma and Bank Governor Marah are fully aware that it is not the role of the Governor to be involved in and use the Banks' resources to fund and implement projects in the financial sector, especially when such projects are politically motivated. But it is important to recognise that the action of the Central Bank Governor is not unique in the context and nature of domestic politics in Sierra Leone.

In fact, the negative and unprogressive political culture prevalent in the country expects the Bank Governor to behave this way, i.e., use official/public resources for personal gains in the manner of Jean Francios Bayart's *'politics of the belly'*. The Bank Governor's action reflects the prevailing political mindset and neo-patrimonial culture amongst the ruling and governing elites who have a rather callous, primitive and uncivilised attitude to governance and respect for social contract. The Bank Governor's action is not different from the President sacking of his Vice President, Sam Sumana, in contravention of the 1991 constitution. The ruling and governing elites in Sierra Leone believe and behave as if they are above the law of the land and any social contact constitution in the country. The contradiction is that, some of these political elites who have held important roles at western institutions and have attained remarkable good governance reputation. But the moment they are in Sierra Leone and appointed to public office, they become or revert to being *'uncivilised'* political elites interested only in primitive accumulation with complete disregard for social contracts. The Bank Governor's action, like that of President Koroma's 'unconstitutional' action, explains why it will be difficult to build and sustain a resilient social contract in post-war Sierra Leone.

By all indications, this status quo cannot build and maintain peace, security, stability, inclusive national development and democratic consolidation. This realisation led to the review of the 1991 constitution by the CRC. The proposed recommendations to be approved in a national referendum will significantly shift the nature of governance in post-war Sierra Leone by creating, on a justiciable basis, inclusive socio-political and economic institutions as well as constitutionally guaranteeing rights, access and entitlement for all sections of society in the country. This is a liberal, inclusive and progressive constitutional review informed by the torturous and chaotic history of the country and with the determination to make the social contract between the rulers and the ruled/the state and society/people work in partnership to deliver the common good for all. The CRC recommendations illustrate that all is not lost in post-war Sierra Leone, but the real challenge is what the ruling and governing elites will do to the revised progressive social contract constitution to serve their extractive and predatory interests. That will be the litmus test as to whether Sierra Leone will emerge in the coming decade as a developed, effectively governed, inclusive middle income country as peace within and without.

References

Acemoglu, D. and Robinson, J. (2012) *Why Nations Fail. Why Nations Fail: The Origins of Power, Prosperity, and Poverty*. USA/Turkey: Crown Business.

Bradshaw, S. (1996) 'The Coming Chaos?', *Moving Pictures Bulletin*, (25), p. 18.

Collier, P. (2000) 'Doing Well Out of War: An Economic Perspective', in Berdal, M. and Malone, D. (eds) *Greed and Grievance: Economic Agendas in Civil Wars*. Boulder: Lynne Rienner.

Cramer, C. (2006) *Civil War is not a Stupid Thing: accounting for violence in developing countries*. Hurst Publishers Ltd.

Francis, D. (2012) *When War Ends*. Ashgate.

Francis, D. J. (2001) *The Politics of Economic Regionalism: Sierra Leone in ECOWAS*. Aldershot: Ashgate. Available at: http://hdl.handle.net/10454/3064.

Hobbes, T. (1999) *Leviathan*. Oregon: The University of Oregon Renascence Editions.

Kaplan, R. (1994) 'The Coming Anarchy', *Atlantic Monthly*, February.

Keen, D. (2006) *Conflict and Collusion in Sierra Leone*. Palgrave macmillan.

Koroma, A. K. (1996) *Sierra Leone: The agony of a nation*. Canada: Andromeda Publications.

Locke, J. (1690) *The Second Treatise of Government*. Indianapolis: Bobbs-Merrill.

Luttwak, E. (1995) 'Great Powerless Days', *Times Literary Supplement*, 16 June, p. 9.

Macaulay, Lord (1835) *Address to the British Parliament in 2 February, 1835, Historum*. Available at: https://historum.com/threads/lord-macaulay's-address-to-the-british-parliament-in-2-february-1835.26268/ (Accessed: 20 February 2019).

Meredith, M. (2005) *The State of Africa: A History of Fifty Years of Independence*. London: The Free Press.

Reno, W. (1995) *Corruption and State Politics in Sierra Leone*. Cambridge: Cambridge University Press.

Richards, P. (1996) *Fighting for the Rain Forest: War Youth and Resources in Sierra Leone*. Oxford: James Currey.

UNDP (2016) *Human Development Index Report.*

World Bank (2016) *Environmental and Social Standard 5 Land Acquisition, Restrictions on Land Use and Involuntary Resettlement (ESS5)*. Washington, DC, USA: World Bank. Available at: http://www.ifc.org/wps/wcm/connect/topics_ext_content/ifc_ext ernal_corporate_site/ifc+sustainability/our+approach/risk+manage ment/performance+standards/environmental+and+social+perform ance+standards+and+guidance+notes.

World Bank Group (2015) 'Leveraging Oil and Gas Industry for the Development of a Comparative Private Sector in Uganda'. Washington D. C: World Bank.

Yew, L. K. (2000) *From Third World to First: The Singapore and the Asian Economic Boom*. Singapore: Marshall Cavendish Editions.

CHAPTER FOUR

Breaking the Conflict Trap in Uganda: Constitutional and Legal Reforms

Nicholas Opiyo, Arthur Bainomugisha and Barbara Ntambirweki

Introduction

Promotion of rule of law and good governance in post conflict situations requires, inter alia, building the capacity of state institutions to address the root causes of conflict, building institutions for the delivery of services such as health, education, justice and dispute settlement, and the police and correctional services to maintain law and order. In sum, rule of law and good governance entail, first and foremost, a government that lives up to its responsibilities by ensuring effective delivery of public goods and services, the maintenance of law and order, and the administration of justice. It also involves the creation of an efficient and dynamic market that secures economic growth and property, as well as a vibrant civil society, which facilitates interaction between the state and economic and social actors within the state" (Ndulo, 2009).

When the National Resistance Movement/Army (NRM/A) captured power in 1986, it immediately embarked on a constitutional reform process. Through its Ten Point programme, the National Resistance Movement (NRM) sought to establish democratic governance, constitutionalism and the rule of law. As early as 1989 with the establishment of a constitution commission that sought views from the population throughout the country and drafted a constitution. The draft constitution was to form the basis for discussion and subsequent promulgation of a new constitution in 1995. Unlike its predecessor, most observers hailed it as a progressive constitution (Kanyeihamba, 2005).

This was partly because it was a result of a countrywide consultative and inclusive process, its gender responsiveness, and sensitivity to other marginalized groups such as persons with disability, workers, minority groups and youths. Most critically, the framers of the 1995 constitution were informed by the country's political history and set out to make a constitution that would stand the test of time, promote political unity and stability and heal the past political wounds (Republic of Uganda, 1995). However the much-hailed constitution was quickly to be amended even before some of its provisions had been tested.

The first amendment was by way of a referendum, which returned the country to political pluralism, which had been suspended by the NRM upon capture of power. Upon ascent to power NRM/NRA in 1986 suspended political party activities on the basis of the need to promote national unity, reconciliation, stability and reconstruction. Political parties were blamed for being divisive and sectarian and responsible for the past political woes that had afflicted the country.

While the constitutional amendment in 2005 was positive to the extent that it restored political pluralism, it was largely interpreted by analysts and the political opposition as an attempt to water down the sanctity of the constitution Kanyeihamba (2005), an allegation that government denies. It was also viewed as political opportunism by the NRA/M that had remained opposed to political pluralism in favour of the movement political system of governance. There were three other amendments subsequent to the 2005. These amendments have not only been contentious and controversial in their contents and manner of passing but were also rushed through parliament in the months preceding elections. These amendments inter alia scrapped presidential term limits (the famous article 105 (2)) and introduced the position of leader of opposition in parliament). Deeper reflections of their consequences were replaced by political expedience and convenience. Political consensus and ownership were not sought and in cases where they were proposed, completely ignored.

It is against this background that this chapter is written in the hope that it can facilitate a participatory, inclusive and issue based constitutional reform proposals to deepen democratic governance in Uganda. This chapter proposes key constitutional reforms to trigger discussion of civil society leaders to pave way for a national constitutional reform process. The process is intended to facilitate a progressive, broader, participatory and inclusive constitutional reform process that will address the country's democracy deficits, resolve political conflicts and widen the democratic space for political processes in Uganda.

The paper is structured into four major sections. Section one is the background and a brief constitutional and political history of constitutional reforms in Uganda. Section two is the conceptualization of constitutionalism and rule of law which is the expected outcome of the process, section three examines the past constitutional reform processes and draws lessons for the current process. Section four focuses on the constitutional reform proposals while section five focuses on constitutional trends in the East Africa Community region and ends with the conclusion.

An Overview of the Political History of Uganda

> Recalling our history which has been characterized by political and constitutional instability; recognizing our struggles against forces of tyranny, oppression and exploitation; committed to building a better future by establishing a socio-economic and political order through a popular and durable national Constitution based on the principles of unity, peace, equality, democracy, freedom, social justice and progress; exercising our sovereign and inalienable right to determine the form of governance for our country, and having fully participated in the Constitution-making process; do hereby in and through this Constituent Assembly solemnly adopt, enact and give to ourselves and our posterity, this Constitution of the Republic of Uganda, this 22nd day of September, in the year 1995 (Republic of Uganda, 1995).

The political and constitutional history of Uganda has been characterized by political violence, dictatorships both military and civilian, contested electoral outcomes, civil wars and military coups (Golooba-Mutebi, 2008). There were eight changes of government within a period of twenty-four years of independence (from 1962-1986), five of which were short termed, violent and unconstitutional. The preamble to the constitution captures this turbulent past and sets out the overarching goal of the constitution, which is a commitment to building a better future by establishing a socio-economic and political order through a popular and durable national Constitution based on the principles of unity, peace, equality, democracy, freedom, social justice and progress. Although pre independent Uganda was characterized by ethnic conflicts, the foundation of political and constitutional [dis] order in Uganda can be traced to the independence constitution. It was a constitution superimposed in a situation where neither a constitution nor constitutionalism had attained any significant growth.

The Independence Constitution has been described as a mere 'Elastoplast' over a system that had been held together largely by a mixture of force and occasional expeditious compromise (Onyango, J, no date). It lacked political legitimacy and did not last long before it became unworkable. It was described as a triumph of hope over experience (Karugire, 1980). Post-independence civilian governments were proto- democratic civilian governments, which were experimental, inefficient, corrupt and incapable of creating any kind of political culture. They therefore bequeathed a political culture that was to become the root of contemporary democratic challenges. Soon after independence, Uganda was plunged into political and constitutional chaos as the implementation of the independence constitution became impracticable. The fusion of a cultural leader as a political head of state with an executive prime minister presented a conflict of interest in respect to the lost counties of Buyaga and Bugangaizi which subsequently led to the abrogation of the independence constitution.

The Constitution was suspended and replaced with the interim constitution popularly known as the Pigeonhole Constitution of 1966 which itself was replaced with the Republican Constitution of 1967.The Constitutional order ushered in by the Republican Constitution was violently replaced by the rule by decree under the Idi Amin's military dictatorship of 1971-1979 and the equally repressive civilian regimes of Obote II of 1980-1985 respectively. It is discernable from the above that while the independence constitution provided a foundation for constitutional instability, the immediate post independent governments made little if any attempt at generating an acceptable constitutional order. Instead most of the post-independence leaders became pre-occupied with regime perpetuation and entrenching their grip on power. The Constitutional order vested executive powers in the ruling class to ensure their longevity in power.

Unfortunately, these actions have always plunged the country into political instability and undermined rule of law and constitutionalism as evidenced by the abrogation of the independence constitution by Obote in 1966, the 1967 by Idi Amin and the repressive Obote II regime (1980-1985). It is no wonder that the obtaining constitutional order designed to serve individual interests of seating leaders has consistently delivered flawed or contested electoral outcomes. For example, the 1980 general elections were widely viewed as flawed. A hotly contested Uganda People's Congress (UPC) victory led to a guerilla war that brought into power Yoweri Museveni's National Resistance Movement (NRM) government five years later which was heralded as a 'fundamental change' (Kanyeihamba, 2002) in the governance of the country.

The political victory of the NRM arguably produced a shift from a vicious to a virtuous circle in Uganda (Bret, 2006) and the greatest of which was the making and promulgation of the 1995 Constitution (Kanyeihamba, 2005) which vested all powers in the people of Uganda who must be governed according to their will and consent expressed through regular, free and fair elections (Republic of Uganda, 1995).

The new constitutional dispensation thus became the ambulatory instrument for good governance and the exercise of the rule of law. It provided the parameters for the protection, promotion and guarantee of fundamental human rights. A stable constitutional order was established through a constitution arrived at after countrywide consultations by the Odoki Commission. It set the stage for the first presidential and parliamentary elections paving a way for the return to a system of checks and balances among the three arms of government (Onyango, J, 2005). However, elections held under the new constitutional order have also been contested as being unfair. The Supreme Court has on two occasions found the elections to have neither been free nor fair (Mwesige and Muyomba, 2007).

The above notwithstanding, the constitution was found needing of amendment only ten years later. In 2005, the process of deconstructing the constitution commenced in July 2005 with an amendment to pave way for the return of the multiparty democracy and to address other political issues and challenges that had come up in the course of its implementation. This was indeed ironical for a constitution that had been hailed as the finest and most progressive to require a comprehensive review 10 years later. Political analysts have for example observed that the sighs of relief and jubilations expressed after the promulgation of the Constitution were suddenly silenced by a series of legal, political and administrative decisions that watered down the quality of the Constitution (Republic of Uganda, 1995, 2000; Kanyeihamba, 2005).

In February 2001, Government of Uganda set up the Constitutional Review Commission that was chaired by Prof. Fredrick Ssempebwa. Legal Notice No. 1 of 2001 issued by the Minister of Justice and Constitutional Affairs established the commission. The need for setting up the Constitutional Review Commission was justified on the basis of experience, which showed that operating the 1995 Constitution had several defects and several areas of inadequacy that needed to be addressed in the interest of proper governance of the country (Republic of Uganda, 2003).

It should be noted in spite of the weaknesses inherent in the 1995 Constitution, the country had enjoyed relative peace, stability, economic growth and stable predictable constitutional order. Hope had been restored in the rule of law. Nonetheless the work of the commission set in motion the process of amending the constitution.

Past Constitutional Reform Processes: Lessons for the Proposed Reform Process

The immediate post-independence constitutional amendment was in 1967 when the then Premier abrogated the constitution and replaced it with a pigeonhole constitution. The legislature was threatened to adopt a new constitution, which exalted the executive prime minister into the presidency abolishing the rotational arrangement between cultural leaders that had been agreed to before independence.

In 2005, ten years after its promulgation, the 1995 Constitution was amended to pave way for the return of political parties. Following the decision of the National Executive Committee of the Movement, of March, 2003 to open the political space, Government set up the Constitutional Reform Commission (CRC) with the mandate to review the entire constitution. Unlike the pigeonhole constitution and the 1967 constitution making processes, the CRC was consultative and collected views from across the country. The CRC was mandated to examine the consistency and compatibility of the constitutional provisions relating to the sovereignty of the people, political systems, democracy and good governance and make recommendations   as to how best to ensure that the country is governed in accordance with the will of the people at all times.

The CRC was a first attempt at reviewing the 1995 constitution. However, from the very onset the opposition largely interpreted the CRC as a political ploy by government aimed at responding to a political sentiment during an election cycle. Critics of the CRC have argued that the process lacked the competence to execute its mandate, as it was largely constituted by NRM sympathizers (Onyango, J, no date).   These critics further observe that in respect to key political issues, the CRC proposals were ignored and a parallel process initiated which came up with possible amendments. For instance on the matter of which political system to adopt, the NRM set up a Movement Committee (chaired by Dr. Crispus Kiyonga) to consider whether to revert to a multiparty system of governance or not. This was in spite of the fact that the issue of opening up the political system was a key term of reference for the CRC.

The Kiyonga committee submitted its report at the end of 2002 in which they recommended the retention of the Movement Political system. The committee's report was however opposed by President Museveni who argued for the restoration of the multiparty political system. The main reason underpinning his proposal was to be delivered at the NRM retreat in Kyankwanzi in 2003 in which the third term debate was also introduced. President Museveni argued that in order to satisfy the demand of the donor community and to rid the Movement of internal dissenters, it was necessary to open political space and restore a multiparty political system. The Government subsequently developed a government White Paper, which was submitted to the CRC, the very body it had set up to explore recommendations for amendment. The government white paper included the proposal to lift the presidential term limits. The CRC final report submitted in 2003 was largely seen as a failure to address serious constitutional issues that would help consolidate democracy, rule of law and constitutionalism in Uganda (Onyango, J, no date). The process nonetheless, set in motion a process of constitutional amendments, which changed the constitutional landscape in Uganda, (Onyango, Oloka, 2005) which most observers interpreted to constitute a democratic reversal of the democratic gains. Critical among the constitutional amendments was the lifting of presidential terms limits. To some observers, in several respects, the CRC was a missed opportunity for meaningful reform of the constitutional order. As Kanyeihamba (2005) noted, the amendments were manipulative, transitory and in some instances motivated by personal reasons.

It could be argued that the post 1995 constitutional amendments were in their nature no different from the immediate post-independence abrogation of the constitution. They were manipulative and aimed at perpetuating the rule of the powers of the day. While the post-independence change exalted the premier to the presidency and concentrated powers in the executive, the post 1995 removed terms limits for the sole benefit of the sitting president. All of these amendments have not enjoyed the support of the majority and failed to rally consensus across the political aisle. They did not entrench constitutionalism but personal rule through legalese. The opposition political parties have always expressed misgivings about the independence and competence of the EC. The manner in which the EC was constituted, its conduct in administering elections has eroded the citizen's trust that it is a neutral body (Makara, 2007).

The nomination, appointment and removal from office procedures are but the most critical means to guard against impartiality, ensure greater independence and attainment of acceptable levels of competence of the EC. A review of these processes will not only enhance confidence in the democratic process but also ensure that elections reflect the true will of the citizens.

The Nomination and Appointment of the Commission

Besides the conduct of its functions, the process of constituting the commission under a multiparty political system has a direct bearing on how the political actors, civil society and the general voting public perceives the EC. Under the current constitutional framework, the nomination and appointment of members of the EC is a preserve of the President. Although parliamentary approvals are required for actualization of the appointment, this has often than not been a formality devoid of any critical evaluation of the appointees. This kind of procedure for nomination and appointment makes members of the commission serve at the pleasure and pressure of the executive in the conduct of its functions. It is such pleasure and pressure that the EC has been accused of being unwilling to upset. Analysts argue that in the obtaining framework of appointment of the EC, it cannot be any less than rubber stamp for the incumbent president.

Indeed, reviews of past nomination and appointment process of the members of the EC lend some credence to the criticism above. For instance, the process of appointing the Kigunddu led EC was riddled with accusations of bias and incompetence. Save for one addition, the entire EC was retained by the executive in spite of the scathing findings by the Supreme Court ruling in respect to its conduct of the 2006 elections.

In order to ensure the independence of the EC, the nomination and appointment of its members should be subjected to a much more open and critical process that takes into account individual person's antecedents, their suitability for the performance of the functions entailed as well as their ability to subject their political interest to the general good of the country and or their ability to resist political interference during the execution of their duties. It is also important that such a process be taken in consultation with all key political actors including political parties and CSOs. The second way of ensuring independence of the EC is the inclusion of members of professional organisations and political parties on the commission and in appointment process of commissioners. Including political opposition and civil society voices in the appointment process increases the legitimacy of the commission and is likely to achieve greater consensus (European Union, 2011).

Uganda can also learn from the experiences of other countries in regard to the manner in which they constitute their commissions. In Ghana, the procedure of appointing members of the commission is consultative in nature. The Council of State recommends to the president the members for appointment. The Council of State itself is a representative body comprising of a cross section of the political actors. The members are then appointed by the President and confirmed by the parliament (Republic of Ghana, 1992). Wider consultations rather than an exclusive appointing process ensure acceptability of the results of elections and could build confidence of the people in the electoral Commission and the entire electoral process.

Consequently, article 60 of the constitution should be reviewed to ensure that the nomination of members of the commission should be done through a consultative process with civil society organisations and political parties. Consideration should also be given to the expansion of the numbers from seven to 11 in order to accommodate representatives of political parties, civil society and professional organizations.

Competence of Commissioners

The appointment to office of the members of the commission should be based on clearly defined criteria that ensure competence and accountability. Although the constitution provides that members of the commission shall be persons of high moral character, proven integrity and possess considerable experience and demonstrated competence in the conduct of public affairs Republic of Uganda (1995) such qualifications have rarely informed the nominations and approvals by the President and Parliament. Rather, political underpinnings have always appeared to take greater considerations. In other jurisdictions, the chairperson of the commission should be a person qualified to be a judge of the High Court. In Mozambique for instance the commission consists of twenty-one members whose professional and personal qualities afford guarantees of balance, objectivity and independence in relation to all political parties participating in an election. In Tanzania, the Chairperson of the commission must be a person qualified to be a judge of the High Court or Court of Appeal (Kanyeihamba, 2005). In contrast to other statutory bodies such as the Directorate of Public Prosecution (DPP), chairperson of the Human Rights Commission (HRC), the Inspectorate of Government (IGG) whose chairperson must be a person eligible for appointment as a High Court Judge, the chairperson of EC is not subjected to such standard.

Proposals for Constitutional Amendment

> We the people of Uganda, recalling our history which has been characterized by political instability … Do hereby, in and through this Constituent Assembly solemnly adopt, enact and give to ourselves, our posterity, this Constitution … this 22nd day of September, in the year of 1995 (Republic of Uganda, 1995).

The first quotation is a snapshot of what democracy is all about. It serves to inform the proposed constitutional reform process to focus on the highest quality of democracy than 'mere' regular and periodic elections. The second quotation is also important in a sense that it reminds us of our political history characterized by political anarchy which greatly inspired the framers of the 1995 Constitution to try and bequeath to the country a constitution that would heal and resolve political grievances and differences and set the stage for the country's economic growth and sustainable development. The ambulance to the free expression of the will of the people is the Electoral Commission (EC), which is mandated by the constitution to organize and conduct free and fair elections (Republic of Uganda, 1995). In order for the free expression of the people's will and consent, the EC is supposed to be independent and not subject to the control or authority of any person.31 In other words, the people's will on how to be governed cannot be freely expressed if the elections are presided over and conducted by a partisan [and incompetent] EC (Republic of Uganda, 1995). The past history of Uganda points to the fact that the failure to conduct free and fair elections is due to either partial or incompetent ECs and has led to violent confrontations and wars. It is therefore imperative to have an EC that can deliver a free and fair election and breakdown the vicious cycle of election induced conflicts.

While this does not make the position any less important, it does make qualification to the post a little less demanding compared to other statutory bodies. Consequently, the provision of article 60 (3) of the constitution should be amended to provide for qualification of the EC Chairperson to preferably be a retired judge or a person with equal or similar qualifications. Similarly, the process of appointment should be more open, inclusive and democratic so as to ensure public scrutiny and accountability and not at the pleasure of the President. The process of nominations, vetting, approving and appointment should provide for public participation.

Tenure of office

The security of tenure empowers the holder of the office to perform his/her function with some degree of comfort and shields them against any undue interference. In terms of the EC, the constitution provides that members of the EC can only be removed from office by the President for physical and mental incapacity, misconduct or misbehavior and incompetence. The import of that provision is that members of the EC hold their office at the President's calling. They can therefore be subject to the overbearing pressure of presidency to which they hold their office. This can negatively impact on their impartiality and independence.

This provision has not been put to test in recent history but it remains a threat hanging over the members of the EC and its reform is necessary and urgent. The proposal in this case is to draw lessons from other statutory commissions such as the Human Rights Commission and the Judicial Service Commission. In the case of the Human Rights Commission, the removal of its commissioners is similar to the removal of a judge of the High Court that requires a tribunal hearing (Republic of Uganda, 1995).

Members of the commission should enjoy similar security of tenure as is the case with the other constitutional commissions. Article 60 (8) should therefore be amended to ensure that the removal from office of the members of the commission should be through a process that accords fair hearing, transparency not at the pleasure of a political party or individual. A judicial process through a tribunal in much the same manner as that of other constitutional commissions would not only bring parity but ensure the security of tenure of the commissioners, shield them from interferences and influence and enhance their independence. It is recommended that the EC commissioners should be appointed for a period of seven years renewed for one term. Two terms of 14 years is intended to give commissioners security of tenure to exert their independence over undue interference from the executive arm of government.

Restoration of Presidential Term Limits

Nothing is more perilous than to permit one citizen to retain power for an extended period. The people become accustomed to obeying him, and he forms the habit of commanding them; herein lays [sic] the origins of usurpation and tyranny…. Our citizens must with good reason learn to fear lest the magistrate who has governed them long will govern them forever (William, 2009). Term limits are a typical feature of a presidential system of governance in contrast to a prototypical parliamentary system in which the executive may be removed by the legislature at any time. Its origin dates back to the ancient Republics. In one of the earliest definition of democracy, Aristotle listed a key definition of democracy that 'no office should be held twice by the same person (Aristotle, 1976). It has thus become a common feature of many democracies across the world. It ensures a smooth transition of government.

The 1995 constitution imposed term limits of the presidency. The debate about term limits received an almost unanimous approval. In its report, the Uganda Constitution Commission (the Odoki Commission) concluded that an overwhelming majority was in favor of limiting the term of office of the president to a two-year term of five years each. It thus included in the draft constitution article 108 (2), which provided that 'no person shall stay in office for more than two terms.' The commission observed that the danger of an indefinite election system was due to personal ambitions of leaders. The commission noted that there had been concerns about orderly transitions of governments. The recommendation of the commission was adopted by the Constituent Assembly (CA), which enacted article 105 (2) limiting the terms of the president to a two-year term of five years each.

The considered observations of the constitutional commission and the people of Uganda were however discarded shortly after the promulgation of the constitution when a proposal to lift presidential term limits was made by the Executive in the government White Paper. Although earlier not included in its report, the lifting of presidential term limits was subsequently included in the CRC report at the insistence of the executive. It was subsequently to form the basis of the amendment of article 105 (2) of the constitution paving way for President Museveni to contest for a third term in office in the 2006 elections.

It is important to note that the removal of term limits opened the possibility of a life presidency with all its attendant problems. Commenting on the removal of term limits, Eriya Kategaya, once considered as number two to President Museveni in the NRM leadership observed that he was shocked by the constitutional amendment.

In his book, Impassioned for Freedom, Kategaya observed that:

> In my naïve thinking, I believed that President Museveni will live up to the stature of a statesman and be the first President of Uganda to retire as per the Constitution and thereby set a constitutional precedent. I strongly believe that this should be done for the sake of the future stability of this country. I have spent most of my youth running up and down and even went into exile because of bad politics and I don't wish my children to experience the same problems

Table 2.1: Third Term Amendments in Sub-Saharan Africa Since 1990 (Adapted from Vencosvsky, 2007)

Constitution does not contain a two-term only provision (8 countries)	Constitution does contains a two-term limit on the presidency (30 countries)			
	Two terms not served by any president (12 countries)	Two-term limit was reached (18 countries)		
		Constitution amendment not attempted (8 countries)	Constitution amendment attempted (10 countries)	
Côte d'Ivoire	Angola	Bemi (Kerekou)	Without success (3 countries)	With success (7 countries)
Eq. Guinea	Burundi	Cape Verde	Malawi (Muruzi)	Burkina Faso (Campaore)
Gambia	C. A. R	(Monteiro)	Nigeria	Chad (Derby)
Guinea-Bissau	Congo	Ghana (Rawlings)	(Obasanjo)	Gabon (Bongo)
Mauritania	Djibouti	Kenya (Moi)	Zambia	Guinea (Conte)
Sudan	D. R. C	Mali (Konare)	(Chiluba)	Namibia
Seychelles	Liberia	Mozambique		(Nujoma)
(3-term limit)	Madagascar	(Chissano)		Togo
Zimbabwe	Niger	São Tomé e		(Eyadema)
	Rwanda	Príncipe		Uganda
	Senegal	(Trovoada)		(Museveni)
	Sierra Leone	Tanzania (Mkapa)		

The proposed constitutional amendments therefore should be able to revisit the issue of presidential term limits with the intent to restore the two presidential term limits. The two term limits has two advantages for the democratization process. First, the two-term limit has the potential of ensuring certainty that by this date a leader will leave office and this is essentially useful for proper planning. The second advantage is that term limits ensure peace, security and stability as it gives hope and possibilities to people with political interests to wait. In Africa, it has become very difficult to compete with the incumbent president for political power. They always use state resources to retain power and in the process create many enemies, which makes them fear to leave power because of possible repercussions. It is against this background that the proposed reforms should also grant general amnesty to leaders from possible prosecution, which would allow a smooth political transition.

Figure 2.1: Map of Africa Showing third term Amendments in Sub-Saharan Africa Since 1990

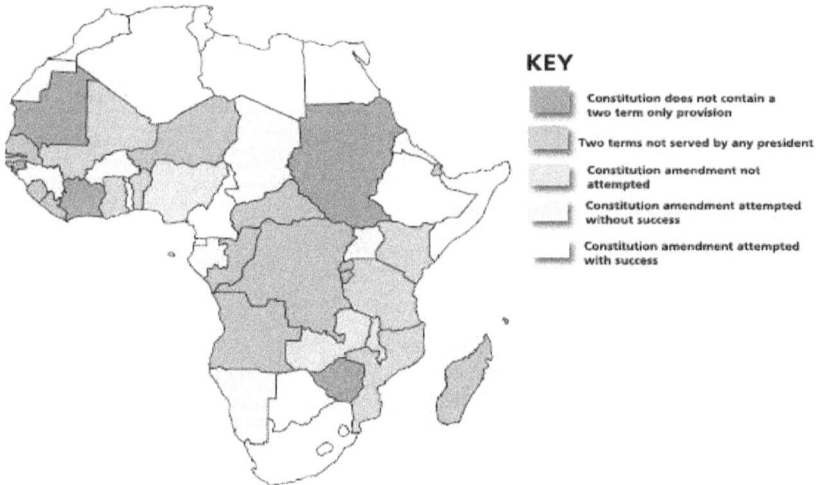

KEY

Constitution does not contain a two term only provision

Two terms not served by any president

Constitution amendment not attempted

Constitution amendment attempted without success

Constitution amendment attempted with success

Separation of Powers

The other reform that will need to be considered is the separation of powers. The principle of separation of powers is premised on the basis that when a single person or group has a large amount of power, it can threaten citizens. Separation of power is a method of checking the amount of power in any institution, individual or group's hands, making it more difficult to abuse such power. Protection of the people against misuse of power by the state itself is, in the first instance, secured when the functions of the government are kept separate and when ultimate power of the state vests with the people, who exercise it through election of representatives in regular, free and fair elections. The principle of separation of powers relates to the very heart of a constitutional government, which structures political institutions with the requisite powers and independence to make judgments that respect equal rights of free people, while at the same time promoting the public good.

Separation of powers means that the legislative, executive and judicial branches of government are independent in exercising their discretionary powers. They are essentially measures and mechanisms calculated to inhibit the tendencies for the excessive use of power and regulate the exercise of discretionary authority of the institutions of governance within the constitutional provisions and political culture of a country.

The constitution of Uganda sets out three arms of government i.e. the executive, legislature and the judiciary (Republic of Uganda, 1995). At a practical level however, it is apparent that the separation of powers between the executive and legislature is blurred. Although complete separation of power is not an attainable virtue in modern day democracies, measures to ensure its near attainment are necessary if we are to avoid an overbearing and controlling tendency by one arm of government over the other. In the Ugandan Parliament, members of the executive sit, deliberate and vote on the floor of the house. Only ex-official members, appointed to cabinet from outside of Parliament cannot vote but are also involved in the deliberations in Parliament. With a bloated cabinet size, the same people who initiate policies and laws in cabinet, not only debate over them again in Parliament but have a numerical number that makes it almost certain to pass in Parliament hence fusing the legislature and executive in the performance of their functions. There is therefore an overlap in function and composition between the executive and the legislature. For instance, the president is empowered to appoint members of the cabinet from among members of parliament or any other person qualified to be a member of Parliament (Republic of Uganda, 1995).

Secondly, the composition of Parliament includes ministers; the unelected being ex- official members of parliament (Republic of Uganda,

1995). This undermines the independence of the legislature and erodes the principle of separation of powers. The other issue that has undermined the independence of parliament in the current political dispensation under NRM leadership is the increasing transfer of debate from the floor of the legislature to caucuses. Members of parliament are summoned by their party and they are cajoled into adopting a party position that should not be contradicted on the floor of the house.

An attempt by two members of Parliament, the Hon Mugisha Muntu and Hon. Onapito Ekomolit to move a motion that bars MPs from being appointed ministers was defeated in the 6th Parliament. There is need to revisit the Onapito/Muntu motion during the proposed constitutional reform process so as to give the principle of checks and balances any meaning in the constitutional framework.

Role of the Army in Elective and Partisan Politics

The constitution provides that the Uganda People's Defence Forces (UPDF) shall be non-partisan, national in character, patriotic, professional, disciplined, productive and subordinate to civilian authority (Republic of Uganda, 1995). This provision would presuppose that the army should not get involved in partisan politics much less in a multiparty political system. And yet, the very same constitution makes the army part of the legislature (Republic of Uganda, 1995). The presence of the army in a largely partisan parliament raises concerns on whether the army is indeed non-partisan. Most critical is that MPs representatives of UPDF are on record for always siding with the executive positions in parliament, which puts into question their independence and neutrality. Compared to past armies in Uganda, the UPDF is highly reputed to be a disciplined army.

However, since the return of political pluralism, its role in elections where some officers committed some electoral abuses raises the question of sustainability of their discipline and professionalism. Most crucially, the UPDF has continued to dominate the political life of Uganda and if not controlled could become a single most threat to democracy. While their presence in parliament was motivated by the desire to regulate and control them, their partisan nature dashes these expectations.

Consequently, it is proposed that the UPDF should be phased out of parliament to protect them from partisan politics. Alternatively, the army representatives could be retained in parliament without voting powers or the right to debate any partisan issue to avoid being drawn into divisive politics.

Size of Parliament

Currently, Parliament has over 400 MPs representing various constituencies around the country. Going by the size alone, this Parliament is too large and an expensive burden to the taxpayers. Ironically, it continues to increase with the trend of creation of new districts which to a large measure serves political expedience rather than ensuring effective legislative representation. Over the years, creation of districts has been justified on the basis of striving to bring services nearer to the people. Yet in most cases, the creation of some districts has not been translated into improved service delivery but rather loss of revenue to the mother district, increased public administration expenditure and conflicts over district borders that always follow the ethnic divide which constrain service delivery. Most noteworthy is that the creation of a new district would mean an additional woman member of parliament.

Structurally, the parliamentary building was built to accommodate only 80 MPs but now has to accommodate over 400 MPs leading to most of them never attending the sessions. But more importantly than the sitting capacity of the house, the quality of representations is impeded by the near crowd in the house. It makes it difficult for the speaker to conduct effective business and provide space for effective and meaningful deliberations by all Members of Parliament. The parliament is simply too big, an unnecessary burden of the taxpayers and does not provide effective representation of the people of Uganda. Consequently, it is recommended that the size of Parliament should be reduced and that constituencies of members directly elected should be based on a population quota of two hundred thousand (200,000) people per constituency as was originally proposed by the Constitutional Review Commission. A small, well-equipped and facilitated Parliament will be able to be effective and to exert its independence. Also related to the size of Parliament is the remuneration of members of Parliament. The current status quo is that Members of Parliament should determine their emoluments. Experience has shown that it is not easy for Members of Parliament to rationally determine their remuneration without provoking public anger and loss of trust among the citizens which also impacts on their performance. Consequently, it is proposed that Members of Parliament remuneration should be determined by an independent commission.

Proposal to Establish a Two Chamber Parliament

A two Chamber (Bi-Cameral) Parliament is being proposed as one of the safeguards for the principle of separation of powers, particularly, the independence of Parliament. Most crucially for Uganda as a conflict prone country, a two chamber Parliament is likely to act as a conflict management mechanism, stabilize and set the country on a path to durable peace. The ideas on which bicameralism which is the practice of having two legislative or parliamentary chambers is based can be traced to the theories developed in the Ancient Sumer and later Greece, ancient India and Rome (Bicameralism, 2011). Recognizable bicameral institutions first arose in medieval Europe where they were associated with separate representation of different estates of the realm. For example, one house would represent the aristocracy and the other would represent the commoners. The framers of the Constitution of the United States of America also favored a bi-cameral legislature. The idea was to have the Senate that was wealthier and wiser. The Senate was created to be a stabilizing force, knowledgeable and more deliberate – a sort of republican nobility - and a counter to what Madison saw as the 'fickleness and passion' that could absorb the House (Bicameralism, 2011).

Madison further noted that the use of the Senate is to consist in its proceedings with more coolness, with more system and more wisdom than the popular branch (lower house or congress). This argument led the framers of the US Constitution to grant the Senate prerogative in foreign policy, an area where steadiness, discretion, and caution were deemed very important. Initially, the Senate was chosen by state legislators, and the Senators had to possess a significant amount of property in order to be deemed worthy and sensible enough for the position. In 1913 the 17th Amendment was passed which mandated that Senators would be elected by popular vote rather than chosen by the State legislatures. In the case of America, a rationale was invented for bicameralism in which the upper house (Senate) would have states represented equally, and the lower house would have them represented by population.

The relationship between the two houses varies from country to country. In some cases both houses have equal power, while in others one house is clearly superior in its powers. There are two schools of thought about bi-cameralism. Critics believe that bicameralism makes meaningful political reforms more difficult to achieve and increases the risk of gridlock especially in cases where both chambers have similar powers. Proponents of bicameralism argue that the merits of the checks and balances provided by the bicameral model help to prevent the passage into law of ill-considered legislation. Kenya, Rwanda, South Africa and Burundi have both houses. Other countries with bicameral legislatures are USA, Canada, Argentina, Australia, Brazil, Germany, India, Switzerland etc. In the United States, Australia, Mexico each state is given the same seats in the upper house. While the difference in population size is taken into account, deliberate effort is taken to ensure that smaller states are not overshadowed by larger states which have more representation in the lower house.

Election of Senators

In Uganda, the election of Senators could borrow from the Canadian model. In Canada, Senators are not elected by all the voters but are elected by the Governor General on the advice of the Prime Minister. The Senate does not originate most legislation although a small fraction of government bills are introduced in the Senate and Senators may introduce private members bills in the same way as Members of

Parliament. The Senate acts as a chamber of revision; almost passing legislation approved by the House of Commons made up of Members of Parliament who are elected. In bi-cameral systems, the Senate must pass legislation before it becomes law and can therefore act as a wise facilitator. Senate does not have to endure the accountability and scrutiny of parliamentary elections. In Germany and India, the upper houses are more closely linked with the federal system and are either appointed or elected directly by the governments or legislatures. The Indian upper house does not have the states represented equally, but on the basis of their population.

It should be noted that bicameralism exists in countries that are not federations where the upper houses representation is based on territorial basis. A good example of a country with a bi-cameral system is South Africa where the National Council of Provinces has its members chosen by each Province's legislature (Republic of Uganda, 2001). Many bicameral countries that have unitary systems such as Netherland, Philippines and Republic of Ireland, the upper house generally focuses on scrutinizing and vetoing the decisions of the lower house.

Why a Bicameral System for Uganda?

Uganda is a conflict-prone country. For most of the 49 years of post Uganda's independence, the country has experienced protracted violent conflicts with the LRA conflict as the longest and still going on. While, there are quite a number of underlying causes of the conflicts in Uganda, lack of constitutionalism and rule of law is central to the history of violent conflicts and political instability in Uganda. Secondly, right from independence in 1962, almost all leaders have pursued the winners take it all model which has meant political exclusion of some people from power forcing some to pursue armed struggle to access political power. Thirdly, the first independence constitution provided a federal arrangement for the four kingdom areas, which were abolished in 1966 together with the constitution. The spirit of federalism especially in Buganda that had tasted its benefits continues to hover around and remains a challenge to national peace and stability.

More so, while the current constitution provides for the principle of separation of powers, in practice, government has greatly undermined and eroded the independence of both parliament and judiciary. The bicameral system is intended to strengthen the independence and protect the sanctity of parliament. Apart from the bicameral system offering checks and balances to the executive and judiciary, the system will act as a conflict management mechanism to prevent future conflicts that bedevil the country's stability. Most crucially, a bicameral system will help to utilize the country's eminent elder statesmen and women who are accomplished and wise enough to provide guidance to the country.

Locating Constitutional Reforms in the Context of the East African Community

Uganda is a member of the East African Community. The East African Community treaty provides for the establishment of a political federation ('The Treaty for the Establishment of the East African Community', 2006). In terms of constitutionalism, the treaty provides that 'in order to realize the objectives of the EAC, the Treaty directs partner states to observe fundamental principles such as good governance, which includes adherence to the principles of democracy; the rule of law; accountability; transparency; social justice; equal opportunity; gender equality, and the recognition, promotion and protection of human rights, in accordance with the provisions of the African Charter on Human and Peoples Rights ('The Treaty for the Establishment of the East African Community', 2006). The need to harmonize the legal framework within the community will be central to the achievement of a political federation. Further, the harmonization of the broader constitutional framework in each of the federating states is also crucial. To this end, any constitutional reform must as of necessity take into account the regional constitutional development in the partner states.

The developments in the region indicate a move towards a more independent electoral commission, presidential term limits and creation of a more independent judiciary. These developments cannot be ignored in the process of amending the constitutional order in Uganda if we are to move towards a political federation. After its traumatic and violent experience arising from election violence, Kenya has undergone a comprehensive constitutional reform with fundamental changes in its constitutional order. One of the key reforms is the establishment of an independent Electoral Commission (Republic of Kenya, 2010). Tanzania has had the most relatively stable electoral process over the years providing for free and fair elections and ensuring an orderly transition of governments. The other important matter for the constitutional development in the region is the question of presidential term limits. The new Kenyan constitution provided for a two-term presidency of five years each (Barkham, 2011). Similar provisions are contained in the constitutions of Rwanda (Barkham, 2011), Tanzania and Burundi. While Rwanda will see a transition of power when the term of President Kagame ends, Tanzania has had many transitions in terms of presidents that have been peaceful. The challenge for Uganda, the country has never had any peaceful transition from one president to another and many people wish to see that happen under President Museveni.

Currently, President Museveni is the longest serving head of state in the region and most observers predict that if the political transition is not well handled, it could plunge the country into political violence (Barkham, 2011). The other regional trend that is worth noting is the matter of separation of powers between the executive and the legislature in order to ensure checks and balances. The Kenyan constitution is very instructive. It has provided a clear delineation of roles and responsibilities between the executive and the judiciary. It should also be noted that among all the five member countries of the EAC, Uganda is the only country without presidential term limits. The preamble to the EAC treaty recognizes the lack of participation by civil society and the private sector as one of the reasons for dissolution of the original East African Cooperation.

The Treaty therefore provides for the creation of opportunity for civil society and private sector participation. In Chapter 25, the Treaty emphasizes the "creation of an enabling environment for the private sector and the civil society", "strengthening the private sector"; and providing for "cooperation among business organizations and professional bodies". The desire to involve civil society in the affairs of the East African Community (EAC) is further given effect by Article7, which describes civil society as one of the crucial actors in the EAC. Article 127 envisages the creation of an enabling environment for both civil society and the private sector to participate in the affairs of the Community and specifically demands the promotion of the roles of non-governmental organizations (NGOs). Civil Society will therefore be crucial for the success or failure of the EAC to execute its mandate. The creation of linkages and development of common programs and strategies under the EAC framework in order to shape the political and democratic developments in the region will be essential. The proposed constitutional reform process driven by civil society to a large extent falls into the framework of the EAC. It is hoped that government of Uganda that has been at the forefront of fast-tracking the EAC integration will embrace this initiative and support it for it to succeed.

Conclusion

In this chapter, we have stated the case for constitutional reforms in Uganda which is mainly intended to deepen the democratization process and consolidation of democracy. The chapter has analysed the constitut-ional history of Uganda to demonstrate the need for democratization and steer the country away from a history of violence and political anarchy. The chapter identified and analysed constitutional issues for reform and justified these reforms in the context of regional integration. It is proposed that while this initiative is driven by civil society, it must be owned by the government since it has the constitutional mandate to review the constitution. We propose a participatory, inclusive and people-centered process that will not only deliver an amended constitution but also issue-based civic education to its citizens.

References

Aristotle (1976) *The Politics of Aristotle.* Edited by E. Baker. London: Oxford University Press.

Barkham, D. J. (2011) *Assessing Risks to Stability.* Washington D.C.

Bicameralism (2011) *Wikipedia.* Available at: https://en.wikipedia.org/wiki/Bicameralism (Accessed: 13 October 2011).

Bret, E. A. (2006) *State Failure and Success in Uganda and Zimbabwe: The Logic of Political Decay and Reconstruction in Africa.* London: Crisis State Research Centre, LSE Working Paper.

European Union (2011) *Election Observation Mission Report.*

Golooba-Mutebi, F. (2008) *Collapse, War and Reconstruction in Uganda: An analytical Narrative of State Making.* London: Crisis State Research Centre (LSE), Working Paper 27 Series.

Kanyeihamba, G. W. (2002) *Constitutional and Political History of Uganda: From 1894 to the Present.* Kampala: Fountain Publishers Ltd.

Kanyeihamba, W. G. (2005) *Constitutionalism and Political History of Uganda: From 1894 to the Present.* Kampala: Centenary Publishing House Ltd.

Karugire, S. R. (1980) *The Political History of Uganda.* London: Heinemann Publishers Ltd.

Makara, S. (2007) 'Deepening Democracy through Multipartyism: The Bumpy Road to Uganda's 2011', *Africa Spectrum,* 45(2), pp. 81–94.

Mwesige, P. and Muyomba, L. (2007) *Deepening Democracy in Uganda: Legislative and Administrative Reforms Ahead of 20II Elections.* Kampala: ACODE Policy Briefing Paper.

Ndulo, M. B. (2009) *Rule of Law Programs, Judicial reform, Development and Post Conflict Societies.* ANLEP Working Paper. Available at: www.sum.uio.no/research/networks/anlep,.

Onyango, J, O. (2005) 'From Whence We Come and Where Exactly are we Going?', *The Politics of Electoral Struggles and Constitutional Non Transition in Uganda.* Kampala: HURIPEC, Rights Democratic Working Paper Series, (1).

Onyango, J, O. (no date) 'Judicial Power and Constitutionalism in Uganda: A Historical Perspective', in Mamdani, M. and Onyango, J.

O. (eds) *Uganda Studies in Living Conditions, Popular Movements and Constitutionalism.* JEP books.

Onyango, Oloka, J. (2005) *Liberalisation without Liberation: Understanding the Paradox of the Opening of Political Space in Uganda.* Kampala: HURIPEC Rights Democratic Working Paper Series.

Republic of Ghana (1992) 'Constitution of the Republic of Ghana. Accra: Government of Ghana'.

Republic of Kenya (2010) 'Constitution of the Republic of Kenya'.

Republic of Uganda (1995) *The constitution of the Republic of Uganda.* Entebbe: UPPC.

Republic of Uganda (2000) 'The Constitutional (Amendment) Act, Act No 13 of 2000'. UPPC.

Republic of Uganda (2001) *Col (Rtd) Dr. Kizza Besigye Vs. Electoral Commission & Yoweri Kaguta Museveni, Presidential Election Petitions No. 1 of 2001 and 2006.* Kampala: Courts of Judicature.

Republic of Uganda (2003) *Government White Paper on the Report of the Commission of Inquiry, (Constitutional Review) and Government Proposals not addressed by Commission of Inquiry.* Kampala: Cabinet Office.

'The Treaty for the Establishment of the East African Community' (2006).

Vencosvsky, D. (2007) 'Presidential Term Limits In Africa', *Journal of Democracy,* 18(3). Available at: http://www.africafiles.org/printableversion.asp?id=17065.

William, C. S. (ed.) (2009) 'TheReelectionDebateinLatinAmerica', in *LatinAmericanDemocraticTransformations: Institutions, Actors and Processes.*

CHAPTER FIVE

Democracy and Enhancing Sustainable Livelihoods in Uganda: Lessons from Performance of Special Interest Groups in the Sixth and Seventh Parliament

Arthur Bainomugisha and Elijah Dickens Mushemeza

Introduction

Uganda, like other East African countries, is going through a political transition process. To most political commentators, this is yet another milestone in the democratic development of a country whose 57 years of post-independence period have been marred by political anarchy and violence. After almost 20 years under no-party political system, Uganda re-introduced a multiparty political system. Most political analysts have observed that the way the political transition and constitutional reforms are handled will determine whether or not Uganda will have a peaceful democratic transition and consolidation of democracy in the context of East African community. Although a number of reforms were carried out after the referendum on political systems in the year 2000, more is yet to be done. In particular different political actors are calling for electoral reforms to facilitate the management and conduct of free and fair elections, an important aspect of democratisation process. Critical in the constitutional and electoral reform and political transition processes is the institution of Parliament which is central to the amendment of the 1995 Constitution to provide for the necessary political reforms.

The legislature in any democratic society is considered the most fundamental arm of the state in promoting democratic governance. Parliament as mostly referred to in commonwealth countries serves to secure the foundations of democracy by translating the will of the people into the law of land. At its core, the legislature is a mirror of society's soul. The question however is how to ensure that the composition of the legislature and the decisions it makes are a true reflection of the will of all people whom this body is designed to represent. The composition of the Sixth and Seventh Parliament of Uganda the case study of this chapter was very diverse. Both parliaments were composed of directly elected members of Parliament and representatives of special interests groups such as women, persons with disabilities, workers, youths and the army elected under the principle of affirmative action to represent the voices of the marginalized.

In this chapter where we assess the performance of Special Interest Groups (SIGs) in the 6th and 7th Parliament, we contend that Parliament is the one important arm of the state and government that can promote environmental governance, protect and advance the interests of natural resource dependent communities. As such, we have argued here that strengthening the parliament to perform its legislative responsibility would ultimately promote environmental governance, peace and sustainable livelihoods. The Special Interest Groups representation in parliament during the period under study created an opportunity for effective representation of issues that directly affect livelihoods of the poor natural resource dependent communities. We have also argued that the SIGs are disproportionately affected by environmental degradation, and environmental scarcity than others in the Ugandan society. Consequently, effective legislative representation of SIGs environmental interests would not only secure their livelihoods but also protect the integrity of the environment and promote sustainable development and peace. However, for parliament and individual legislators to perform effectively, they need to be independent and accountable, with authority to make fundamental decisions.

The analysis in this chapter is premised on the understanding that Uganda is largely a nature based economy with natural resources providing immediate economic and enterprise opportunities for the majority of poor people in rural areas. As such good environmental governance would ensure equity and availability of goods and services to majority of the citizens and therefore guarantee peace and stability not only in Uganda but the entire East African community.

Empirical data for the analysis of this work was mainly collected using qualitative methods while the rest of the data is based on secondary sources. The Parliamentary Hansard, Constitutional Assembly and Constitutional Review reports, newspaper reports, books, the Ugandan Constitution and other pieces of legislation were found to be very useful sources of information during the study. Furthermore, the research team carried out a number of interviews with key selected respondents drawn mainly from the members of the sixth and seventh Parliament, civil society, academia and the general public. This was necessary for comparative analysis. The researchers also used self-administered interview schedules which were found to be handy especially in dealing with very busy respondents such as MPs. The conclusion draws lessons for the rest of the countries in East African community in terms of democratic governance for sustainable peace and stability.

Legislative Representation and Environmental Governance

Agriculture is considered the backbone of Uganda's economy and is the most important sector in terms of food and nutrition security, employment, income, raw materials for industry and exports to regional and international markets (Republic of Uganda, 2015). As a matter of fact, the agriculture sector is one of the priority sectors for investment in Uganda given its great multiplier effect on the economy. About 69.4% of Uganda's 7.3 million households depend on subsistence farming as a source of livelihood with majority of these households (82%) living in rural areas (Uganda Bureau of Statistics, 2016). Subsistence farmers deliver 75-80 per cent of the total agricultural output and marketed agricultural produce (Republic of Uganda, 2015). The agriculture sector contributes 25.3% to Uganda's GDP, employs about 72% of the total labour force (77% of whom are women and 63% are youth) and accounts for 54% of total exports (Republic of Uganda , 2015). This is why; the agriculture sector is regarded as the key determinant in the Uganda's efforts to reduce poverty in the years ahead (Republic of Uganda, 2010). In spite of this recognition, citizens' standard of living remains at the lowest level in most parts of the country. Part of the explanation for a down trend in poverty levels is linked to poor environmental management.

Yet, despite the various opportunities in the environment sector, they cannot be enjoyed by the majority rural poor people unless they have information about such opportunities. Similarly, they cannot participate in making decisions concerning management of those resources and later on seek legal redress in case of denial of those opportunities. It should be noted however, that Parliament in most democracies is an institution where citizens can participate in decision making through their elected representatives. By strengthening Parliament and individual MPs to effectively represent the interests of their constituencies, the practice promotes environmental governance and environmental interests of the majority of the citizens.

Because the majority of Ugandans are dependent on natural resources, most human rights abuses and conflicts revolve around the struggle to access and control of various natural resources. The political problems in the greater Kibale area reported over the years between the indigenous Banyoro, the immigrant Bakiga from Western Uganda and the quest for federalism for Buganda region presented as political issues over decades are known to be driven and fuelled by the struggle to access and control land resources. In such circumstances Parliament is best placed to act as a conflict management and conflict prevention mechanism in natural resource based conflicts. Parliament using the various mechanisms and resources at its disposal can promote environmental rights especially of vulnerable resource dependent communities including access to land, access to protected areas, access to clean water and access to key economic resources such as forests and wildlife concessions.

Furthermore, security analysts see a nexus between natural resources and violent conflicts for natural resource dependent societies arising out of the struggle for access and control of natural resources. Homer-Dixon for example has argued that environmental degradation which leads to scarcities in natural resources is fuelling civil conflicts within the poorest states in the international system (De Soysa, 2000). According to these scholars, a persistent and serious ingenuity gap raises grievances and erodes the moral and coercive authority of government, which boosts the probability of serious turmoil and violence. If these processes continue unchecked, countries with a critical ingenuity gap therefore risk becoming trapped in a vicious cycle of instability and democratic governance deficits. Parliament as a main negotiation mechanism and decision making body in Uganda can play a big role so as to avoid the ingenuity gap and the risk of being trapped in the cycle of violence and lack of peace.

In order for Uganda to deepen the democratization processes, and guarantee peace and stability it requires to focus seriously on democratizing the management of the country's natural resources and fair distribution of scarce resources. Indeed, since 1986 when the NRM came into power, Government has attempted to correct the historical wrongs including political exclusion and disenfranchisement of disadvantaged groups. The 1995 Constitution for instance, undertook to institutionalize the principle of Affirmative Action which provided for representation of marginalized groups in Parliament and other positions of decision making.

Understanding the Concept of Affirmative Action and Representation

The principle of Affirmative Action gained credence in the 1960's at the height of the civil rights movement in the United States. Affirmative action from the civil rights perspective is defined as, attempts to make progress toward substantive, rather than merely formal equality of opportunity for those groups, such as women or racial minorities, which are quite often are under-represented in significant positions in society by explicitly taking into account the defining characteristic- sex or race— which has been the basis for discrimination (Tamale, 1999).

Affirmative Action as a Mechanism for enhancing representation in Uganda

The struggle for independence and representation in the governance of Uganda took a new turn after World War II. The militant Nationalists were in command of the anti-colonial resistance. The Second World War had unleashed forces that loosened the colonial states' hold on political power. Internally, the colonial arrangement which had incorporated the chiefs in colonial governance had to be revised. Efforts were made to satisfy new political demands by democratizing the local government structures which had been manned largely by chiefs and by establishing limited representation in central institutions. Under the African Local Government Ordinance 1949, limited powers were devolved on district councils and a limited number of posts in local governments were elective. By 1952, the LEGCO was almost truly representative consisting of the Governor, nine Ex-official members, eleven cross-bench members and twenty-seven representative members (Kanyeihamba, 2002). In the same year it was announced that each district except Karamoja, would elect a representative on the Legislative Council. The new chamber was also for the first time, to include two women, although both women were European - Mrs Saben and Mrs Boase (Kanyeihamba, 2002).

The rise of political parties in the 1950s consolidated the need for representation within parties and subsequently in government. As representation came to be accepted as norm in the new political dispensation particularly after independence, political parties included special interest groups in their structures and hierarchies namely, the youth and women. The decades that followed independence were characterized by political upheavals and dictatorship narrowed the political space for special interest groups at the national level. In 1967 however, the constitution was amended, where formal provision for representation of the military in the legislature was established. There were also to be ten specially elected members and another ten nominated by the President to represent interest groups.

When the National Resistance Movement took power in 1986 and subsequently instituted the Uganda Constitutional Commission to review the Constitution and make proposals for a new Constitution, the issue of interest groups bounced in the public realm. It aroused much debate in the People's views coming to the Commission. Sections of society opposed any interest group representation, saying it would debase the principle of democratic representation while others noted that direct election of people's representatives would in any event tend to bring people from different sections of society to Parliament including people from interest groups (The Report of the Uganda Constitutional Commission: Analysis and Recommendations, 1988). In the end the Commission recommended inclusion in the Constitution, representation of special interest groups in Parliament namely Women, Youth, Workers, Persons with disabilities and the army.

Constitutional Provisions Supporting Special Interest Groups in Parliament

One of the fundamental achievements of the National Resistance Movement (NRM) was the affirmative action that enfranchised formerly marginalized groups in Uganda by involving them in all positions of decision-making. Objective Six under the National Objectives and Directive Principles of State Policy of the 1995 Constitution provides that, "The State shall ensure gender balance and fair representation of marginalized groups on all constitutional and other bodies". Article 32 (1) of the Constitution is very instrumental on affirmative action in favour of formerly marginalized groups. It states that: "Notwithstanding anything in this Constitution, the State shall take affirmative action in favour of groups marginalized on the basis of gender, age, disability or any other reason created by history, tradition or custom, for the purpose of redressing imbalances which exist against them". Sub-section (2), states that Parliament shall make relevant laws, including laws for the establishment of an equal opportunities commission, for the purpose of giving full effect to the clause" (Uganda constitution, 1995).

Further constitutional guarantees are provided for in Article 36 under the protection of minorities. The article states that, "Minorities have a right to participate in decision making processes, and their views and interests shall be taken into account in the making of national plans and programmes". Other provisions for protection and representation of interest groups can be found in article 21 which guarantees equality of all and provides for freedom from discrimination and article 35 on the rights of Persons with Disabilities. Article 78 on Composition of Parliament is very instrumental on representation of Special Interest Groups in Parliament. Section (a) of article 78 provides for one woman representative for every district while subsection (b) provides for such numbers of representatives of the army, youth, workers, persons with disabilities and other groups as Parliament may determine.

Factors that influence Members of Parliament

Individual MPs are motivated or de-motivated to perform their legislative responsibilities by a numbers of factors. These factors are categorized as autonomy, authority, accountability, personal attributes and the level of civic awareness of the citizens.

Autonomy

One of the motivating or de-motivating factors that significantly affect effective legislative representation relates to the autonomy of the Institution of Parliament and individual legislators to freely exercise their right to perform their duties. For example, one of the responsibilities of Parliament is to provide oversight over the actions and decisions of the Executive and Judiciary. While the three arms of Government are supposed to be interdependent on each other, their effectiveness depends on the ability of each one of them to enjoy autonomy while exercising its duties. In the case of the Ugandan Parliament, autonomy is provided under the law. Key legal provisions related to the autonomy of the Parliament include the power of Parliamentary Standing Committees and Sessional Committees, the method of elections of MPs to Parliament, and legislative powers of Parliament.

The mechanism of committees is the major method by which legislatures conduct their business. The autonomy of Parliament can be assessed based on whether or not the Parliamentary Committees have adequate powers to respond to concerns addressed to them by the electorates. Such concerns may be related to management of environmental resources, budget review, examining the conduct of ministers or any other civic matter that directly affects the livelihoods of the citizens. Article 90 of the Ugandan Constitution grants Parliament powers to appoint or set up Standing Committees. The same Constitution grants Committees extensive powers to enable them perform their functions. For example article 90 (4) provides that in the exercise of their functions under this article, Committees, "may call upon any Minister or any person holding a public office and private individuals to submit memoranda or appear before them to give evidence; Committees shall have the powers of the High Court for (i) enforcing the attendance of witnesses; (ii) compelling the production of documents; and (iii) instituting a commission or request to examine witnesses abroad". There is significant evidence from the records of the 6th and 7th Parliament which indicate that Standing Committees utilized their powers to summon public officials to appear before them and provide evidence or information in government conduct or decisions. For example the Parliamentary Committee on Natural Resources while handling the petition lodged in Parliament by the tree farmers of Butamira Forest Reserve summoned the Minister of Water Lands and Environment, the Executive Director of National Environment Authority and other senior officers from relevant Government departments to give evidence during the hearings.

Electoral Process of Members of Parliament

It should be understood that the Parliament's autonomy or the autonomy of individual legislators can also be influenced by the manner in which Members of Parliament get elected into Parliament. The electoral process of MPs is likely to significantly influence the voting patterns on particular issues and contribution in Parliament. Consequently, their independence, responsibility and effectiveness in Parliament are also affected. While majority of legislators in the 6th and 7th Parliaments were directly elected through the universal adult suffrage that emphasized the principle of individual merit, there existed a substantive number of legislators (91 MPs) who were elected by electoral colleges representing special interest groups. These included: the women, youths, workers, persons with disabilities and the army. It is important to point out here that the way legislators are elected into Parliament greatly determines their performance. For instance the performance of the Special Interest Groups in the 7th Parliament emanates from the way they were elected into Parliament. In what is nationally and internationally acclaimed as an effort to enfranchise formerly marginalized groups, the NRM government introduced the principle of affirmative action that ensured political representation of these groups at positions of decision making. This starts right from the village level to national level. Parliamentary representatives of these groups are elected by electoral colleges. Scholars such as Sylvia Tamale note that because of affirmative action introduced by the NRM administration most of the representatives of the special interest groups find it hard to vote against an issue coming from the Executive (Tamale, 1999).

Most MPs interviewed during the study observed that some representatives of Special Interest Groups and indeed most MPs in the

7th Parliament were reluctant to express their thoughts publicly for fear of not being re-elected in the next Parliament. An MP lamented about the lost golden time before parties were allowed to operate. She said,

> *"you see, the 6th Parliament was based on the principle of individual merit. We could afford to debate and vote according to our conscience. But now under partisan politics, we are controlled by collective responsibility. Once the Movement Caucus takes a position, we all support without questioning".*

Representatives of special interest groups face a fundamental challenge because they are elected by electoral colleges which are small and easy for the Executive to mobilize against any "errant" Members of Parliament

Authority

Political theorists such as John Locke (1632-1704) and Jean Jacques Roseau (1712-1778) observed that the basis of any democratic polity was the social contract between the rulers and the ruled which gives power to the former to enact laws to govern society. At the same time these political thinkers observed that delegated power and authority can be withdrawn by the people. The argument is still valid today and fits in the context of modern world democracy where leaders are periodically elected by the people. The electorate has power to elect MPs or not to re-elect them based on their performance or any other reason. For example, members of parliament and the president under 1995 Constitution are elected periodically for a period of five years after which they are expected to go back to the people to seek fresh mandate.

The constitutional authority of Members of Parliament is provided for under the 1995 Constitution. The constitution mandates Parliament to enact a legislation granting immunity and privileges to members of Parliament and any other person participating or assisting in or acting in connection with or reporting the proceedings of Parliament or any of its committees. On the basis of the existing constitutional provisions, Parliament and individual MPs have sufficient authority to perform legislative roles without undue interference.

Accountability

Underpinning effective legislative representation of the electorate's interests: environmental and other civic issues in Parliament by their MPs, is the whole issue of political accountability. Accountability refers to the answerability of government to law and the people - an essential ingredient of a new democracy (Harris and Reilly, 1998). As long as the Government remains in real terms answerable to the citizens, a self-regulatory process is set in motion. Accountability comes out most clearly in elections in a sense that if voters do not like a government's or MP's record, they can vote it or him/her out of office. In order to enforce accountability of Government and Parliament in particular, it is important to put in place legal and political mechanisms which would monitor progress, review and criticize performance and ultimately compel Government to be accountable to the citizens.

Civic Competence of the Electorate

Another factor that could motivate or de-motivate a legislator to effectively champion the interests of the electorate in Parliament is their level of civic awareness. Where the electorate is knowledgeable about their civic rights, duties and responsibilities and have access to vital information about their Government, they are likely to demand effective representation from their legislator. Likewise, in a situation where the electorate is largely ignorant of their civic rights, obligations and duties, uninformed, with limited access to information on the functions and actions of parliament, it becomes difficult for them to demand effective representation from their representative. This is why for any country that chooses to establish durable democracy it must invest in building civic awareness of the citizens. In Uganda, the Human Rights Commission and the Electoral Commission were set up among other responsibilities, to conduct civic education and build the citizens civic competence to hold their government accountable as well as fulfill their civic duties and obligations (Uganda constitution, 1995).

Transparency

Transparency essentially refers to the openness of the government system. As long as there are no mechanisms for making Parliament transparent in its business transactions, it becomes hard for the electorate to hold it accountable. In Uganda's case the Constitution under Article 41 (1) provides that, every citizen has a right of access to information in the possession of the State or any other organ or agency of the State except where the release of the information is likely to prejudice the security or sovereignty of the State or the privacy of any other person. The law on Access to Information (AI) has also added force to the Constitutional provision on freedom of access to information on Government actions and decisions where citizens could base their decisions to support it

Personal Attributes of a Legislator

The final factor that influences individual legislators to bring the interests of their electorate on the floor of Parliament are what scholars have termed as personal attributes. Some legislators are motivated by the desire to serve the electorate well with honour, zeal and distinction in order to live behind a legacy (Mushi, 2004). Other legislators are motivated by ambition and responsibility. An example is the former Woman Member of Parliament for Mbarara District, Honorable Miria Matembe. She joined Parliament in 1989 through the Local Council structures to rise to Parliamentary level. Because of her being articulate and passionate for the cause of women in Uganda, she was appointed a Commissioner in 1989 on the Constitutional Commission which moved around the country soliciting views for inclusion in the Constitution. She was subsequently elected a member of the Constituent Assembly which debated enacted and promulgated the 1995 Ugandan Constitution. She was appointed a Minister of State for Ethnics and Integrity a post she held for three years. Because of her dedicated service to the women's cause, Matembe is regarded as one of the leading women's activist in Uganda (Matembe, personal communication). Through Matembe's example one can see how personal attributes linked to personal ambition desire to perform better and personal conviction can influence legislators to effectively represent the interests of their electorates.

Functions of a Member of Parliament

In order to measure the performance of members of Parliament, it is important to articulate their functions as representatives of the people. Montesquieu in "The Spirit of the Laws", wrote admiringly about the legislature. He declared, "… since it was impossible in a large state for the people to meet as a legislative body, they must choose representatives to do what they could not do themselves" (Dahl, 1989). Seen from Montesquieu's point of view and from modern democratic practices, people's aspirations and their views are voiced through their representatives to whom power and responsibility has been delegated. In any democratic polity, legislators are elected through popular elections where people pronounce themselves by choosing representatives of their choice for a specific term of office: five years in Uganda's case.

Suffice it to say, that the function of Members of Parliament are very much linked with the function of Parliament: making laws, approving the Government budget, policies and appointments as well as providing checks and balances to the other arms of Government. However, Legislators are also expected to perform a lot of other functions either based on personal initiatives or exerted by expectations from voters against which performance can be assessed.

First, a Member of Parliament acts as a bridge between the Government and the citizens being represented in Parliament. As an MP one is supposed to articulate Government policy and political decisions including legislations to the people in the Constituency. Second, a Member of Parliament is expected to mobilize and attract resources, financial and material for the development of his/her constituency. Hard working and innovative MPs attract projects such as water, health and sanitation to their constituencies

Third, a Member of Parliament is to defend his constituency from unfair Government policy, decision, or legislation. In matters or issues that threaten the existence or livelihoods of the voters/ constituents, the MP becomes a spokesperson in Parliament and a defender of his/her people. The role of MP Frank Nabwiso in the defense of his constituents in the 7th Parliament when they were faced with Government's attempt to degazette Butamira Forest Reserve in favour of Kakira Sugar at the expense of tree farmers is a good example (Tumushabe and Bainomugisha, 2004).

Fourth, a Member of Parliament is expected to mobilize the people in the constituency for development. Mobilizing people for development is a leadership function. Most communities have potential to undertake collective or individual development. The MP can assist the constituency in shaping the development agenda by working with them to identify relevant projects to undertake. The fifth function is what is called self-advertising. Self-advertising is any effort used by an MP to disseminate one's name among constituents in such a fashion as to create a favourable image. A good member of Parliament should establish good relations between his/her constituency and other constituencies to promote harmony and national unity.

Mechanisms for Measuring Performance of MPs

The performance and effectiveness of members of Parliament can be measured in several ways. For instance, Members of Parliament can be assessed based on their contributions during debates on the floor of Parliament on national issues and those issues that affect their constituencies. Secondly, MPs can be measured based on their regular attendance of Parliamentary sessions. One of the noted weaknesses of the 7th Parliament was absenteeism of most MPs and Ministers even during crucial constitutional debates. The climax of absenteeism resulted into Government loss of a critical motion in Parliament: the Referendum Bill, which prompted the Prime Minister, Apolo Nsibambi to impose a travel ban on all ministers (Osike, 2005). The performance of Members of parliament can therefore be assessed based on their regular attendance in parliament which would involve one analyzing the attendance register and their contributions on the floor of Parliament in the Hansards. The third mechanism for measuring performance of MPs is what Winnie Byanyima, the former Member of Parliament for Mbarara Municipality called a track record of gender sensitivity in respect to women MPs. She argued that, 'the performance of a woman representative should be measured by her record of gender sensitivity and (the) equal opportunity legislation she has moved or actively supported. And also by the programs she has initiated or contributed to enhance the status of women (Tamale, 1999, 76).

The fourth mechanism for measuring performance is analyzing the voting patterns of members of Parliament on controversial bills and motions in parliament where the Executive has serious interests. Most opposition groups and political analysts have criticized representatives of Special Interest Groups for always supporting the position of the Executive as a payback for bringing them out of historical marginalization. In such situations representatives of Special Interest Groups in the 6th and 7th Parliaments were always caught in the middle of two opposing sides: the opposition and Government with each one of them wanting their support. It therefore becomes necessary for the MPs to exercise their independence to support a side where the interests of their constituencies are best served. In a situation where Uganda's recent political history has been dominated by the Movement Government, representatives of Special Interest Groups have naturally voted the Government's side. The section that follows attempts to assess performance of Special Interest Groups in Parliaments by analyzing their voting pattern, the circumstances surrounding their participation and the debates they were engaged in.

Term Limits for the Presidency

The 1995 Constitution introduced limitation on the number of times a person can be elected as President of Uganda. In the Constitutional reform after the referendum of 2000, Government proposed that this limitation be revisited with a view to allowing indefinite eligibility for the post of the President. A number of reasons were raised by Government in support of this proposal including the desire to give people the right and freedom to exercise their right of choice in selecting a leader. The debate on the tenure of the president became one of the most controversial issues in Parliament. Three Ministers including President Museveni's closest ally from childhood and former 1st Deputy Prime Minister Eriya Kategaya are believed to have been sacked for opposing the "third term" for President Museveni. The motion to lift the Presidential term limits was overwhelmingly supported by Parliament with majority of the Special Interest Groups MPs supporting the amendment.

Women Members of Parliament form the majority of the Special Interest Groups represented in the Parliament of Uganda. Out of the 305 Members of Parliament of the 7th Parliament, 56 were women representatives elected specifically on affirmative action to represent their districts. At the time, they were elected by an electoral college comprising all councillors at parish (LC11) and Sub-County (LC 111) levels within the district, plus all members of parish women councils within the district. The voting mechanism has however changed because their election is also by universal adult suffrage. The introduction of Affirmative Action in favour of women was hailed by women feminists in Uganda as a tool that would enhance the liberation of women.

Some feminist scholars however, have argued that if affirmative action had been introduced as a result of pressure from the women's movement which is a bottom-up approach, perhaps the rules for participation would have been devised by women themselves or women would have become empowered. The argument here as Tamale has pointed out is that "the beneficiaries of such a policy would hardly regard it as a favour. Neither would the NRM hold women psychologically hostage, engendering the kind of complacency and self-satisfaction that is sometimes exhibited by some women parliamentary-ans" (Tamale, 1999, 105).

The attitude that NRM is a benevolent saviour of women is abundantly clear among female parliamentarians. Most women MPs view the affirmative action policy as a favour (as opposed to a right) and view the NRM as a critical factor in not only the initial enactment of the policy but also its continuation. This view is supported by the views that are expressed by women leaders that have benefited from affirmative action. One of such women leaders is Mary Kamugisha who observed that: We should

> use this chance; it's God's grace that we have this chance. We should use it to consolidate our position so that... you never know; next time the next government might be anti-women. If we don't do it now, we would have missed the chance" (Tamale, 1999, 105).

Further, effective representation of women in Parliament has been hampered by the general poverty among the electorate and of most MPs. Most MPs are not economically empowered enough to fund their elections and for quite some time, some of them who are professed Movement supporters have been funded by the State. Because, of the funding from Government, most of them become compromised to the extent that they cannot oppose any motion/ bill where the Executive has interests. Related to poverty is the whole issue of commercialization of Ugandan politics at the electorate level. The electorate is too demanding from their MPs such that some of them choose not to go back to the constituencies after a torturous election process which makes them loose touch with the constituencies.

In some cases, the electorate does not understand the role of MPs. They demand resources and services from them as if they are the Government. As such most MPs in Uganda end up sharing out their Parliamentary earnings with the electorate which demolarize them with some of the MPs vowing not to run again. The case of Beatrice Kiraso can illustrate the above point. Beatrice Kiraso was a former woman MP for Kabarole district. She hosted a party in her constituency and categorically promised not to run again because of the frustration of the job during the seventh parliament (Kiraso, 2008).

The critical moment however, for effective representation by women MPs will come when they succeed in winning themselves off the support of any government. The recent motions and voting pattern on the referendum and the constitutional term limits for the president clearly shows whether affirmative action women MPs can be independent and autonomous while executing their legislative work. Out of the 54 district women representatives on affirmative action, 49 of them voted in favour of the Government driven referendum that was boycotted by the opposition while five voted against. This overwhelming support for the Government's led referendum by the affirmative women MP tends to confirm the fact that women's "liberation" movement has been exploited to bolster Government numbers in Parliament.

A woman Member of Parliament who did not want her name mentioned and is a National Resistance Movement party supporter confirms this point. She said that women MPs had supported the Government's side with hope that they will be given juicy positions on the executive of the NRM party-led government.

Army Representation in Parliament

The Uganda Peoples Defence Forces (UPDF) is one of the Special Groups represented in the Uganda Parliament. The institution of the army is established under Article 208 of the Constitution which states that, "There shall be armed forces to be known as the Uganda Peoples Defence Forces". Article 209 provides for the functions of the Uganda Peoples Defence Forces among which are to preserve and defend the sovereignty and territorial integrity of Uganda and to foster harmony and understanding between the Defence Forces and civilians. Article 210 provides for Parliamentary oversight or control of the UPDF. The same article makes provisions that mandate Parliament to make laws regulating the management and conduct of the Uganda Peoples' Defence Forces. Article 78 (c) is the most instrumental in respect to the army representation in Parliament. The army has ten MPs elected by the electoral colleges constituted by the Military Council which is chaired by the Commander-in- Chief who is the President of Uganda. The decision to have the army represented in Parliament was born out of the need to control the military by civilian leaders and reverse Uganda's political history where the army has held the democratic development hostage through successive military coups and military rule. Uganda, like most other countries in Africa has suffered successive military coups and its consequences.

Commenting about the tragedy of militarism in Africa and struggle to control armed forces, Kayode Fayemi has observed that, "in a region where military rule and militarism have contributed significantly to the arrest of state building and democratization projects, finding the most innovative mechanism to address the problem of coup d'etats remains a major objective of several constitution-making exercises in Africa" (Fayemi, 2003).

The framers of the 1995 Constitution reflected upon Uganda's past and decided that in order to control the army from overthrowing the elected Governments, it was important for it to be represented in Parliament as a Special Interest Group. During the making of the 1995 constitution the continued representation of the army in Parliament was justified on two grounds: First, the significance of the military in state building historically. It was argued that the military is a political institution and a strong pillar of the state. In pre-colonial Africa and elsewhere in the world, state building involved use of violence where the military was a dominant actor. This is what guided strategic thinkers like Clausewitz a German General and Mao Tsetung the Chinese revolution-ary leader. The two thinkers argued that the objectives in war must be determined by political authorities while at the same time the pressures faced by the military commanders on the battle field invariably give rise to civil-military tensions regarding the best means to be employed. In other words the nature of war, a phenomenon that has historically been part of the development of society is a reflection of the dynamic relationship among the political authorities, the people, and the military,

Following the above argument, the question that arose during the constitution making process was: Is it possible to have a non-partisan army but ideologically committed to defend the common good? The response that was entrenched in Chapter 12 of the Constitution is where a non-partisan UPDF is expected under multi-party arrangement or any other system of representation, not to take sides with the political organizations or political parties particularly during elections.

More so, the representation of the army in Parliament was believed to consolidate the positive civil-military relations that were emerging in the post 1986 era. It was argued that the interaction between society and the military is based on the principle that the military must not be isolated and insulated from civil society. Rather the two must have an active and ongoing exchange. If the military is exposed to the diverse interests and forces within pluralistic civil society, the armed forces begin to understand that their role is not to dominate or influence the civil sector but to be subordinate to it and to protect it from foreign threat. If the military learns to appreciate the broad spectrum of interests that exist, it intuitively realizes that its function is to remain neutral and thus serves democracy (Biddle, 1995). Therefore, civil society and the armed forces must be constantly exposed to one another and maintain an open and transparent dialogue. Representation in Parliament is one such avenue to achieve the desired improved civil-military relations.

The UPDF is widely respected by majority of Ugandans as a disciplined army compared to the past armies that are blamed for holding the country hostage and committing gross human rights abuses. During the Constituent Assembly (CA) debate, it was envisaged that the army needed to be insulated from political controversies. The army was supposed to remain neutral and non- partisan in controversial political matters since the country expects them to protect all Ugandans irrespective of different political persuasions. UPDF representatives such as General David Tinyefuza and Late Colonel Serwanga Lwanga (RIP) were not allowed to express their personal views openly for doing so would create divisions within the army. As such the army representatives in the CA would be constantly reminded that they were there as listening posts. While the army's representation in Parliament is justified, most political analysts argue that its performance in the 6th and 7th Parliaments has been wanting. A close examination of the army members of Parliament attendance and contributions in the house shows that they were irregular, rarely consult their constituency and at times receive directives to behave as 'listening posts'. The experience from the constitutional amendment process confirms this observation. One of the Army MPs abstained from voting on a controversial amendment of Article 105 (2); in respect to the proposal to remove the term limit for the president. The response from both the military and political leadership and the public through the press raised questions about the effectiveness of an army MP in Parliament who is expected to be guided by constituency opinions, rational judgment, consideration of national interest and personal convictions or conscience. While nine out of ten Army MPs voted in favour of the bill to lift the presidential term limits in the Constitution, Colonel Bogere abstained. Asked why he did not vote, Bogere said, "I just complied with the law." The Constitution itself demands that the UPDF shall be national and professional in character and non-partisan. The Political Parties and Organizations Act (PPOA) maintain the spirit of the Constitution. I just complied with the law. There is nothing more I did (Gyezaho, 2005).

Apparently Bogere's actions did not please the military leadership and Government. The Army Commander while passing out soldiers at Kabamba Military Training School warned errant soldiers that, "People who think they belong to the UPDF and also believe that they can do whatever they want... we are going to be firm on discipline. The army's position is one. If you want to represent your own things, you go and form your own army and then represent it" (Gyezaho, 2005). Colonel Bogere's abstinence from voting and the response his decision drew from the army leadership cast doubt as to whether army MPs can exercise independence and promote effective representation in Parliament.

Like is the case of Women, the Army, Workers, and Youth, representatives of Persons with Disabilities operating in an environment dominated by the Executive are also exposed to similar constraints. For instance, just like women representatives, Persons with Disabilities regard the NRM government as a saviour for introducing affirmative action to address their plight especially political representation and participation. The perception was that MPs representatives for Persons with Disabilities find it hard and ungrateful to oppose a motion, bill where the Executive has interests. The operating environment has even become more constrained to most MPs with the introduction of a multiparty political system. According to one woman MP who did not want to be named, "under the Movement system, it was easy to debate and vote according to one's conscience. Today, we are caucused under the NRM party where members are expected to exercise collective responsibility irrespective of the interests of our constituencies". A few examples would perhaps serve to demonstrate the nature of the operating environment of MPs. In order to push through Parliament all the proposed amendments including the controversial lifting of the presidential term limits, Government embarked on a registration of MPs that subscribe to the newly created NRM organization so as to make sure that they have the two thirds in Parliament Before the motions for presidential term limits and the national referendum, Government amended the Parliamentary Rules of Procedure providing for open voting in Parliament. The change in the rules of procedure providing for open voting away from secret voting made it easy for Government to monitor the voting patterns of MPs. One of the negative implications of open voting is that it makes it easy to monitor the voting pattern of MPs especially when they are believed to have been facilitated with funds to support the position of the Executive. Ultimately, such an operational environment does not promote effective legislative representation especially of Special Interest Groups with few numbers, little experience and limited financial base to assert their independence. It is not surprising that during the motion on the presidential term limits, four out of five MPs representing persons with disabilities voted in favour of the motion. Another challenge that is not only unique to MPs of PWDs is meeting the material expectations of the electorate. There is a tendency to expect MPs to cater for the needs of their constituency for instance, school fees, rent, food and debt settlement. Where the MPs have not satisfied such expectations, they are perceived to have failed to provide effective representation. In other words, the conditions of poverty which the MPs operate in make them vulnerable to unfair judgment on their performance.

By and large, representatives of persons with disabilities can be credited for advancing collective interests of their constituencies regardless of their political leanings. James Mwanda (RIP) former MP for Persons with Disability noted,

> On matters of Persons with Disability, we have always stood together. We can act differently on other political issues like the third term issue where four of my colleagues voted in favour and I voted against the motion, but we are united for the cause of our constituencies.

Most importantly, representatives of Persons with Disabilities consistently supported environmental issues because they knew that environmental degradation affects their constituencies badly than any other group.

Contributions of the SIGs in the 6th and 7th Parliament of Uganda

Special Interest Groups in the sixth and seventh Parliament were instrumental in several ways; they were able to bring the interests and issues of their constituencies on the floor of Parliament. Among the SIGs, Women and Persons with Disabilities were the most vocal and prominent; They significantly increased the number of MPs and representation in Parliament; the principle of Special Interest Groups enfranchised formerly politically excluded communities and groups in decision making especially at Parliamentary level; the representation of SIGs also has earned Uganda a name and recognition in the international community as a progressive country. Therefore, as East Africa works for a political federation, the constitution for a new entity might find Uganda's experience worth studying for a possible emulation in some respects.

Special Interest Groups in Parliament faces a number of challenges. Some of the challenges are generally faced by Parliament as an institution while others are specific to Special Interest Groups representatives. The challenges that face Parliament not only in Uganda but the rest of East Africa, generally relate to the issues of autonomy, authority, and accountability in the face of a strong Executive and a low level of civic competence of the electorate. On the other hand, Special Interest Groups face specific challenges which include lack of adequate financial resources, too much expectations, demands by the electorate and inexperience since most MPs of Special Interest Groups have been pioneers of the affirmative action.

Conclusion

This chapter set out to audit the performance of the Special Interest Groups in the 6th and 7th Parliament and draw lessons for other countries in the East African community. Since Uganda is a natural resource dependent economy with over 90% of the population deriving their sustenance to natural resources, the analysis contended that the good governance and management of these resources at higher positions of decision making like Parliament will determine whether Uganda will achieve sustainable livelihoods, peace and development. An attempt was made to ascertain whether representatives of the Special Interest Groups specifically the women, army and persons with disabilities have effectively represented the environmental and other civic interests of their constituencies in Parliament. We also discussed the functions of a parliamentarian and what factors motivates and de-motivates MPs while doing their legislative roles.

By and large, the analysis shows that the representatives of Special Interest Groups tried to bring the issues of their constituencies, such as the environmental or other civic interests to the floor of Parliament. However, we also established that these groups like the rest of the Parliament operate under serious challenges some of them originating from Uganda's political history, and also because of a strong executive which makes it hard for it to exercise autonomy, authority and independence to perform well. Since democratic development is not an event, but a process, one can safely conclude that the performance of the Special Interest Groups and the Ugandan 6th and 7th Parliament is commendable considering the turbulent political antecedents of the country. This why it is important for proponents of the East African political federation to study Uganda's experience on the role of interest groups in promoting positive environmental governance. By strengthening parliament institution in East Africa to perform its legislative responsibility would ultimately promote environmental governance, peace and sustainable livelihoods.

References

Biddle, G. C. (1995) *A Principle Lesson of Civil Military Relations in Latin America, the Democracy Projects, School of International Service*. The American University.

Dahl, R. A. (1989) *Democracy and its Critics*. New Haven, London: Yale University Press.

Fayemi, K. (2003) *Constitutionalism in Transitional in Africa: Balance Sheet & Prognosis*. London: Centre for Democracy and Development.

Gyezaho, E. (2005) 'Col. Bogere martyrdom: So why have Army MPs?', *Daily Monitor*, 6 July.

Harris, P. and Reilly, B. (eds) (1998) *Democracy and Deep-Rooted Conflict: Options for Negotiators*. Stockholm: International Institute for Democracy and Electoral Assistance (IDEA).

Kanyeihamba, G. W. (2002) *Constitutional and Political History of Uganda: From 1894 to the Present*. Kampala: Fountain Publishers Ltd.

Kiraso, B. (2008) 'Establishment of Uganda's Parliamentary Budget Office and the Parliamentary Budget Committee', in Stapenhurst, R., Pelizzo, R., Olson, D., and von Trapp, L. (eds) *Legislative Oversight and Budgeting*. Washington D. C: World Bank Institute.

Mushi, S. S. (2004) 'Historical and Theoretical Analysis of Representation', in Al., M. et (ed.) *People's representatives: Theory and Practice of Parliamentary Democracy in Tanzania*. Kampala: Fountain Publishers.

Osike, F. (2005) 'PM stops ministers travel', *The New Vision*.

Republic of Uganda (2010) *Agriculture Sector Development Strategy and Investment Plan 2010/11-2014/15*. Entebbe: Ministry of Agriculture, Animal Industry and Fisheries.

Republic of Uganda (2015) 'Second National Development Plan (NDPII) 2015/16-2019/20'.

De Soysa, I. (2000) 'The Resource Curse: Are Civil Wars Driven by Rapacity or Paucity?', in Berdal, M. and Malone, D. M. (eds) *Greed and Grievance: Economic Agendas of Civil Wars*. London: Lynne Rienner.

Tamale, S. (1999) *When Hens Begin to Crow: Gender and Parliamentary Politics in Uganda*. Kampala: Fountain Publishers.

The Report of the Uganda Constitutional Commission: Analysis and Recommendations (1988).

Tumushabe, W. G. and Bainomugisha, A. (2004) *Constitutional Reform and Environmental Legislative Representation in Uganda*. Kampala: ACODE Policy Research Series.

Uganda Bureau of Statistics (2016) 'The National Population and Housing Census of 2014: Main Report'.

Uganda constitution (1995).

CHAPTER SIX

Monitoring Legislative Representation: Environmental Issues in Uganda's 7th Parliament

Arthur Bainomugisha, Elijah D. Mushemeza and Sabastiano Rwengabo

Introduction

Over the past few decades, specifically since the United Nations Conference on Environment and Development (UNCED) of 1992, there has been growing appreciation of the need to promote public participation in environment-related decision making. This has given rise to such conceptual and practical innovations as: participatory and multi-level environmental governance (Newig and Fritsch, 2008); "multi-criteria assessment in participatory decision-making contexts" (Antunes et al., 2006); "multi-criteria decision analysis in environmental decision making" (Kiker et al., 2005); "community-based environmental decision making (Jankowski, 2009)"; multi-stakeholder environmental decision making (Thabrew et al., 2009); and several others. In reality, however, rural voters do not have both the opportunity and competencies to participate meaningfully in national policymaking processes. Consequently, legislative representation, a common feature of representative democracy, becomes an inevitable medium through which the common man and woman can elevate his or her concerns and choices at the decision-making levels of government and thereby influence environmental choices of one's society.

Representation relies on the assumption that all citizens cannot participate in the public debate and decision-making at all levels. For efficiency and effectiveness, representative democracy presupposes that representatives have powers and rights allocated to them by a larger group of persons at a given time, specifically during elections. Correspondingly, the values, concerns, interests and actions of representatives should correspond to those of the general public. At the same time representatives are held accountable to the people they represent through reporting mechanisms and elections. Representation, therefore, is a key governance principle in parliamentary democracy.

This chapter assesses the logic of participatory environmental decision making in the context of legislative representation of issues related to environment and natural resources (hereinafter, "ENR") in Uganda's 7th parliament (2001-2006). These issues are important because Uganda's socio-economic future is hinged on ENR governance. The utilization and protection of these resources through multi-level political processes is central to sustainable development of not only the country but the region given the geographical contiguity and interdependence of Nile Valley riparian States. The 7th Parliament is also important because, unlike post-2006 parliamentary processes, which can be contextually assessed as a single continuum of parliamentary processes under a multi-party/multi-organisation political dispensation, the 7th parliament was the last national legislative establishment under the No-Party Movement System of government that ruled Uganda between 1995 and 2005. The parliament, therefore, ended a decade of constitutional rule under a no-party democracy that was unique to Uganda in some respects (Republic of Uganda', 1995; Tripp, 2010).

Both aspects—the country's dependence and its political context— have direct but interlinked bearing on our understanding of ecological security and socioeconomic transformation that may unfold in a different dispensation. Theoretical and practical lessons are drawn for legislative representation of environmental issues under Uganda's current multiparty dispensation. Better management of ENR leads to sustainability. Similarly, sustainability requires that human activity, at a minimum, only uses nature's resources at a rate at which they can be replenished naturally. This measure is only possible when established political institutions regulate the relationship between human and other environmental resources.

The chapter draws on a previous study by the Advocates Coalition for Environment and Development (ACODE) conceived to assess the degree to which the legislative performance of individual MPs, the parliamentary Committee on ENR, and the entire 7th Parliament, represented the interests of natural-resource-dependent poor communities. Emphasis is placed on representation of constituency and national environmental issues in Parliament, namely: (i) contribution during debates on the floor of parliament; (ii) regular attendance of

Parliamentary sessions; (iii) track record of ENR sensitivity; (iv) Private Members' bills; and (v) voting patterns of MPs on controversial bills and motions relating to the environment. The study relies on quantitative and qualitative methods for data collection and analysis, supplanted with literature review to comprehensively analyse existing literature on legislative representation in Uganda. Parliament Hansards; reports of parliamentary committees; the Ugandan Constitution and other laws; national documents related to development that directly affect voters, such as the 2004/05-2007/08 Poverty Eradication Action Plan (PEAP); and legislations passed by Parliament provided useful information.

The findings reveal few challenges that hindered parliament's effectiveness in legislating ENR. First, high levels of members' absenteeism undermined parliament's performance on ENR and other possible issues. Absenteeism resulted in the government losing crucial motions in Parliament. Similarly, the strong influence of the executive somehow undermined members' performance on ENR issues as Uganda's policy shift from ENR interest to industrial/agricultural investments led to the destruction of green belts with limited parliamentary control over the process. Finally, constitutional reforms and political transitional process dominated the 7th parliament over the 2003-2006 period, sacrificing ENR issues at the altar of political transition maneuvers. Nevertheless, seven Bills were passed pertaining to ENR in period of five years, although none of the tabled Private Members Bills directly related to ENR. Some MPs who attended regularly made remarkable contributions because some MPs were apparently motivated by the awareness that particular Bills affected their constituents. In terms of number of Bills passed and ENR sensitivity, the 7th parliament was compliant as the debate on the Land (Amendment) Act 2003 demonstrated high-level participation indicating that MPs considered land to be an important issue to their constituents. Participation also demonstrates MPs' sensitivity to ENR issues, as well as parliamentary autonomy when dealing with sensitive matters.

The rest of the chapter examines the nexus between environment, poverty, and legislative representation. The third section briefly draws a historical perspective of environmental legislation. The fourth section examines the performance of Uganda's 7th parliament on ENR legislative representation. The fifth section draws broader implications for multi-party legislative representation, ecological security, and development in Uganda.

Environment, Poverty and Legislative Representation

Environment and Natural Resources (ENRs) are understood to mean natural capital (the sum total of nature's resources) such as trees, habitat earth, wild life, biomass, fisheries, wetlands, minerals, pollution, waste management, climate change, water and air (Bainomugisha, 2006). Better management of ENR leads to sustainable development—the development that meets current needs of present generations without compromising the needs and interests of future generations. Sustainabi-lity requires that human activity, at a minimum, only uses nature's resources at a rate at which they can be replenished naturally. Thus, the nexus between environment, poverty and legislative representation is this: in natural-resource-dependent economies, livelihoods are drawn from ENR. Poverty is the function of the extent to which ENRs are accessed, controlled, appropriated, extracted, and utilized. In such polities, development priorities and state policy interests are likely to reflect interest in ENR governance for such a country to reach a desired development destination. Other priorities are not unimportant, but in non-industrial, ENR-dependent economies to relegate the ENR sector is to spell doom for the country's development. Since governance determines people's access, control, and appropriation of ENRs, the more the access, control, and ownership of ENRs, or the benefits accruing therefrom, the lower are the levels of poverty.

Uganda is natural-resource dependent. Almost 90% of citizens and the national economy depend on ENR as the basis for agricultural, industrial, tourism, and infrastructural development. ENR is also bedrock of scientific research and progress (Uganda Bureau of Statistics, 2016). Governing the ENR sector is one of the critical determinants of whether or not the country attains development objectives and becomes globally competitive. On the basis of this reality, state representative institutions, especially Parliament, should have incentives to prioritize ENR issues and exhibit a high level of enthusiasm and interest in ensuring that good environmental governance and stewardship is upheld. For Parliament to provide effective environmental representation for the electorates, it must enjoy autonomy, authority and have a transparent mechanism of accountability under the principle of separation of powers (Ackerman, 2000) because separation of powers promotes political accountability (Personn et al., 1997).

From the foregoing, and in order to avoid unnecessary theoretical and conceptual complications, we outline the theoretical nexus between environment, poverty, and legislative representation—that is, we show why one should care about the link between ordinary Ugandans and the interest of the country's parliament with ENR—by outlining the importance of ENR to Ugandan citizens, the legal frameworks regarding ENR governance, and monitoring indicators for tracking legislative representation in order to make our theoretical postulation more akin to the empirical question at hand.

Importance of the ENR to Ugandans

Over 90 per cent of Ugandans directly or indirectly depend on products and services from the ENR sector. Over 90% of energy used is extracted from ENR sector. The sector is the major contributor to GDP, in both monetary and non-monetary terms. It is the leading employer of the country's labour force since over 80% of the population depends on agriculture. Raw materials for industries are drawn from ENR. The country's food security and sovereignty, livelihood security, revenue generation, foreign exchange earnings, and household incomes, are drawn from this sector. At the time the 7th parliament was in force, and till now, majority of Ugandans depended on subsistence agriculture for their livelihood and their standard of living remained low (Uganda National NGO Forum, 2009). Part of the explanation for this continued dependence on ecological wealth, concurrent with limited wealth accumulation is poor environmental management. The importance of the ENR sector was highlighted in the country's 2006/2007 budget, where the decline in economic development and Uganda's failure to achieve economic projections was attributed to prolonged drought and energy crisis. This indicates that addressing environmental concerns is central to the country's priorities (Republic of Uganda, 2006).

Environmental security analysts predicted that unless Uganda reverses the situation, its development rates would not be sustainable as the present generation would bequeath an ecological debt to the future generations. By 2016, the country's growth rates, which were 8.1% in

2007, fell to 4.7% in 2016. The energy crisis in the country, which was in part due to the declining water levels in Lake Victoria and the River Nile, slowed down economic growth to 5.3% in financial year 2005/2006 (Republic of Uganda, 2006). The total environmental loss was quantified: some sources estimate the cost of annual degradation of ENR to range from 4% to 12% of GNP (MWLE, 2003). Other studies estimated this loss to about 17% (MoFPED, 2004). This annual environmental loss is enormous and presents a gloomy picture of the future, hence the demand for prudent stewardship over natural resource management. At the centre of the problem is the whole question of governance. Most ENR decisions have been, and continue to be, taken at highest levels of government: in the national legislative body and executive levels.

In theory, parliament and the executive make such decisions on behalf of the citizens, yet most rural communities who are mostly affected by such decisions lack the opportunity and capacity to influence meaningfully in decision/policy-making processes as promised by proponents of democracy. The executive seems to undermine parliamentary oversight. The president is increasingly involved in the allocation of land and forest reserves for investors to carry out large scale commercial farming, such as Butamira, the attempt to allocate Mabira forest reserve in 2007-2009, and debates on new forest giveaways in 2016 (Alweny, 2007). The weak oversight role played by Parliament fails to balance investment needs and ENR sustainability to tame the country's worsening environment crisis (The East African, 2006). It is not uncommon for political executives, driven by the desire to attract foreign investors, foreign capital, foreign technology, and foreign networks, to sacrifice the wellbeing of their local populations at the altar of promoting local economic growth, hence the difficult balance between ENR-dependent livelihoods and large-scale investments (Anyuru et al., 2016).

This obsession for investments, in many cases, results in unwanted destruction of ENR and other forms of ecological colonization that marginalizes local communities without necessarily improving their living conditions as Uganda's recent experience has shown (Carmody and Taylor, 2016). How, then, can citizens take part in ENR governance and have a voice in decision making? The theory of participation is accommodative of these loopholes: representatives carry with them the participation desires of those who assign them. In principal-agent theory, legislative representatives are agents assigned by their constituents to advance their interests within an established framework of legislative representation (Strøm, 2000). Therefore, the starting point for understanding the possible role of parliament in promoting and protecting the interests of citizens in ENR is a critical analysis of the legal framework.

The Constitutional Basis of ENR Legislation

In modern countries, policies, laws, and other governance instruments and powers are derived from national mother-laws commonly known as Constitutions. The analysis of the constitution in this sub-section is not to be construed as implying absence of any pre-1995 ENR-related legislation but to underline the political-constitutional context within which the 7th parliament legislated on ENR issues. Our focus is on the legislations related to ENR, which form the empirical basis of this chapter. The constitution is the basis, not the subject, of such legislations. The 1995 Constitution of the Republic of Uganda has been upheld for returning the power and sovereignty to the people. According to Article 1(1), "all power belongs to the people [of Uganda] who shall exercise their sovereignty in accordance with this Constitution" (emphasis added). Accordingly, the state derives and exercises its power and authority from the people. National objectives and directive principles of state policy stress this people-centered governance to guide, inter alia, all state organs and agencies including parliament.

Principle II (i) provides that the State shall be based on democratic principles which empower and encourage the active participation of all citizens at all levels in their governance. This objective, analyzed along with Article 1, emphasizes that power belongs to Ugandan citizens. The Article further provides, under Clause 4, that "the people shall express their will and consent on who shall govern them and how they should be governed, through regular, free and fair elections of their representatives." These representatives obtain at different levels of government—local and national. The highest level of participation is through popular representation in the national Parliament through elected representatives, majority of whom were elected and hence mandated by universal suffrage (Article 78).

Monitoring Legislative Representation: Environmental... (147-175)

In theory, through the various MPs the needs and priorities of the people they represent are brought to the highest echelons of power. Each MP must make his priority the needs and interests of his/her people and take legislative decisions in their best interest. The Constitution initially provided, under Article 84, that the people had a right to re-call MPs who failed to deliver on the people's behalf, a check mechanism upon agents by the principals that would ensure due representation and legislators' accountability to the electorate. This provision was rendered only applicable under the movement political system through a constitutional amendment. It is, therefore, inapplicable in the post-2006 multiparty dispensation.

From the foregoing, post-7th Parliament MPs, who are elected under a multi-party dispensation, have a lee-way. There is no claw-back against them until the expiry of their term when they are due for re-election, unless political parties recall them or they are forced out of parliament through a court process. This further provides justification for our focus on the 7th parliament. How effective was this representation? How is this to be determined and measured?

Monitoring and Tracking Effective ENR Representation

Effective representation in, case of the 7th parliament, entails articulation of the key ENR issues outlined at the beginning of this chapter: contribution during debates on the floor of parliament; regular attendance of Parliamentary sessions; track record of ENR sensitivity; Private Members bills; and voting patterns of MPs on controversial bills and motions, relating to the environment.

The monitoring indicators for tracking effective representation of constituency and national environmental issues in Parliament, as outlined above, may not be exhaustive but is useful for analytic purposes. It is our basis for evaluating the performance of MPs as individual representatives and Parliament as a state institution. This measures representative participation in ENR at different levels at which participation is to be gauged. Practically, our monitoring mechanism can enable the principal, the electorate, to measure the performance of individual agents, the MPs, and inform decisions on whether or not such agents deserve further delegation to represent their principals in subsequent legislatures. Any agent that does not represent the views of his/he principal is, in our assessment, less helpful in the fight against poverty in an ENR-dependent economy. The reverse is true of a legislator who prioritizes ENR.

Performance of the 7th Parliament: Handling of ENR Bills

Precolonial representative bodies in the various states scattered around the Great Lakes Region were named according to the cultural-linguistic traditions of the area. In Nkore it was called Ishengyero. In Bunyoro-Kitara it was *Orukurato*. In Buganda, it was *Lukiiko*. When these and other states were merged through colonial conquest, what became Uganda emerged with colonial-constituted arms of government. The British introduced as a Legislative Council (LEGCO) by the Orders-in-Council in 1902 and later 1920 to serve their interests. LEGCO was exclusively non-African until 1945 when the first African legislators joined (Bainomugisha and Mushemeza, 2006). The Royal Instructions of 1921 made provisions the membership for the LEGCO, which excluded representation for Africans (Kanyeihamba, 2002). After independence in 1962, Parliaments—especially between 1962 and 1970; and 1981 and 1985—were characterized by factional fighting which did not enable them performs their legislative roles. Despite these shortfalls, there was some semblance of ENR-related legislation, which is traceable from the LEGCO-enacted Forests Ordinance of 1947. Several Ordinances have since been passed but have had little bearing on environmental protection, preservation, and conservation.

At independence in 1962, Uganda adopted a multiparty representative democracy, which was, unfortunately, interrupted by the 1966 constitutional crisis, abrogation of the constitution, the 1967 republican constitution, and then the 1971-1979 military dictatorship under which representative democracy was unimaginable. Though reintroduced after 1979 liberation war, representative democracy did not regain its meaningful place and impact until during the 1990s. The National Resistance Army/Movement (NRA/M), upon capturing power following a gruesome 1980-1986 civil war, established representative politics through a kind of multi-level governance structure which stretched from grass root (village/cell) to parliament/national level. This was entrenched in the 1995 constitution—hence the preceding analysis on the constitutional basis of ENR legislation.

Constitutionally, the people's will and consent to governance is expressed through election of representatives and the legislative bodies (local government councils and parliament) the elected constitute. Simultaneously, representatives are held accountable through elections and the recall process. Legislators are mandated to ensure that government choices and actions address constituents' ENR demands and priorities (Prudence and Oyono, 2004) in keeping with the country's national and international ENR commitments. International commitments to promote public participation in environmental decision making are contained in Principle 10 of the Rio Declaration to which Uganda is signatory (Tumushabe et al., 2003). The performance of the 7th Parliament is therefore important for understanding the efficacy of representative participation in post-1995 Uganda.

Table 4.1: Uganda's Parliaments since Independence

Legislature	Speaker	Period
1st Parliament (National Assembly)	John Bowes Griffin	1962—1963
2nd Parliament (National Assembly)	Narendra M. Patel	1963-1971
No Parliament	Idi Amin military dictatorship	1971-1979:
3rd Parliament (National Consultative Council)	Edward Rugumayo	1979-1980
4th Parliament (National Assembly)	Francis K. Butagira	1980—1985
5th Parliament (National Resistance Council)	Yoweri Museveni (Chairman)	1986—1996
6th Parliament (Parliament of the Republic of Uganda, PRU) 1996-2001	James Wapakhabulo	1996-1998
6th Parliament [continued]	Francis Ayume	1998-2001
7th Parliament (PRU) 2001—2006	Edward Ssekandi	2001—2006
8thParliament (PRU) 2006—2011	Edward Ssekandi	2006—2011
9th Parliament (PRU) 2011—2016	Rebecca Kadaga	2011—2016
10th Parliament (PRU), 2016-2021	Rebecca Kadaga	2016—to-date

Source: Daily Monitor (2011)

Chapter Six | Bainomugisha, Mushemeza and Rwengabo

The 7th Parliament debated and passed 104 Bills into Laws. Out of 104 Bills tabled, debated, and passed, only 9 Bills were related to ENR. This represented 8.2% of the total Bills. Below we consider some of the bills which attracted interest from some of the MPs.

Table 4.2: Bills, Motions, Petitions and their Relationship to ENR

	Not Related to ENR	Related to ENR	Total
Bills	95 (91.8%)	9 (8.2%)	104
Motions	149 (84.2 %)	28 (15.8)	177
Motions (Private members Bills	3	0(O %)	3
Petitions	-	3	3

Source: Hansard

Table 2 summarizes the number of bills, motions and petitions and their relationship to ENR issues. Only 8.2% of the bills tables in the 7th parliament (nine out of ninety-five) are ENR-related. This indicates that the parliament gave less than 10% of its time and resources and energy to ENR legislation.

Table 4.3: Attendance and Contributions of MPS on ENR-Related Bills

Title of the Bill	No. of MPs in Attend-Ance	No. of MPs contributed to the debate	Pro- ENR submissions	Submissions not related to ENR	Total submissions
The Nile Water Initiative Bill, 2002	88	19	11	18	32
The National Forestry and tree Planting Bill 2002 * First sitting	N/A	15	21	1	22
** Second Sitting	N/A	26	148	4	152
*** Third Sitting	N/A	16	61	-	61
The Petroleum Supply Bill	N/A	19	82	82	82
The Land	N/A				

(Amendment) Bill 2003 * First Sitting		24	43	4	47
** Second Sitting	N/A	18	56	-	56
*** Third Sitting	N/A	39	156	-	156
**** Fourth Sitting	N/A	3	4	-	4
*****(Fifth Sitting	N/A	16	48	-	48
****** Sixth Sitting	N/A	13	38	-	48
****** Seventh Siting	N/A	17	36	-	36
The Mining Bill 2003 First Sitting	N/A	28	167	1	168

Source: Uganda Parliamentary Hansard

Table 4.3 summarizes the attendance and participation of MPs during debate on some of the ENR-related bills. We discuss details of legislative work on these bills in the coming sub-sections.

The Nile Water Initiative Bill, 2002

The Nile River is one of the world's greatest strategic rivers and the longest. Throughout history, this unique waterway has nourished livelihoods, supported multifarious ecosystems, and enriched cultural-existential diversities along its valley. It traverses more than 6,800 kilometers from the headwaters of its farthest known tributary, River Ruvyironza in Burundi, through Kagera River in Rwanda and Uganda into Lake Victoria, and on to its delta on the Mediterranean Sea in present-day Egypt via Khartoum, Sudan, where it is joined by the Blue Nile originating in the Ethiopian Highlands. The Nile River Basin is international, shared by eleven countries. These countries have been working toward cooperation, establishing the Nile Basin Initiative (NBI) in 1999, as an agreed basin-wide framework to promote economic development in the Valley. The Initiative, a transitional plan aimed at achieving "sustainable socio-economic development through the equitable utilisation of, and benefit from, the common Nile Basin water resources" until a permanent framework would be in place, remains critical to the management of the Nile.

As part of the institutionalization of the Initiative, Uganda's 7th Parliament enacted the Nile Water Initiative Bill, 2002. Issues under this bill were not divisive within Parliament—so, debate and passing took one day. We prepared a statistical tally from the Hansard indicating (i) the MPs who were present; and (ii) those who contributed toward debating the Bill with legitimate concerns on ENR issues of an international nature. The attendance register of 18th September 2002 indicates that out of the 305 total number of MPs, only 88 were present. Only 19 out of the 88 present contributed to the Bill. Whereas only 26% of the total MPs were in attendance, only 6% participated in debating the Bill. The accountability issue is this: a very small percentage (less than one-third) was in attendance when an important environmental bill was being discussed, pointing to limited interest of the MPs in the subject. And a paltry percentage took part in debates, indicating dismal interest in ENR issues. Whether or not their constituents would hold them accountable over the Nile's fate is a different question. Yet passing the bill was crucial for Ugandans who derive their livelihood from the Nile.

The National Forestry and Tree Planting Bill, 2002

In 1998 Uganda sought to restructure the forestry department which had failed to manage the country's forest resources partly due to lack of clear policy and good regulatory mechanisms. Government decided to establish the National Forestry Authority (NFA) to manage forest resources, and developed policy plan to guide the sector. A Bill was drafted as a step toward operationalization of the policy plan and legalise the NFA.

The Bill was tabled in late 2002 for the First Reading, and submitted to parliament's Natural Resources Committee for scrutiny and improvement. The Committee prepared and submitted a report to the House on 8 May 2003 for consideration and adoption, and tabled for the Second Reading by Kezimbira Miyingo (RIP, then State Minister for Environment. In his submission Miyingo observed that: 96% of the country is dependent on wood for energy, and therefore, the sooner this Bill is passed, the sooner the country will have an effective force to control the forest sector not only for the economic gains but also environmental gains of this country (Kezimbira-Miyingo 2002, personal communication, Kampala).

The Bill sought to provide for conservation, sustainable management and development of Forests; engender sustainable use of forest produce and the enhancement of productive capacity of forests; and consolidate the law relating to the forest sector and related matters. During the debate, 15 MPs made supportive submissions. Only one submission was not related to the Bill. Hence, few MPs participated in debating the Bill and Committee report. Some MPs like Muzoora-Kabareebe made pertinent contributions to the debate, arguing that stakeholders should mind about the regeneration of natural forests rather than concentrating on the artificial ones: "Emphasis should be placed on natural forest regeneration where possible as opposed to artificial forests" (Kabarebe 2003, personal communication, Kampala). The house adjourned to 13 May 2003. During this debate, 26 MPs participated. 148 contributions were made in support of the Bill. Only 4 were unrelated to the merits of the Bill. The House constituted itself into a Committee of Natural Resources, and the Committee Chair guided the House to debate and pass the Bill—a very crucial stage at which decisions on the various clauses in the Bill are taken; where participation and quality contributions guided by principles of accountability, autonomy, and ambition are easily recognized. At this point 16 MPs submitted on the Bill making a total of 61 submissions. Some MPs could submit more than once on the Bill.

After all the clauses were passed, the Minister moved a motion to resume the House so that the whole Committee of the House could to report to the August House. At this point Jack Sabiiti requested to make an amendment on clause 95(2) of the bill. He was over ruled by the Deputy Speaker, who then allowed the Minister to move a motion for adoption by the House. This was agreed upon. The minister read the Bill for the third time and it was passed as "The National Forestry and Tree Planting Act, 2003" (Republic of Uganda, 2003b).

Analysis of MPs' contributions to the Bill

The MPs' level of contribution is negligible compared to a total of 304 MPs in the 7th Parliament. Only 57 MPs contributed on the floor of Parliament when the Bill was being debated. Of the 57 MPs who participated, very few contributed more than twice. Most submissions were in form of points of inquiries, information, order, and clarification. Few followed the debate. Table 2 above reveals that MPs contributed to the debate only 22 times, by the 15 MPs who participated. Hon. Jack Sabiti took the lead: four submissions during the first sitting of the Second Reading. MPs' participation increased in subsequent sittings, with Nandala Mafabi, Ken Lukyamuzi, Loote Ogwel Sammy, Ogenga Latigo, and Wangoda Muguli contributing.

The statistical analysis indicates that only 16 MPs participated in the actual debating of the Bill. Perhaps most MPs were in agreement with the issues submitted by the few, or most MPs lacked good grasp of the issues under this sub-sector to a degree that would arouse their interest. The track record of MPs' participation and representation on this aspect of ENR is unimpressive.

The Petroleum Supply Bill, 2003

This Bill was intended to provide for supervision, monitoring, importation, exportation, transportation, processing, supply, storage, distribution and marketing of petroleum products; to establishment a Ministry responsible for the petroleum sector and for the licensing and control of petroleum-related activities and installations; to provide for safety and protection of public health and the environment in petroleum supply operations and installations; to encourage and protect fair competition in the petroleum supply market; to repeal certain related laws; and to address other connected matters. Petrol carriers in Uganda had been involved in several fatal accidents. These accidents, beyond human life, destroy property, cause destructive fires, and pollute the environment.

Daudi Migereko, then State Minister for Energy, tabled the Bill in Parliament on 15 May 2003, after the First Reading the Bill was submitted to the Natural Resources Committee for further scrutiny. The petroleum supply sector had been regulated by many instruments: transportation and storage by the Petroleum Act under Ministry of Energy and Mineral Resources; the Importation of Fuel by Trade (Licensing) Act; and External Trading Act under the Ministry of Trade, Tourism and Industry. The construction of fuel stations was regulated by the Petroleum Station Filling Rules under the Ministry of Local Government (Republic of Uganda, 2000). These legal instruments were weak, outdated, and could not properly regulate profit-oriented operations of private firms.

The Bill would synchronize these instruments, and foreground key principles: setting up of national petroleum standards and code of practice to ensure public health, safety and environmental protection; establishing of a Technical Petroleum Committee consisting of petroleum industry players as an advisory body to the Ministry and the petroleum Industry; and establishing a monitoring and information system. The Natural Resources Committee observed that: fuel stations were concentrated in urban areas and neglected the remote areas; and that these mushrooming fuel stations, in urban areas, and close to one other, threatened the population. It recommended fast implementation of the Uganda-Kenya Pipeline Project to reduce costs and increase safety in transporting petroleum products; and Environmental Impact Assessment (EIA) before petrol stations are constructed.

During the debate, Hon. Kibaale Wambi, MP Budadiri County East urged his colleagues to support the Committee's recommendations on the Bill. In total, 19 MPs participated making 82 submissions in favor of the Bill. None was against it. Thus, the Bill was debated and passed based contributions of only 6% of 305 MPs. Possibly non-resistance to the bill indicated appreciation of the environmental interests but does not account for non-participation.

The Land (Amendment) Bill, 2003

This Bill was introduced when the Land Act of 1998 suffered implementation problems. Baguma-Isoke, the then State Minister for Lands, introduced the Bill to Parliament at the end of 2002 for the First Reading. At Committee level, this Bill caused disagreements, leading to a Minority Report. The Committee, however, made several recommenda-tions. The committee that land was an important means of production, a direct source of livelihood for most Ugandans, and that, therefore, laws governing the ownership, management and use have a direct impact on the agriculture-dependent economy. John-Ken Lukyamuzi authored a minority report arguing that the annual UGX 1,000 ground rent explains the cause of failure to implement the 1998 Land Act, since landlords never demand this paltry fee. He submitted that the high number of institutions, designed to regulate and manage land issues, were not the problem but the scrapping of the Busuulu and Envujjo Laws of 1928 by the Land Reform Decree of 1975. Lukyamuzi claimed to have made consultations in Mukono district, where many people suggested that the Land Act, 1998 be repealed. He also made some recommendations.

Although Lukyamuzi's arguments do not show concern with the state of the environment, they views represent the interest of some of his constituents in Buganda. In another reflection of the interests of the constituents, Tungwako Twarabireho submitted that lack of land policy had led to eviction of people from Kyambura Game Reserve, Katerera Sub-County in Bunyaruguru, between 1993 and 2001. He called for a clear land policy to provide for a mechanism to handle land conflicts already created by the 1998 Act. The debate was adjourned to 10th April, 2003, when a Select Committee was formed to study the report of the Natural Resources Committee and report back within two weeks on the status of Sections 32 and 95 of the Bill. The MP's who contributed to the debate on 10th April 2003 were 18 in number, making a total of 56 pro-bill submissions.

The debate continued on 14 April 2003. A total of 39 contributed a total of 156 submissions in support of the Bill but the House also adjourned to 24 April 2003 when the house would appoint a Select Committee to study clause 95. The House was adjourned to early June when the Select Committee would report back, and resumed business on 14 June 2003 to debate the report of the Select Committee. On resumption, 3 MP's participated in debating the Select Committee's report, making 4 pro-bill submissions. The house did not accomplish the Select Committee's Report, and adjourned to 17 June, 2003 when 16 MPs Participated and made 48 pro-Bill submissions. That was Third Reading, and the House constituted itself into the Natural Resources Committee to pass clause by clause. 13 MPs participated in the debate and made 38 supportive submissions. It got late and the House adjourned to the following day, 18 June 2003—when 17 MPs participated and made 36 pro-bill submissions.

This Bill attracted many MPs compared to other Bills brought to Parliament during the same session. It forced Parliament to form a select committee to scrutinize the report of the Natural Resources Committee, and Lukyamuzi's Minority Report, with a view to harmonizing the positions of both reports. The debate in parliament demonstrated high-level participation. This indicated how much importance the MPs attached to land issues. Participation and non-interference from the executive also showed ENR sensitivity of the MPS and how much autonomy the parliament should enjoy when dealing with sensitive matters.

The Mining Bill, 2003

Mining has a significant impact on the environment. Extraction of minerals involves excavating the land and destabilization of land-stability. ENR suffer greatly during mining and mineral processing. For example, areas surrounding Kilembe Cement Factory face too much dust. The wildlife around Queen Elizabeth National Park faces a problem of poisonous emissions from the factory. The need for regulatory mechanisms for regulating these processes was clear. When Kamanda Bataringaya, minister of State for Mineral Development, brought this Bill before Parliament for the Second Reading on 14 May 2003, it had been last reviewed in 1964. Derived from pre-independence Mines Ordinance that implemented colonial policy, the law had become outdated in many respects. The Law/Mining Ordinance favoured mineral exploitation for export. Little mention was made on building local capacity. Issues like environment, gender, and labour conventions were hardly addressed. Therefore, the proposed new Bill would repeal this old law (Republic of Uganda, 2003a).

The Committee found that prospectors, explorers and miners were poor at restoration of the environment after completing their activities. It cited a company called Branch Energy, which was mining gold in Karamoja and left glaring pits after their activities, and "several examples prevailed countrywide" (Republic of Uganda, 2003a). The Committee made several recommendations related to expansion of the minerals' list and environmental safeguards.

During debate some members disagreed with the Committee on inclusion of stones, sand, clay and murram on the list of minerals. Oliver Wonekha submitted that

> ... Some members of society especially women, youth and the disabled would be left out in terms of being engaged in income generating activities. People pick any opportunities that are available at their disposal of which mining and extracting the above items is their main

occupation, and putting a cost on them would force them out of their business.

Their inclusion on the list of minerals would require a constitutional amendment (Republic of Uganda, 1995). The Natural Resources Committee report to Plenary Session on the 8 May 2003 reflected these views. During the 2nd Reading, the debate involved 28 MPs making 167 submissions in favor of the Bill. There was more active participation of Achilla John Roberts (Jie) and Ogola Akisoferi (West Budama). After the Third Reading the Bill was passed. The participation of MPs and contention on what constitutes minerals and their utility again demonstrated the ENR sensitivity of the legislators and concern of the people's livelihood that they represent.

Private Member Bills

In the 7th Parliament, there were only three motions originated by Private Members' Bills. Rule 102(1) of the Parliamentary Rules of Procedure provides that

> all bills shall be accompanied by a certificate of financial implication setting out: the specific outputs and outcomes of the bill; how those outputs and outcomes fit within the overall policies and programs of government; the costs involved and their impact on the budget; the proposed or existing method of financing the costs related to the Bill and its feasibility27.

None of the three motions seeking leave to present private members' Bills concerned ENR: (i) The Access to Information Bill, 2004—Abdu Katuntu; (ii) The Abolition of Graduated Tax Bill – Okullo Epak; and (iv) The Copyright and Neighboring Rights Bill, 2004—Jacob Oulanyah

Assessment of Environmental Representation

The 7th Parliament has been viewed by some sections of the electorate as below average compared to the executive, indicating real or perceived unequal performance between the two arms of government. The high levels of absenteeism undermined parliament's performance.

Absenteeism resulted in government's loss of a crucial motion in Parliament: the Referendum Bill, 2005. This prompted the Prime Minister to impose a travel ban on all ministers in order to attend the proceedings in Parliament (Osike, 2005). Similarly, the strong influence of the executive over parliament undermined performance on ENR issues. For instance, the change of political interest from ENR interest to industrial/agricultural investments creates incentives to destroy green belts. Further, the constitutional reform and political transition process dominated the 7th parliament, occupied more space than ENR issues, and two most vocal green MPs were apparently targeted by the executive and other political forces: these did not make it back to the 8th Parliament. One of them was technically thrown out of the 7th Parliament.

Nevertheless, there were remarkable contributions from some MPs who attended regularly. This was possible because some MPs seem to have been motivated by the fact that particular Bills directly affected people from their constituencies. The available statistics show that it was almost unthinkable to raise 50% of the 305 MPs during the debate of ENR Bills. The low number of Bills passed and ENR sensitivity reflected during these legislative processes clearly demonstrates that the 7th parliament was compliant but less enthusiastic about ENR issues given members' absences. With seven Bills passed pertaining to ENR in five years we can safely submit that largely the ENR concerns have, in one way or the other, been taken care of. With none of the motions tabled as Private Members Bills touching ENRs issues, parliament seems to have waited for the executive alone to initiate ENR policy and legal issues.

The 7th Parliament handled 177 Motions. Of the 177 Motions, only 28 (16%) motions related to natural resources. The remaining 149 motions (84 %) were not related to ENR (Tables 2 & 3). Among the motions that were moved on the floor of Parliament in relation to ENR, three are good examples, namely: (i) The motion for a resolution of parliament to authorize government to borrow money to finance Kafu-Masindi Road; (ii) Motion for resolution of Parliament to authorize government to borrow money to finance Lake Victoria Environmental Management Project (LVEMP); and (iii) The Motion for resolution of Parliament on the status of pre-independence agreements on the Nile Waters. There were also petitions, all related to natural resources: (a) the petition, submitted by ACODE on 7 November 2003, on de facto de-gazettment of Butamira Forest Reserve, Uganda Wildlife Society (UWS), Butamira Pressure Development Group and Buyego Sub County concerning Butamira Forest Reserve, (ii) Power Tariffs Petition submitted by the Uganda Electricity Distribution Company Limited (UEDCL) seeking tariff increase in vain; and (iii) the Kibale Petition concerning land wrangles in Kibale between immigrants and indigenous Banyoro, which did not make any headway because of its sensitivity as government immediately appointed a Commission of Inquiry to conduct investigations in these ethnic conflicts. For space reasons we cannot go into details of these petitions and motions.

Implications for Multi-Party Legislation, Ecological Security, and Development

We can now consider the implications of the observed limited participation and representation of elected people's ENR interests, in the 7th Parliament, for multiparty legislation, ecological security, and development in Uganda and the region. The 7th parliament was a unicameral parliament in which opposition and ruling parties were not clear-cut. It operated with a not-unfamiliar intra-organisational opposition in which opposing views—if any and if instances such as Ken Lukyamuzi's minority report can be thus conceived—were not considered to have legitimate organisational origin but were more of idiosyncratic convictions of the legislator. This implies that as Uganda transitioned to multi-party dispensation in 2005, new legislative dynamics have emerged which have direct bearing on ENR issues: the possible partisanship of ENR legislations vis-à-vis broad strategic national development interests; the perceptional implications based on party identity and membership; and limitations on private members' bill.

Partisanship over ENR legislations affects broad strategic national development interests. When ENR issues appear to threaten the ruling party, it may have incentives to keep such issues out of the public domain—or just bring them to the public domain through parliament in order to gather public opinion and guide policy strategies of the ruling party. In the process, pertinent issues may be compromised. For instance, Uganda has been seeking to legislate the "The National Biotechnology and Biosafety Bill, 2012."

Civil society groups have observed that the Bill covers genetically-modified organisms more than it does the broad biotechnology issues, while also conflating biosafety with biotechnology. This generated protracted debates between government and civil society groups, including ACODE, partly because the Bill has environmental and other ENR-related implications. But the government, aware of the sensitivity of the bill, seems to have allowed the process to unfold and become protracted until these stakeholders either give up or lose interest without significantly altering the content of the bill (Republic of Uganda, 2012). Given the tendency for MPs to be absent when important bills are being legislated, Uganda may suffer limitations in checks and balances mounted by the opposition in parliament. Similar afflictions may hinder effective legislation on land-related governance frameworks in the country, as well as frameworks for governing the nascent oil and gas sector which has direct implications on ENR in the country and beyond (Republic of Uganda, 2008). This indicates that effective legislation of ENR requires bipartisan interest which remains limited given the dominance of the ruling NRM in Uganda's post-2005 parliament. The numerical and capacity weaknesses of the opposition in post-2005 Ugandan Parliament may adversely affect strategic legislations as MPs' absence and limited participation may allow the numerically dominant party to have uninterrupted sway over certain ENR issues.

The perceptional implications based on party identity and membership is this: belonging to political parties creates political identity for members of such parties, which may affect the ways in which legislators respond to each other's opinions. Though this may have personal and other aspects, and may not be generalized, it is well known that human beings tend to agree faster with the people with whom they share identity (politico-ideological, ethnic, etc) than those from non-groups members. Mobilization and sensitization of MPs takes place within party caucuses, which creates intra-party cohesion and inter-party division. This in-group—out-group perception limits interactions and understandings between the different groups.

If opposition MPs raise issues of ENR, such as the proposed reforms of land governance frameworks (constitutional amendments, development of the Land Acquisition, Resettlement, and Rehabilitation Policy, or debating future reports from the Land Inquiry), MPs from the ruling NRM may just dismiss it as opposition politics instead of looking at the strategic development implications of the issue. Similarly, the limited parliamentary autonomy and independence from the executive implies that once the ruling executive sways the opinion of its MPs the rest of the parliament is captured. This implies that is relevant ENR issues, however controversial and contentious they may be, will still depend merely on the ability of the ruling party caucus to convince its member MPs.

Uganda imposes limitations on private members' bills. A private MP can only table a bill with no serious financial implications. Only ministers are allowed to initiate and table bills with financial significance. This implies that opposition MPs, who would be checking the powers and interests of the ruling coalition, are constrained in using the legislative platform to advance ENR interests that may be in contradistinction with the interests of the executive. This is because in an era of heightened natural resource exploitation, the evolving oil and gas and mining sector (Auty, 2004), and increasing interest in massive land-based investments, the incentives of Uganda's ruling party to protect the interests of the people remains limited (Anyuru et al., 2016). Were private MPs allowed to meaningfully engage the parliamentary infrastructure to cause policy and institutional changes necessary to regulate ENR exploitation in the country, the health, quality, and intensity and extensity of parliamentary debates and processes would be improved upon, thus giving rise to legislations with more pro-people interests unlike the failing 1998 Land Act.

The implications of the parliamentary behavior and legislative business for ecological security and development are clear: first, limited parliament interest in ENR resources sows seeds of natural-resource conflicts, as the land conflicts have demonstrated in post-2005 Uganda. Second, disinterest in, or inattention to broad ENR issues, and the tendency to confine interests to MPs' specific constituencies, narrows the picture with which MPs view ENRs. This may limit the attention with which MPs may research, legislate, and task the ruling party on such issues as ENR-related border conflicts with neighbours (for instance over Rukwanzi and Migingo islands with DRC and Kenya respectively), as well as prevention of environmental damage caused by natural resource exploitation. It is clear that the extraction of stones, sand, clay and murram, while not categorised as minerals, has contributed to ecological destruction in the country. As a result, the failure of parliament to include them in the list of minerals without simultaneously developing a law on the regulation of their exploitation leaves the country open to environmental damage wrought by the exploitation of these resources. Similar observations can be made about forestry and wetland governance which is partly responsible for the climatic changes, disasters like floods and landslides, and other forms of ecological insecurity (NASA, no date; CNN, 2010).

Finally, the development implications of the changing dynamics of parliamentary legislation on ENR in Uganda are both political and socioeconomic. Politically, in a multi-party democracy, opposition MPs provide alternative policy options and compete with the ruling party for voters' support. Genuine political representation consists not in just articulating the individual interests of a constituency but in broadly articulating ENR interests as they affect the whole country and as they are articulated in party policy. These considerations would demand of MPs to periodically refer to their parties' policy standpoints on ENR. It remains unclear whether political parties in Uganda pay serious attention to ENR issues. This issue is addressed in more detail by Bainomugisha and Ntambirweki-Karugonjo's chapter on the degree to which manifestos of Uganda's political parties manifestos reflect ENR issues. But as Khisa and Rwengabo have demonstrated in another study, the opposition in Uganda remains too weak to mount meaningful challenge to the ruling NRM, which further stifles the development of multiparty democracy in the country.

Socioeconomically, the post-2005 parliamentary focus on anti-ENR policy and development choices, such as oil and gas and mineral resources exploitation, creates unique demands upon parliament on the sustainable management of ENR resources for the country's development. As of 2016 significant strides have been made in developing governance frameworks in the oil and gas sector, but there are inadequacies that need to be addressed. The land governance spectrum remains riddled with inconsistencies in laws, inadequate policy provisions, unresolved land-governance issues, weaknesses in land-governance institutions, and impunity in the land sector (Republic of Uganda, 2017). These afflictions also affect other land-based investments and may slow down the pace of Uganda's socio-economic transformation.

Conclusion

Representation has limitations in the extent to which it ensures that the needs, concerns, and interests of citizens in a given polity are brought to bear on policymaking processes. This chapter has revealed that when it comes to ENR in Uganda, the 7th parliament (2001-2006) passed little legislation, received few petitions, and initiated no private member's bill on ENR. This is so despite the centrality of ENR to the country's agriculture, extractive industry, energy security and sovereignty, and food security and sovereignty. The 7th Parliament, as the last legislative arm under the No-Party Movement System transition to a multi-party/multi-organisation political dispensation, demonstrated limitations in (i) individual contributions during parliamentary debates; (ii) absenteeism from parliamentary sessions; (iii) constituency-tailored, seemingly narrow, ENR sensitivity; (iv) absence of private Members bills on ENR; and (v) pro-bill voting patterns and behaviours. Parliament was unable to meaningfully challenge the executive in ENR issues It remains difficult to determine whether there would have been any legislature-executive stalemate on such issues. Perhaps the post-2005 multiparty dispensation will present new developments, but in any case to a limited extent due to executive excesses as the NRM's long stay evolves to an increasingly personalized form of rule.

Our findings reveal that: high levels of members' absenteeism undermined parliament's performance on ENR and possibly other issues; absenteeism was common in all the ENR bills legislated; and the strong influence of the executive undermined members' performance on ENR issues as it engendered a policy shift from ENR interest to industrial/agricultural investments with direct bearing on ENR and constraining parliamentary opposition to such developments. The obsession with attracting investments in ENR areas has also had direct bearing on the livelihoods of the people as well as exacerbated threats to the environment led to the destruction of green belts with limited parliamentary control over the process. The political transitional process dominated the 7th parliament over the 2003-2006 period, sacrificing ENR issues at the altar of political transition. Nevertheless, seven Bills were passed pertaining to ENR in period of five years—even though none of the Private Members Bills directly related to ENR issues. Some of the MPs who regularly attended parliamentary sessions made remarkable contributions because particular Bills affected their constituents—as the debate on the Land (Amendment) Act 2003 demonstrated.

The degree and extent of participation demonstrates MPs' sensitivity to ENR issues, as well as parliamentary autonomy when dealing with sensitive matters. This has direct bearing on the nexus between environment, poverty, and legislative representation in a multi-party order. First, the non-partisanship of ENR issues does not necessarily imply that in multiparty politics MPs will not be divided along party lines in legislating these issues. Second, broad strategic national development interests may be lost if party legislative politics prevents consensual standpoints on ENR sustainability. Third, party identity and membership may prevent inter-party interfaces with disastrous consequences for ENR legislations on sensitive issues like land, oil and gas sector, mineral exploitation, and ecological security. Finally, limitations on private members' bill hinder the possible channels though which citizen groups, such as civil society groups, may advance broad people's interests to the highest echelons of policymaking and legislation.

The foregoing observations lead to few recommendations. Apart from additional inquiry in the evolution of ENR legislation in post-2005 Uganda, under a multi-party dispensation, there is need to explain MP absenteeism in the 7th, previous, and subsequent parliaments, as well as uncovering underhand forces that impact upon legislative standpoints on ENR issues. In terms of practical interventions, there is need for stronger advocacy for access to information by the public; civic education to the electorate on the extent to which their interests are advanced by their representatives; improvements in parliament's record-keeping function; increased whipping to reduce MP absenteeism; improvements in technology to monitor MP performance and effectiveness; capacity building and facilitation for MPs; and development and implementation of a sanctioning regime targeting MP absenteeism under a multiparty dispensation. These interventions will have a direct bearing on the development of institutional infrastructure for guaranteeing the country's ecological peace and ENR-based socioeconomic transformation.

References

Ackerman, B. (2000) 'Separation of Powers', *Harvard Law Review*, 113(3), pp. 633–725.

Alweny, S. (2007) *Forest Giveaways to Cost Uganda Dearly*. Kampala: Africa News Service.

Antunes, P., Santos, R. and Nuno, V. (2006) 'Participatory decision making for sustainable development—the use of mediated modelling techniques', *Land Use Policy*, 23, pp. 44–52.

Anyuru, M. A., Rhoads, R., Mugyeni, O., Manoba, J. A. and Balemesa, T. (2016) 'Balancing Development and Community Livelihoods: A Framework for Land Acquisition and Resettlement in Uganda. Environmental Democracy Programme', *ACODE Policy Research Series*. Kampala, 75. Available at: http://www.acode-u.org/Files/Publications/PRS_75.pdf.

Auty, R. (2004) 'Natural Resources and Civil Strife: A Two-Stage Process', *Geopolitics*, 9(1), pp. 29–49.

Bainomugisha, A. (2006) 'Political Parties, Political Change and Environmental Governance in Uganda. A Review of political Parties Manifestoes', *Policy Research Series*. Kampala: ACODE, No. 16.

Bainomugisha, A. and Mushemeza, E. D. (2006) 'No TitleDeepening Democracy and Enhancing Sustainable Livelihoods in Uganda: An Independent Review of the Performance of Special Interest Groups in Parliament', *Policy Research Series*. Kampala: ACODE, No. 13.

Carmody, P. and Taylor, D. (2016) 'Globalization, Land Grabbing, and the Present-Day Colonial State in Uganda: Ecolonization and Its Impacts', *Journal of Environment & Development*, 25(1), pp. 100–126.

CNN (2010) *More than 100 bodies recovered after massive landslides in Uganda*, *CNN*. Atlanta, Georgia. Available at: http://www.cnn.com/2010/WORLD/africa/03/02/uganda.landslide/index.html (Accessed: 31 August 2017).

Daily Monitor (2011) 'Speakers of Parliament since 1962', *Daily Monitor*. Available at: http://www.monitor.co.ug/News/National/-/688334/1166118/-/c1gr8uz/-/index.html.

Jankowski, P. (2009) 'Towards participatory geographic information systems for community-based environmental decision making', *Journal of Environmental Management*, 90(6), pp. 1966–1971. Available at: http://www.sciencedirect.com/science/journal/03014797/90/6.

Kanyeihamba, G. W. (2002) *Constitutional and Political History of Uganda: From 1894 to the Present*. Kampala: Fountain Publishers Ltd.

Kiker, G. A., Bridges, T. S., Varghese, A., Seager, T. P. and Linkovj, I. (2005) 'Application of Multicriteria Decision Analysis in Environmental Decision Making', *Integrated Environmental Assessment and Management*, 1(2), pp. 95–108.

MoFPED (2004) *Post-conflict Reconstruction: The Case of Northern Uganda*. Available at: www.finance.go.ug.

MWLE (2003) 'Guidelines for Mainstreaming ENR issues in other sectors and programmes'.

NASA (no date) *Large Landslide in Uganda, NASA*. Washington D.C. Available at: https://earthobservatory.nasa.gov/NaturalHazards /view.php?id=43130.

Newig, J. and Fritsch, O. (2008) *Environmental governance: Participatory, multi-level - and effective?* Liepzing: Helmholtz Centre for Environmental Research – UFZ, UFZ Diskussionspapiere.

Osike, F. (2005) 'PM stops ministers travel', *The New Vision*.

Personn, T., Roland, G. and Tabellini, G. (1997) 'Separation of Powers and Political Accountability'. Available at: ftp://ftp.igier.unibocconi.it/wp/1996/100.pdf.

Prudence, G. and Oyono, P. R. (2004) 'Legislative Representation and The Environment: Lessons From a Case Study of Cameroon'.

Republic of Uganda (2000) 'Petroleum Act Cap 149 Vol. 7 Laws of Uganda'. UPPC.

Republic of Uganda (2003a) *The Mining Bill, 2003*. Kampala: arliament of the Republic of Uganda.

Republic of Uganda (2003b) 'The National Forestry and Tree Planting Act, 2003', *Uganda Gazette*. Entebbe: UPPC, XCVI(37).

Republic of Uganda (2006) *Budget speech by Minister of Finance, Planning and Economic Development*. Kampala: MoFPED.

Republic of Uganda (2008) *National Oil and Gas Policy for Uganda*. Entebbe: Ministry of Energy and Mineral Development.

Republic of Uganda (2012) *Biosafety and Biotechnology Bill*. Kampala: Parliament of the Republic of Uganda.

Republic of Uganda (2017) 'Commission of Inquiry (Effectiveness of Law, Policies, and Processes of Land Acquisition, Land Administration, Land Management and Land Registration in Uganda)', *Uganda Gazette*. Entebbe: UPPC, CX, 3rd(7).

Strøm, K. (2000) 'Delegation and accountability in parliamentary democracies', *European Journal of Political Research*, 37, pp. 261–289.

Thabrew, L., Wiek, A. and Ries, R. (2009) 'Environmental decision making in multi-stakeholder contexts: applicability of life cycle thinking in development planning and implementation', *Journal of Cleaner Production*, 17(1), pp. 67–76.

'The Constitution of the Republic of Uganda' (1995).

The East African (2006) 'Uganda Power Crisis worsens as L. Victoria water levels drop', *The East African*, pp. 18–24.

Tripp, A. M. (2010) *Museveni's Uganda: Paradoxes of Power in Hybrid Regime.* London: Lynne Rienner.

Tumushabe, G. W., Bainomugisha, A., Makumbi, I., Mwebaza, R., Manyindo, J. and Mwenda, A. (2003) 'Sustainable Development Beyond Rio + 10- Consolidating Environmental Democracy in Uganda Through Access to Justice, Information and Participation', *ACODE Policy Research Series*. Kampala, (5).

Uganda Bureau of Statistics (2016) 'The National Population and Housing Census of 2014: Main Report'.

Uganda National NGO Forum (2009) *Civil Society perspective on the progress and challenges of attaining the Millennium Development Goals in Uganda.* Kampala: NGO Forum.

CHAPTER SEVEN

The Dilemma of Natural Resource-Dependent Pastoral Communities in Africa: The Case of Teso - Karamoja Border Conflict

Arthur Bainomugisha, John Bosco Ngoya and Wilson Winstons Muhwezi

Introduction

> Land lies at the heart of social, economic and political life in most of Africa, but across much of the continent, there is a lack of clarity regarding property rights and everywhere, land tenure is contested (Huggins and Clover, 2005).

Pastoral communities in the Greater Horn of Africa and indeed across much of Africa have always experienced violent conflicts which arise because of the harsh climatic conditions in which they live. However, it is important to note that conflicts in Africa's natural-resource dependent pastoral societies are part of the Africa-wide conflict trap that has since 1990s engulfed the continent with debilitating consequences, which marginalize the African people (Department for International Development (DFID), 2001). This chapter examines the plight of natural resources-dependent pastoral communities in Africa with specific focus on Teso and Karamoja ethnic communities located in north-eastern Uganda. The two communities have endured decades of ethnic based violent conflicts fueled and sustained by cattle rustling, as well as competition for access and control of scarce natural resources especially water and pasture. This historical conflict involves Karimojong pastoralists forcefully grazing their cattle, sheep and goats in Teso region during the dry season and returning to their traditional grazing areas with stolen animals whenever it rains and pasture sprouts.

The conflict pits two ethnically related communities; the Itesots and Karimojong over the Katakwi-Moroto districts border line. Both groups claim large chunks of land on either side of the border and accuse each other of land grabbing. This border conflict has often resulted in internal displacement of mostly Itesot's in Katakwi district where conditions of living are appalling. Before the disarmament by the Government of Uganda, this conflict was lethal because of the availability of small arms and light weapons in the hands of the Karimojong. These weapons gave the Karimajong power and undue advantage over neighbors. While disarmament removed the bulk of the guns, the Karimojong continued to possess some arms, mostly acquired from war zones in Somalia and South Sudan (Teso Initiative for Peace, 2010; Odong, 2016). This has always been complicated by competition for access and control of water and pasture.

Using the case of the Itesot and the Karimojong in Katakwi-Moroto districts, the chapter elucidates the linkage between land scarcity, security and ethnic conflict and identifies options on how to resolve the conflict. The chapter is premised on the realization that the land question among pastoralists and their livelihood issues deserve more attention by policy makers. In Uganda, pastoralists as an interest group are known to be generally marginalized in development. This results in escalation of natural resource-based conflicts (Bamuturaki, 2011). The causes of Katakwi-Moroto border conflict revolves around environmental scarcity and stress, colonial marginalization and the post-colonial containment policy towards the Karimojong people, lack of a clear border demarcation along the Katakwi and Moroto districts and the transhumant nature of the Karimojong. Other causes include; politicization of border issues by political elite seeking political mileage during elections; general political instability in Uganda; inadequacies in the land policy epitomized in unclear land conflict management mechanisms and the availability of small arms in the region which makes people opt for the use of force, rather than peaceful resolution of the conflict.

Background

Uganda is a natural resource dependent country with land as the most strategic and contested of all the natural resources. As the country recovers from political and governance failure-driven conflicts, a preview into the future of peace and security point to the possibility of a new wave of protracted conflicts revolving around the struggle to access and control land by different ethnic communities, between government and communities as well as between Government and conservationists. Incidentally, most conflict management and prevention measures pursued by Government, the international community and stakeholders focus largely on the political dimensions of conflicts without looking at ecological underpinnings and future implications. This chapter adduces evidence to fill that information gap.

The increasing population, poor agricultural practices, decreasing acreage of land, environmental degradation and declining food stocks are some of the leading factors causing ethnic clashes over land resources. Examples of areas with such pressures include Kigezi (Kabale, Kanungu, Rukungiri and Kisoro districts) where landlessness and declining food stocks as well as hunger are forcing people to migrate to other district like Kibaale and Kyenjojo in Uganda. It is known that these immigrants end up conflicting with indigenous Banyoro and Batooro over land. Similarly, environmental scarcities in the form of lack of water, pasture and food security partly explains the struggle between Katakwi and Moroto districts, pitting the Itesots against the Karimojong.

Land is key in a country's stability as it supports the most basic needs of rural communities as well as a strategic resources needed for national economic development. Current statistics show that over 90% of Uganda's rural populations depend on land for food and food security, employment and other forms of income generation as well as spiritual and cultural nourishment. For quite a long time,, there has been a consistent escalation of land and natural resources-related conflicts notably from the rangelands of Karamoja through the grasslands of Northern Uganda and the cattle corridor, cutting across the country to the highlands of Kigezi. Land and other natural resource related conflicts have been evolving and often coalescing into violent confrontations among communities and between communities and the state. The unending feud between the Karamjong and the Itesot over grazing and water rights, the displacement of the Benet, the Basongora and the Batwa from their ancestral lands and conflicts between the Banyoro and the Bakiga immigrants in Kibaale, and the threat by Acholi Members of Parliament to spear investors are but a few examples of land and other natural resource conflicts in Uganda.

Consensus abounds in literature that land and resource scarcity is both a cause and a driver of conflicts (Bardal and David, 2000). However, most of this literature is generalized often focusing on particular resources, like range lands, fisheries, oil, and water. Secondly, comprehensive studies on land and natural resources conflicts that give a complete picture of the situation in Uganda is rare. The few existing literature concentrates more on selected resources like wildlife, forestry and generally armed conflicts and lack theoretical and practical grounding. The resulting effect has been that these conflicts are analyzed in a proper socio-economic, political and governance contexts which provide the appropriate framework for conflict mapping, prevention and mitigation.

In areas with land-driven conflicts, Government's response is in most cases reactive and suppressive rather than proactive which simply postpones the problem. In Kibaale district for example, the inter-ethnic political confrontation between the indigenous Banyoro community and the immigrant Bakiga is a clear manifestation of the underlying conflicts over land ownership and access to land. In Katakwi district, state responses to the continuing confrontation between the Karimajong and the Itesot has only focused on short-term solutions such as temporary travel authorizations for pastoralists and livestock without addressing the long-term dimensions of the conflict. In the meantime, the conflict resulted into internal displacement of people. For over six years, people in Katakwi lived in congested camps where susceptibility to diseases like cholera was very high. Like in many other violent conflicts around the world, the worst affected are the rural and poor communities who are largely dependent on land-based resources and often have limited social safeguards and technological capacity to cope with the resulting scarcities and the associated disenfranchisement.

Data collection methods for research in this chapter

A qualitative research approach was used to collect, analyze and interpret material in this chapter. Primary and secondary data was collected in 2005 and 2006 for this research. The primary data collections methods were: in-depth interviews (IDIs), key informants (KIs), observations and focus group discussions (FGDs) in both Karamoja and Teso regions.

The KIs were organized for key stakeholders on both sides of the conflict including Members of Parliament (MPs), Local Leaders, elders and youth leaders. The FGDs were useful since problem solving techniques were employed. The design of FGDs ensured that participants identified the root causes of the conflict, negative effects and how it could be resolved peacefully. The secondary data collected and used included key documents such books, reports, newspaper articles, government policy papers and Internet sources.

This research for this chapter was part of a bigger project titled, "Land Conflict Mapping and Environmental Security in Uganda" whose overall objective was to identify potential land conflicts that could threaten peace, stability and sustainable development and propose policy responses to manage and prevent such conflicts. The specific objectives of the research were:

a. To find out traditional use of the borderlands and root causes of the border land and natural resource-based conflicts between the Iteso and Karimojong

b. To establish the social, economic and political consequences of the conflicts on the affected peoples' livelihoods and propose appropriate interventions

c. To influence the on-going national land policy making to address land conflicts in the country and promote sustainable development; and

d. To inform future programmatic and development agenda of DanChurchAid on conflict resolution and peace building in the Teso and Karamoja regions.

Historical synopsis of Katakwi-Moroto Border conflict

The Iteso and Karimojong belong to the Nilo Hamitic group who are closely related to the Jie and Toposa of Sudan and Turkana of Kenya. The Iteso, Turkana, Toposa and Karimojong lived together in Abyssinia (Ethiopia) as one ethnic group about 500 years ago (Gray et al., 2003). They owned and depended on large herds of livestock. As people and the number of livestock increased, the necessity of moving away from their ancestral lands became inevitable. This culminated in a large tribal movement southward. The Turkana moved and settled in northern

Kenya. The second group also left Ethiopia around 1600 and attempted to join the Turkana but were repulsed by the Turkana who had earlier on settled around Lake Rudolf (now Lake Turkana) (Cisternino and Karamoja, 1979; Opuli-Watum, 1980). This group decided to move westwards and settled around Mount Moroto. Their settling in the new area was made uncomfortable by drought and famine. This state of affairs caused internal and external conflicts. To worsen their predicament, there were outbreaks of human and cattle diseases.

Consequently, people began to discuss the possibility of moving out to new places. The young men were in favor of migrating to other places. The older men urged them not to do so. They were worried that the young men would be killed by hostile tribes or be eaten by wild animals. In their arguments, the young men mocked their fathers (elders) as "Akar Imojong" where the word "Akar" means "stay behind" and "Imojong" meaning "old man". In other words "The old men stay behind". Akar Imojong in turn called the young men "Atesia" meaning graves. The word "Atesia" also meant children. From that day, the Akar imojong remained and settled near Mt. Moroto, presently known as Karamoja sub-region. Later, they acquired the name Karimojong (tired old men). The young men who were called Atesia moved southwards and finally called themselves Iteso (Amodoi-Okoboi, 2016). Before British colonialists arrived on the scene, the people of Karamoja were a collection of tribes (the Dodos, Jie, Labwor, Bokora, Pian, Matheniko and the Upe) with historical links. Their way of life was communal. A person was an individual only to the extent that he was a member of a family, a community or a clan. The means of livelihood was cattle and cultivation of land and these were never owned by an individual but by all the people. No single individual could dispose such communal survival means. It is important to note that before colonialism, pastoralists in Karamoja and the neighboring regions were accustomed to free possession of firearms which for many decades had been obtained from Ethiopian gun-runners and Arab and Swahili slave traders, poachers and merchants from the East African Coast.

In the first half of 1888, the East African coast was a conduit for as many as 3,744 assorted firearms, mainly Breech-Loaders and Winchester rifles. By 1910, a private army operated in Turkana border lands with Ethiopia and Sudan, which was organized in units of between six hundred and one thousand fighters. They were mainly armed with single shot rifles and they operated in smaller tactical units. Therefore, Britain had to "pacify" Karamoja and Turkana regions before they could claim full administrative control of this sphere of influence.

After the transfer of Uganda's Rudolf Province to Kenya in 1926 and the creation of Kenya and Uganda as they are known today, the British tried to confine the Turkana and Karimojong within the newly created states. Before the arbitrary colonial delimitation sliced their grazing areas, the Turkana and Karimojong had lived within the Rudolf province where they shared natural resources under a system of social reciprocity. After the partition of Kenya and Uganda, these transhumant societies were expected to respect the invisible meridians that delineated the newly created states.

In order to get protection from the colonizers, each ethnic community was expected to lay down arms they had acquired over many decades and stop cross-border livestock rustling. When they refused to surrender guns peacefully, Britain conducted a disarming campaign codenamed "Operation Tennis" from the Turkana side of the Kenya/Uganda common border. The operation was unsuccessful due to lack of proper coordination and the evasive agro-pastoralists simply relocated to rugged mountainous terrain, out of reach of colonial patrols. Consequently, Karamoja and Turkana regions were declared "closed districts" where movement within and outside was restricted if one had no valid pass. This decision was ostensibly aimed at containing the spread of livestock diseases down south, particularly render-pest and pleuro-pneumonia. In addition, by restricting transhumance, the policy had the impact of impoverishing the two communities who previously had a thriving agro-pastoral economy and barter trade in grain, iron ware, and livestock. It also insulated them from mainstream nationalism and fervor of patriotism that was going on in the southern half of each country. It remains to be seen whether the cattle rustling and violence the Karamojong have meted on their neighbors is related to the effects of this confinement.

The History of Karimojong Cattle Rustling in Teso

Accounts by most people in Teso, especially the elders, indicate that Karamoja cattle raids into Teso started between 1945-1950. Strict measures were put into place by the then colonial District Commissioner with patrols of Kings African Rifles to control these raids. A post was established at Omoro which was part of Teso to curb cattle raiding. Cattle raiding in Karamoja started as a local tribal affair limited in area and scope, but later went out of hand leading to humanitarian emergencies. Initially, the two tribes enjoyed a cordial relationship where the Itesots allowed the Karimojong the privilege of grazing and watering their livestock in Teso during dry seasons.

However, this relationship soured in early 1950s when the British government imposed restricted movement of livestock in and out of Karamoja due to the outbreak of the contagious Borbine plural pneumonia disease. The Karimojong stubbornly refused to vaccinate their cattle against the killer disease, prompting the Government to prohibit their cattle from grazing in Teso land. The cattle that crossed the border into Teso were captured under quarantine regulations. The sick animals would be burnt to destroy the disease while some would be eaten by the Iteso, although the quarantine regulations did not permit that. When the Karimojong learnt their cows were being eaten, they became very angry.

The Karimojong blamed the Iteso for having been behind the plan by the government of confiscation of their cattle. They did not appreciate the fact that the quarantine was intended to make them vaccinate their cattle. When the practice continued for a long time, the Karimojong reacted and started raiding sub-counties in Teso land that neighbored Karamoja notably; Ngariam, Usuk, Magoro and Kapelebyong with the aim of recovering the lost cattle. Apart from the quarantine, harsh climatic conditions set cattle rustling off around 1955, as several Karimojong herdsmen sought water and pasture in Teso. In 1955 for instance, a group of Karimojong herdsmen forcefully crossed the border line at Olilim and Palam villages in order to find green grass and water for domestic use and animals. These herdsmen were grazing cattle that belonged to two of the richest and most respected Karimojong leaders. About 350 heads of cattle were captured including

Geno's biggest bull named "APAIRIONO ETOME". It was the biggest bull in the whole of Karamoja district (now Moroto district) comparable to almost the size of an elephant. Geno used to worship his bull and valued it as a god which had given him fortune for riches. This angered Geno and his in-law Labwok who went back to Karamoja and organized their people to come for the bloody raid. The raid covered Nagrian, Magoro, Toroma and Usuk Sub-counties. The raiders burnt the wooden bridge at Komolo inside Katakwi district to prevent security personnel from coming to challenge them. For so many years, the raids remained concentrated within Usuk county since at the time, there was a balance of power since both Iteso and Karimojong were using spears and shields as weapons. With the acquisition of guns, the Karimojong became militarily stronger and were able to raid far and wide in the whole of Teso and other neighboring regions.

Katakwi-Moroto Border Conflict: A Socio-Economic Description

Socio-Economic Description of Katakwi

Katakwi district is one of the eight districts that make up Teso sub-region located in North Eastern Uganda. The district gained its district status in 1997 through an Act of Parliament. It first became a district in 1970s having been curved out of Soroti district when it was known as North Teso district but this status was cancelled in the 1980s. Katakwi District is bordered by the districts of Napak to the north, Nakapiripirit to the east, Kumi to the south, Ngora and Soroti to the southwest; and Amuria to the west. The district's 'chief town', Katakwi and is located approximately 55 Kms, by road, north of Soroti, the largest town in the sub-region. Katakwi Town Council is about 380 Kms East of Kampala. At the time of doing research for this chapter, Kotido was one district to the west of Karamoja sub-region up to July 2010 when it was divided into Napak, Nakapiripirit and Kotido districts.

Katakwi district is generally a plateau with gentle undulating hills, resting at 1,036m-1127m above sea level. The district experiences two rainy seasons a year. The wet season runs from March to October while the dry season runs from November to February. The mean annual rainfall varies from 1000 mm to 1500mm. At present, the rainfall pattern is unreliable and unpredictable with the December-February period being the driest season. The soils are mainly sandy sediments and sandy loam. The bottom land contains widespread deposits of alluvium. Though not very fertile, the land is productive with agricultural production becoming the major economic activity and employing activities in the district. Geological surveys have revealed that rocks of basement complex such as granite, magnalite, gneiss, schists and quartzite underlie most areas. The vegetation is savannah grassland dotted with shrubs and trees. There are two minor lakes (Lake Bisina and Lake Opeta) along its border with Kumi district and River Kiriik- a seasonal river that flows from neighboring Karamoja. It also has large swamps of water on both sides of the district. Human beings, livestock and wildlife animals depend on water from these sources. Compared to other regions in Teso, Katakwi district, from which Amuria district was curved in June 2005 has historically suffered most at the hands of Karimojong cattle rustlers. The predominant ethnic group is Itesot who are the indigenous people. The district also has a sizeable number of Langis, Karimojongs, Bagisu, Baganda, Basoga, Banyoro, Banyankore herdsmen.

Socio-Economic Description of Moroto

Karamoja region and Moroto district (used to include Napak and Nakapiripirit) in particular lies in the North-eastern part of Uganda where the northern Savannas meet the western shoulder of the Great Rift escarpment. This scarp line forms the frontier with Kenya and the watershed of westward and eastward flowing river systems. Most of the area comprises a gentle sloping plain at 1,050m broken only by steep-sided volcanic inselbergs such as Kadam, Moroto, Napak and Toror. The whole region lies within categories which the East Africa Royal Commission considered marginal for settled cultivation. Only the west, near higher ground as in Labwor, is suited for settled agriculture that can be carried out without irrigation. To the west, the red sandy soils give way to heavier black cotton soils (clay) broken by lighter red-sand ridges. The drainage lines in this western area are seasonally waterlogged and swampy becoming permanent swamps in the Teso and Acholi district lines (Randal, 1977). Moroto, part of former "Karamoja province", in

Northeastern Uganda has traditionally had three main ethnic groups – Karimojong, the main inhabitants of the rangelands, as well as the Pokot and the Tepeth, who live in mountains of Moroto and Napak. While these people have differences in language and culture, they share a similar socio-economic lifestyle of being agro-pastoralists. They practice subsistence crop production along with semi nomadic animal rearing.

Within the described exists strips of land which do not fit the situation described above. These are zones that border with Teso, Lango and the Acholi regions to the west, and the zones occupied by the Pokot and the Sebei to the south, where agriculture is possible. These contested border areas currently do not only provide pasture and water for livestock of the Karimojong but also provide wild foods, medicines and building materials.

Features of the Borderline

According to the information obtained from Karamoja side, the Acacia tree marks the border line between Katakwi and Moroto districts and has a milestone that runs through to Sising hill and bares a straight line up to Lotukei Mountain. Also, along the same axis can be traced the old mark of sign posts which were inscribed South of Karamoja in 1963. These border marks can be found adjacent to the same acacia tree and during the dry season, the straight lining can be seen from above in an aerial view. However, this information is contested by the people from Teso who want a fresh border demarcation by the Government.

Nature and Description of the Conflict

The border conflict that separates the old geographical districts of Katakwi and Moroto revolves around claims and counter claims of land on both sides of the border by people in the two ethnic groups; the Itesot and the Karimojong. While the conflict revolves around the border land claims by each side, it has been complicated by cattle rustling by the Karimojong whose motivation besides land seems to include cattle, pastures and water resources found in Teso sub-region, notably Katakwi. Consequently hundreds of people in Teso sub-region used to be internally displaced and to live in Internally Displaced Persons'

Camps (IDPs), where living conditions were appalling. Though the IDPs phenomenon dissipated with time, there are still occasional skirmishes that displace people.

Issues and Views about the Conflict: Voices from Fieldwork

During FGDs and IDI conducted in Katakwi and Moroto districts, the following issues and proposals were raised concerning the border conflict. The causes of the Border Conflict were diverse:

Water Scarcity:

It emerged that lack of water for both cattle and human beings on the side of Moroto in Karamoja region drives people to migrate to where there are permanent sources of water. Changing climactic conditions in Karamoja sub-region were also cited as a cause and propeller of the border conflict. People in Katakwi observed that weather changes make conditions in Karamoja unbearable and unsuitable for both cattle and human beings which force them to look outside of their geographical area.

The Culture of the Karimojong towards Cattle

A culture of keeping large numbers of cattle among the Karimojong was identified as a cause of border conflicts. It was pointed out that keeping the border conflict alive allowed cattle rustlers a chance to continue carrying out raids. It was for instance pointed out that among the Karimojong, the number of cattle one accumulated bestowed on somebody high esteem and status.

Politicization of the Border Conflicts by Politicians

Political interests by politicians who capitalize on keeping the border conflict alive in order to win elections were also identified as a cause and sustainer of the conflict.

Inferiority Complex and Superiority Complex

Inferiority complex and superiority complex of both ethnic groups was identified as an issue. The Karimojong commonly accused the Itesot of a superiority complex since they were more educated. This factor was seen both as a cause and sustainer of the conflict.

Availability of Small Arms

The availability of guns in the hands of Karimojong sustained the conflict. Their belief in violent resolution of conflicts was higher. For instance, there had been attempts by officials from the Ministry of Lands of the government of Uganda to survey the border but they had been chased away by warriors from Karamoja side. It looks like they resorted to force as a result of power that the gun confers to the holder.

Poor Politics and Lack of a Culture of Negotiations

In Uganda, most politicians thrive on political manipulation of the electorate in order to be elected into political positions including into Parliament. Hence, politicians drum up ethnic sentiments and present themselves as defenders of their communities' land and other resource rights hence sustaining conflicts. More so, there is a general absence of a culture of peaceful negotiations over contested issues, interests and needs in Uganda. Most parties in a conflict always pursue a zero-sum game instead of win-win situation. This culture explains why most conflicts in Uganda never end.

The Social, Economic and Political Marginalization of Karamoja Region

Karamoja is one of the poorest regions in Uganda. The region has the worst socio- economic indicators in the country and the population is largely dependent on relief aid from humanitarian agencies. As long as the people in Karamoja continue living on the margins of life, conflicts between themselves and with their neighbors can never be resolved.

Critical Actors in the Conflict

Any effort to end the Iteso-Karimojong conflict or even the conflict within the Karimojong must depend on the extent to which the main actors are identified and their roles in sustaining and ending the conflict recognized.

Women as Actors in the Conflict - The unmarried women whose desire is to be married renders them one important category of actors in the conflict. Their marriage is premised on payment of bride price of up to at least 40 herds of cattle, yet many marriage suitors do not have such numbers of cattle. They resort to cattle resulting to raise cows for bride price. Marriage is important for their recognition and respect in community. Therefore, while the young Karimojong men participate in cattle raiding, women bless them before going out on raiding missions and praise them when they come back successfully. Therefore, women have a position of influence in fuelling the conflict. They inspire husbands to raid by either beating children to portray poor household welfare (example lack of food, treatment) or minimizing/belittling their husbands considered a humiliation. This forces men to go and raid in order to defend their status. Women also cook special meals for warriors, keep and give ammunition to warriors and stage prestigious welcome ceremonies on return of the raider warriors. They also benefit from milk and other products. Women only want a lover or a husband who is a successful raider.

Military Personnel - The Ugandan army particularly stands out as a key actor because of its role in combating cattle rustling, disarmament and sometimes its involvement in illegal activities in the region. The army is blamed for sometimes conniving with cattle rustlers or indifference in combating cattle rustling.

Non-Governmental Organisations (NGOs) and Community Based Organizations CBOs) - The NGOs and CBOs provide development and humanitarian assistance to the people in Karamoja and IDPs in Katakwi district. Some of the NGOs are directly involved in peace-building and reconciliation of the two ethnic groups.

The Church - Both the Catholic and Anglican Churches are highly respected and have great influence in Teso and Karamoja regions. Both institutions are involved in evangelism and development activities in both regions. Any attempts to resolve the conflict between Teso and Karamoja must involve both churches.

Ngikaracuna or youthful warriors who are the active warriors and the implementers of the decisions taken directly or indirectly by elders and women have a role too. Their interests are in forced acquisition and expansion of herds as well as personal fame.

Witch Doctors who perform rituals and ceremonies aimed at instilling fearlessness

Ngimuu which means twins and *Ekediany* referring to a left-handed person smearing earth mud on the warriors going for raids, thus evoking greater brevity and supposedly immunity from attack.

Ekungut who are persons that were conceived or born as a result of mother not experiencing menstrual period that are believed to have natural powers of being able to mix and spy on the enemy without being suspected. Their findings are taken very seriously.

Political Leaders - Political leaders protect or conceal the raiders so as to maintain their political positions and avoid annoying the electorate. It is also alleged that some of the political or tribal leaders have private armed groups whose sole purpose is to carry out raids and therefore do not cooperate in the recovery of raided cows. They also conceal culprits since they are beneficiaries, politically and materially.

The Kraal Leaders in Karamoja have a lot of influence on the warriors given the powers and respect they command.

Government - Government is a key actor in the conflict because it is responsible for providing security to its citizens in a holistic manner. Government is supposed to develop Karamoja and is supposed to keep law and order which surprisingly in this case, it has failed to keep. Government should be blamed for failing to check the illegal possessions of firearms by Karimojong.

External Actors - Countries such as Sudan, Ethiopia, Somalia and Kenya have been singled out as sources of small arms that fuel and sustain the conflict in both regions. Kenya is particularly a key external actor as it is a country where the Turkana and the Pokot pastoralists are found. These two are involved in cattle rustling in Teso and Karamoja.

Consequences of the Conflict

Poverty and Insecurity on both sides- The conflict has resulted in underdevelopment of concerned districts. On Katakwi side, the conflict undermines people's livelihoods. People who used to feed themselves and fend for their families were reduced to depend on relief by NGOs. It is also important to note that land conflicts coupled with cattle rustling restricts movement for most Karimojong. They are generally criminalized as cattle rustlers and risk being lynched publicly if sighted within Teso region. This has greatly affected the Karimojongs' ability to look for work outside their region. The region cannot attract foreign investment which would create jobs and other opportunities because of insecurity.

Ethnic Hatred - The conflict has served to rekindle traditional hatred and amplify rivalry between the ethnically related tribes. This greatly undermines the regions' ability to engage in joint development necessary to propel the region forward.

Food Insecurity - The insecurity in the region undermines people's ability to produce adequate food stocks for subsistence and for sell. Consequently, the region especially Karamoja is chronically hit by food shortages.

Collapse of the Traditional Authority of Elders - In Karamoja, the conflict has partly led to the collapse of traditional authority and other cultural institutions that held the society together and ensured peace and tranquility. Availability of guns in the hands of able-bodied Karimojong has reduced the authority elders used to enjoy over the youths. Consequently, anomie and lawlessness abounds since power lies in the holders of guns.

Breakdown of Law and Order - Communities have slowly lost trust in the leadership (formal leaders) and increased their determination and desire to defend land by whatever method (violent or non-violent means).

Further Isolation and Marginalization of Karamoja - The border conflict and other associated insecurity in Karamoja has also made it difficult to access the region by people from other regions. Consequently, the region has further been isolated and marginalized which makes people poorer.

Chapter Seven | Bainomugisha, Ngoya and Muhwezi

Previous Attempts to Resolve the Conflict

Moroto district Political leaders and Members of Parliament led a delegation in the 1966 to reclaim the land which Hon. Cuthbert Obwangor allegedly wanted to grab from Karamoja. The delegation met the then President Milton Obote to complain about border boundary alteration by Hon Obwongor who was a minister for Local Government in the Central Government at that time. President Obote declared the border drawn by Obwongor illegal and arbitrary. The Moroto Local Government in 2005 came up with a position paper on the border issue which they presented to Government. In 2004/05, the Central Government and Local Government tried to resolve the border conflict but their efforts did not materialize into much. The "Magoro Accords" of elders crafted for the purpose of promoting peaceful coexistence and sharing of resources especially water and pasture between the two communities did not materialize into much. Another attempt to resolve the conflict in the recent past was when the leadership in Moroto and Katakwi with support from the officials from Ministry of Lands agreed to survey the border. The surveying exercise is known to have been stopped and the surveyors chased away by Mr Achila, a former LC V Chairman of Moroto district with the support of Karimojong warriors.

General Findings and Analysis of the Causes of Katakwi - Moroto Border Conflict

Several probable causes have been advanced to explain the border land conflict between the Karimojong and Iteso over Katakwi – Moroto districts. These causes whether historical/colonial, environmental or political have had a violent face and led to displacement of hundreds of people and continue to fuel traditional hatred between people that are ethnically related. Some of probable causes of the conflict include:

Lack of a clear border demarcation, constant border shifts and gazettment of most potentially productive land in Karamoja. While the link between land and conflict in Karamoja and Teso regions is complex, research found that in Karamoja, communities never understood anything about boarders. The reason behind this was that there had been border shifts from Komolo, Angobo, Orungo to the current contested Acacia tree without people ever raising their voices.

Environmental scarcity and stress leading to pressure to acquire land:- The underlying struggle to control land on either side of Katakwi and Moroto districts is by Karimajong due to the desire to access water and pasture for cattle. Karamoja is largely semi-arid and is increasingly becoming unable to sustain livelihoods. Consequently cattle rustling and pastoralism become the most immediate coping mechanisms for survival. Unfortunately, the two coping mechanisms are in conflict with sustainable environmental use of natural resources.

Scholars have confirmed the nexus between environmental scarcity and the various conflicts within the Karimojong ethnic communities with neighboring tribes like the Itesots, Acholis and the Sabiny. For instance, one of the likely causes for the current border conflict between Katakwi and Moroto districts was believed to be the bigger problem of environmental stress and scarcity faced by Karamoja. Drought and hunger has been described as the defining characteristic of this region (Quam, 1996). During periods of dry seasons, herdsmen leave their permanent settlements and move with their cattle to temporary encampments near pasture and watering places located to the west and south of the central plains, often crossing over into the territory of neighboring groups and districts. The main thesis is that competition for scarce resources, particularly water and pasture, and the high value placed on cattle continue to produce a culture of raiding and warfare.

Another commentary proposes that inadequate pastures and water during periods of drought coupled with the pressure and accentuated by the spread of tsetse flies, is likely to continue forcing people like the Karimojong to look for more land (Becker, 1977). This pressure coupled with increasing population forces most people from marginal lands to fertile lands hence causing conflicts with the farming communities. More so, the need to find new grazing grounds drives people to take their livestock where grass and water are relatively abundant (Novelli, 1988) This leads various groups to scatter in different directions where water, pasture and fertile land can be found. Consequently, competition arises among adjoining groups for pastures and watering, leading to violent confrontation.

Another commentary suggested that resource pressure made the people of Karamoja to move outwards towards the peripheries of the settlement belt, where they normally lived; into the barrier between themselves and their neighbours: - the Acholi, Iteso and Suk (Randal, 1975). In comments about the border conflicts in a book titled *"Aspects of Karimojong Ethno-Sociology"* (Novelli, 1988), it was argued that the establishment of borders, which had among its aims the ending of ivory and arms trafficking while reaching certain results in this field, did nothing but worsen the situation of the pastoral peoples, since it led to a loss of not only men and livestock, but also of "a permanent peace." This led to competition for the few pastures and water resources that remained resulting into acute fights among the Karimojong groups.

Greed for Land and Manipulation by Teso Politicians

Among the Karimajong, it is a generally believed that greed for land by Itesot politicians led by Mr. Cuthbert Obwangor (former Minister of Local Government in Obote 1 Government) is responsible for the current stand-off between them over the Katakwi- Moroto border. The leadership in Karamoja allege that being a Minister of Local Government in 1960s, Obwangor and other Itesot leaders took advantage of the little education among the Karimajong and altered the border boundary in favour of the Itesot. Most people in Karamoja attribute the conflict to laxity of the Local Administration of Moroto district and its failure to follow up matters of land or even document records. According to Hon. Terence Achia, MP for Bokora County in 2006, the demarcation of the border between Katakwi and Moroto districts departed from the original one dating back to 1926. According to Achia, the unofficial drawing which brought the unnecessary conflict could be traced from the drawings made in 1938 where the Cartographer at that time inscribed on the map, 'District Boundary here uncertain'. Mzee Abednego Achia - a respected elder in Karamoja, corroborated Hon. Achia's view. Abednego Achia was a member of the delegation of Councilors who went to meet President Obote over the border issue. Others on the team included; Bakari, Logwe Peter; Mudong Mathew; Napakori Peter and Naburi; - when the border conflict started. A group of MPs from Karamoja led by Hon. Lobunei went to see President Milton Obote in

1966 to explain to him the changes in the boundaries by Hon. Obwangor Cuthbert, then an MP from Teso. President Obote subsequently made a pronouncement to the effect that the new boundary was illegal and dismissed Obwangor from Parliament.

In 2004, the border issues resurfaced when the former LC V of Moroto District, Mr. Terence Achia and former LC V Chairman of Katakwi Ilemukorit went into confrontation over parts of Napak, Kodike and Alekilek which the latter claimed belonged to Katakwi. This recent claims and counter claims by politicians threatened to inflame the conflict and was about to result into generalized violence.

Administrative Policies

Administrative policies in Karamoja that pursued containment instead of development and empowerment alienated the Karimajong. People from Karamoja and Teso agree that there has been a deliberate policy by all successive governments in Uganda to maroon and contain the Karimojong in dry, marginal areas. This view is not without basis. Past research points out that authorities imposed a more apocalyptic ruling on the Karimojong when they started to define the boundaries of the districts and to frame legislation on the basis of "these new and ill-conceived delineations" (Randal, 1975). The authorities then proceeded to allocate dry-season grazing which had formerly been the domain of some of the Karimojong groups, but appeared 'unused', to other communities. On the west, Suk County was handed over to Kenya hence depriving the Bokora of their best hedge against drought. Much more seriously, on the eastern side between the Kanyangareng River and the Chemerongit hills, a tract of 3,700 Km2 was handed-over over to the Suk of Kenya. Initially, this was thought to be a temporary arrangement made during the drought conditions in Suk county in 1927. The giving away of Suk county deprived the Karimojong, particularly the Matheniko and the Pian of their dry season grazing land, leaving them with the option of either moving south wards where they threatened the cultivators of Sebei or to the west where they intensified the problems of the newly confined Bokora (Onyango, 2010).

Other analysts have observed that British imperialism pursued a land policy that deprived the Karimojong of their best land (Opuli-Watum,

1980). Colonialists turned a large part of fertile land into a game park for animals and another part was turned into game reserves and government (crown) land. Accordingly, the best land was given to animals and the people were crowded into semi-arid areas! This resulted into land exhaustion and its attendant consequences of social instability.

Lack of Participation in Decision-Making

Most interviewees, especially elders and opinion leaders in Karamoja link the land problem to lack of political and administrative participation by the affected people. Successive Governments that have ruled Uganda have not involved the Karimojong in decision-making matters that affect them. Consequently, most of the decisions are handed over 'from above'. The net effect of this is that most of the Karimojong leaders have not been socialised in matters of participatory leadership. The argument is that increased participation in public affairs and decision-making of communities would create civic awareness among people about their rights, duties and obligations. Low public participation of Karimojong in the affairs of Uganda, is evidenced in the low percentage of people participating in politics. For example, in 1961 elections, only 4% of the population of Karamoja participated in elections and this was replayed in the 1982 elections with 23.6% participating. In the same period, only one Minister from Karamoja was in cabinet. Analysts further note that peoples' participation increases channels of communication and reduces conflict. They conclude that unless the Karimojong participate vigorously in the political processes, their pastoral and other problems caused by semi-arid conditions will continue to be given scanty attention.

Politicization of the Border Conflict by Politicians

Politicians on both sides of the conflict are known to have found it politically expedient to politicize the border dispute to gain political capital in the electorate. Such conflicts always escalate during elections and de-escalate thereafter. Some politicians have personalized the border issue and the electorate as "my people" for the sake of votes which fragments communities. Leaders in Karamoja often point out that the problem is because of incitement by the leadership in Teso. It is alleged that leaders in Teso once remarked that the Karimojong should not be seen anywhere near Teso. As a result, the elected political leaders on both sides of the divide have not been able to provide the kind of leadership that would be useful and effective in managing and resolving the border conflict and insecurity in the region.

Political Instability

Political instability and civil wars including the Uganda People's Army (UPA) rebellion in Teso (1987-90) and the inconsistent implementation of the disarmament programme have been cited as responsible for the current land conflict in Katakwi and Moroto. Adduced data indicated that political instability creates insecurity which confines people to the unproductive dry lands, leading other tribes to take advantage of this situation and grab their land. According to opinion leaders in Karamoja, settlements in Karamoja were based on where the church establishments were located, notably; Kangole, Namalu, Amudat, Iriir - because of the need to be close to basic services like food, prayer, security and psychological support. This fed into the narrative for any claimant that land belonged to none.

Erosion of the Traditional Authority of Elders

The acquisition of sophisticated weapons especially, contemporary guns by the Karimojong dealt a blow to traditional authority of elders in society. Time came when guns defined Karamoja to the outside world. Not only did guns define the way the Karimojong relate with their neighbors, but has also the way the Karimojong lived amongst themselves. The gun redefined social and political relations within the community and is a major factor mediating the relations between the Karimojong and the government of Uganda. The gun dynamic shifted power to whoever had it in his/her possession. Unfortunately, the erosion of traditional authority of elders occurred in the absence of strong institutions of government. Consequently, issues such as the border disagreements that could easily be handled by elders basing on history have been inflamed by politicians and young people to a violent level. Modern institutions especially those meant to administer justice and enforce law and order have proved inadequate. This is recognized by government at the highest level. President Museveni when visiting Moroto on 5th December 1998 acknowledged that the modern judicial system centralized in Moroto was totally inadequate to the task of administering justice in the district. The President noted that there was need to increase government presence in the area to prevent communities from taking the law in their hands.

Absence of Effective Government Structures and Institutions

One of the reasons that explain the causes of the conflict is the absence of an effective government and the absence of a clear development policy on Karamoja. The isolation and hostility that marked the relations between the Karimojong and successive governments in Uganda left a legacy where Government presence is always ineffective which makes Karamoja look like it is not part of Uganda. Consequently, the Karimojong faced with insecurity decided to acquire guns to protect themselves against government and their neighbors out of fear and mistrust.

The absence of effective government at the local level in Karamoja has serious implications for the maintenance of law and order. For example, the whole of Moroto and Nakapiripirt districts, have one operational court which sits at Moroto district headquarters in the municipality. It simply cannot cope with the administration of justice in the vast districts. Similarly, there are few police outposts in the entire region to enforce law and order. Equally important, there is a problem of underdevelopment which is directly linked to security and how the Karimojong relate to their neighbors. In some parts of Karamoja, there are no social services to speak of. The few that exists are provided and maintained by the international NGOs. As such, the region is linked more to the international donor world than to the Government of Uganda which ultimately erodes Government legitimacy among the communities.

Conclusion

The escalation of natural resource-based conflicts especially revolving around the struggle for access and control of land, pasture and water resources is unnecessary and uncalled for. Unless quick and relevant conflict resolution and peace building measures are put in place, a conflict like the one between Itesot and Karimajong can escalate, breed more violence and destruction. Negative effects of the conflict are enormous, and therefore, peace-building interventions are needed. For too long, many pastoral communities in Uganda and elsewhere have been ignored and marginalized. The transition of pastoral societies from peasantry defense systems to militarization is not only a threat to their survival but a threat to peace elsewhere. Civic and national consciousness demands social justice and equity in the treatment of all citizens irrespective of race, tribe, sex , color and occupation and national leaderships needs to design and implement peaceful coexistence for attainment of the common good.

The conflict between Karimojong and Itesots negatively impact on both parties. It is vital to resolve such a conflict and ease the suffering of the people. Attempts at resolution through peace-building should address the root cause and strengthen capacity to manage future conflicts. It is necessary to pursue confidence building by carrying out genuine and sustained development. It is important to avoid top-down approach interventions because all people have a contribution to make. There is need to transparently revisit colonial boundary mark-stones to the comfort of all stakeholders.

Affirmative action like in the case of having a Ministry for Karamoja Affairs is positive development but it should be capacitated to cause impact in society. Efforts like creation of Anti-Stock Theft Unit and the Arrow Group could be helpful in managing cattle rustling. However, care must be taken not to significantly militarize the region. The presence of many guns in the hands of civilian people is known to be taken advantage of by criminal elements to rob and settle personal disputes. As part of the interventions to resolve the border conflict, there is a need to increase Government presence by deploying trained police and army officers to maintain security.

Civil society and other stakeholders in peacemaking could do better if they supported initiatives that enable conflicting leaders and people to re-establish contact, trust, confidence and engage in face to face dialogue. There is a need for undertaking peace-building initiatives like reconciliation, peace education and development activities in the region. Leaders should champion social-economic development and mobilize the population accordingly. Government should be at hand to provide adequate judicial services for maintaining law and order.

It is impotent to facilitate exchange visits by the leadership to learn from one another and demystify biases and misperceptions. Peer-to-peer visits provide opportunities for learning lessons essential for building a culture of tolerance and co-existence. Such conflicting communities need to be opened up to the outside world to enable interaction, appreciate strangers, and create jobs to improve their livelihoods.

References

Amodoi-Okoboi, J. (2016) *The genesis, development and impact of cattle rustling in Teso sub-region, 1600-2001: A case of Katakwi district, Uganda.* Available at: http://ir-library.ku.ac.ke/bitstream/handle/2006 (Accessed: 19 October 2014).

Bamuturaki, M. (2011) 'How Do We End Conflict over E. Africa's Natural Resources', *Daily Monitor*, 25 December.

Bardal, M. and David, M. M. (2000) *Greed and Grievance. Economic Agendas n Civil Wars.* London: Lynne Rienner Publishers, Inc.

Becker, L. C. (1977) *Property Rights: Philosophic Foundations.* London: Routledge and Kegan Paul.

Cisternino, M. and Karamoja (1979) 'The Human Zoo (The history of the Planning for Karamoja with Some Tentative Counter-planning)', *Dissertation, Center for Development Studies.* Swansea: University of Wales.

Department for International Development (DFID) (2001) 'The Causes of Conflict in Africa: Consultation Document'. DFID. Available at: http://webarchive.nationalarchives.gov.uk/+/http:/www.dfid.gov.u k/pubs/files/conflict-africa.pdf (Accessed: 14 September 2017).

Gray, S., Sundal, M., Wiebusch, B., A.Little, M., Leslie, P. W. and Pike, I. L. (2003) 'Cattle Raiding Cultural Survival, and Adaptability of East African Pastoralists', *Current Anthropology*, 44(5), pp. 3–30.

Huggins, C. and Clover, J. (eds) (2005) *From the Ground UP: Land Rights, Conflict and Peace in sub-Saharan Africa*. Pretoria: Institute for Security Studies.

Novelli, B. (1988) *Aspects of Karimojong Ethnosociology*. Verona: Museum Combonianum.

Odong, J. (2016) *Cattle rustling once a valued cultural practice now a trigger of conflicts in Uganda's northern east*. Teso-Karamoja Journalists Association (TEKAJA).

Onyango, E. O. (2010) *Pastoralists in violent defiance of the state: The case of the Karamajong in north eastern Uganda*. University of Bergern.

Opuli-Watum, D. R. (1980) *The Karamoja Problem is a land question*. Kampala: FORWARD.

Quam, M. D. (1996) 'Creating Peace in an Armed Society: Karamoja', *The Online Journal for African Studies*. Uganda. Available at: http://web.africa.ufl.edu/.

Randal, B. (1975) 'Development and the Pastoral People of Karamoja, North Eastern Uganda. An example of the treatment of symptoms', in Monod, T. (ed.) *Pastoralism in Tropical Africa*. Oxford: Oxford U.P.

Randal, B. (1977) 'Polarization', in Philip, O. and Ben, W. (eds) *Land Use and Development*. London: International African Institute.

Teso Initiative for Peace (2010) *Building Peace between and within Teso and Karamoja*. Available at: https://tipsoroti.wordpress.com/.

CHAPTER EIGHT

The Legislature and Politics of Budget Oversight: A Comparative Study of Selected Countries in the East African Community

Elijah Dickens Mushemeza

Introduction

This chapter takes a comparative perspective in which it unravels the legislative arms of government and their oversight role on the budget process in selected countries forming the East African Community. The budget is a political process in which scarce resources are allocated to various sectors of the economy for production and service delivery. It was conceived that the budgetary oversight function is part of a checks-and-balances system that ensures presence of accountability in the utilisation of scarce resources. When such process has been properly managed, the citizens would be in a position to appreciate democratic governance. The analysis in this chapter brings out lessons for good governance and particularly a more effective legislature in terms of budget oversight, equitable distribution of resources, and ultimately peace and stability of the country.

The central thesis of this chapter is that the legislature and its budget oversight function are critical for democratic governance in East Africa. This central preposition is supplemented by three subsidiary prepositions: (i) that government accountability becomes successful when public officials are answerable for their actions and their unbecoming behavior is corrected well in advance and (ii) for the government to manage public resources efficiently and effectively, parliamentary oversight committees as well as the national audit institution, both entrusted by the people should work independently but complementary to ensure value for money. (iii) equitable distribution of scarce resources at national level facilitates peace and stability of society. It is argued therefore that positive outcomes on democratic governance are achievable if the administration of the legislature focuses on continuous training and other capacity- building activities for the MPs and Parliamentary technical staff on how to analyse budget documents and audit reports; provides the necessary Information Technology (IT) infrastructure for quick access to information; fights corruption; and timely checks the executive from crossing its boundaries. The chapter also argues that such above actions would positively affect utilisation of scarce financial resources and service delivery; and provide the overall socio-economic transformation that is urgently needed in East Africa for peace and stability.

The comparative analysis perspective in this chapter follows these themes: (i) parliamentary strengthening as a pre-requisite to effective oversight; (ii) the budget process (legal and institutional framework, role of oversight committees e.g. Public Accounts Committee before (PAC) PAC) and the budget cycle; and effectiveness of East Africa Parliament in budget oversight; (iii) challenges that legislatures face in East Africa.

On the whole, the analysis brings out facts that attempts have been made by the legislatures to carry out their budget oversight function amidst numerous challenges and shortcomings. These were found to range from; capacity and competence limitations; interference by other branches of government to limited financial resources for operations purposes. In particular, PAC one of the leading budget oversight committee in the three parliaments of selected East African countries was widely perceived by the citizens as an institutional organ that 'barks more and bites less'. This is in spite of the fact that in order for PAC and other oversight committees to effectively deliver on their responsibility, the other organs of the state – the Controller and Auditor General, Police, Inspectorate of Government, Courts of Judicature - must do their part to ensure value for money and where appropriate enable the tax payers to recover the resources wasted by corrupt officials.

Parliamentary Strengthening: a prerequisite for Legislative Oversight

It is a widely known that responsive and effective elected bodies are the foundation of good governance (Inter-Parliamentary Union, 2004; Bainomugisha and Mushemeza, 2006). However, these bodies need to be buttressed in order for them to carry out their roles as effectively as possible. The world over, parliaments need support in order to carry out their work. The principle behind legislative oversight is to ensure that public policy is administered in accordance with the legislative intent, and by inference, the citizens' aspirations. In this context, the legislative function does not cease with the passage of a Bill. It is, therefore, only by monitoring the implementation process that Parliamentarians uncover any defects and act to correct misinterpretation or maladministration. In this sense, the concept of oversight exists as an essential corollary to the law making process (Institute of Economic Affairs, 2009).

Tsekpo and Hudson (2009) observe that traditionally, parliaments have three primary roles; legislation, representation and oversight. Legislation deals with passing laws which make up a country's legal framework. Representation is about collecting, aggregating and expressing the concerns, opinions and preferences of the country's citizens. Oversight is about keeping an eye on the activities of the executive and holding the executive to account on behalf of the country's citizens. Oversight may take different forms; including summons and hearings in established Committees. Parliament's oversight of the budget process involves monitoring and review of the entire budget process including the broad fiscal challenges facing government, expenditure controls and budgetary tradeoffs that affect present and future spending. Overall, the budgetary oversight function is part of a checks-and-balances system that ensures that there is accountability in the utilisation of financial resources (Madhidha, 2011), thus enhancing good governance and stability of the state. Globally, an accountable state is one that responds to its citizens, particularly in situations where they demand appropriate action to promises previously made. In the budget process, the Executive has the responsibility of drafting and implementing the budget but the role of checking whether this responsibility is successfully fulfilled rests with parliament. Parliament has potential to assist

Government departments to plan and implement budgets more effectively and efficiently through provision of the checks and balances. It has potential to help in curbing corruption, reducing gaps between planned and actual budgets, and even leading to greater efficiency in Ministries/Departments' delivery of services within the shortest time possible (Institute of Economic Affairs, 2009). Ideally, parliaments (a concept used interchangeably with the legislatures) are key institutions of the state that promote democratic governance which is achieved through legislation, oversight and representation. In practice, however, parliaments in many developing countries are always seen as being weak, ineffective and contributing little to good governance .

Parliamentary strengthening therefore enhances the effectiveness of parliaments through institutional development, builds the capacity of parliamentary staff, Members of Parliament and committees, and puts in place the nuts and bolts of infrastructure and equipment. It also involves improving staffing needs to be rigorously linked to size, typologies, membership, composition, mandate and investigatory requirements of specific committees. In addition, changes in the reporting mechanisms, the drafting of quality reports and implementation of parliamentary resolutions are necessary (AFRICOG, 2012). An effective parliamentary committee system also ensures that different parliamentary interests and points of view are taken into account when the House makes its decisions. They provide avenues for meaningful probe and debates; management of complex parliamentary business, and above all, mechanisms for parliamentary accountability (Institute of Economic Affairs, 2009).

Parliamentary Strengthening in East Africa

A number of international agencies have shown great interest in parliamentary strengthening in East Africa. These include development partners such as the United States, United Kingdom, Canada, Sweden, Austria, Belgium, Denmark and Germany, inter alia. This is alongside multilateral organizations such as the World Bank, the United Nations (UN) and European Union. In addition, there are a number of national and international parliamentary organizations and networks including the Parliamentary Centre, the Inter-Parliamentary Union, Commonwealth

Chapter Eight | Elijah Dickens Mushemeza

Parliamentary Association, and European Parliamentarians for Africa (AWEPA), the Parliamentary Network on the World Bank (PNoWB) and the Global Organization of Parliamentarians against Corruption (GOPAC). All these have contributed to parliamentary strengthening and providing support to the Parliaments in the three East African countries in order to enhance their oversight roles over budgets, along with the Constitutions of the respective countries (Tanzania Constitution, 1977; 'Uganda constitution', 1995; Kenya Constitution, 2010; Tsekpo and Hudson, 2009).

In Uganda, a number of development partners have engaged in parliamentary strengthening since 1996, with international organizations such as United Nations Development Programme (UNDP) and United States Agency for International Development (USAID) playing particularly important roles. From 1996, the focus was on the provision of equipment and training for MPs and parliamentary staff while from around 1998, considerable efforts were made to put in place some key parliamentary institutions including the Parliamentary Commission, the Parliamentary Service and the Parliamentary Budget Office.(SUNY/CID, 2003; Tsekpo and Hudson, 2009).

In Kenya, USAID is one of the very active international agencies that are promoting parliamentary strengthening in the country. For instance, the agency, together with the Department for International Development have funded a Parliamentary Strengthening Programme to further enhance the Kenya National Assembly's (KNA's) key legislative, budget oversight and representation functions and to consolidate the body's growing links to academic and civil society expertise and resources. Implemented by the State University of New York and the Centre for International Development (SUNY/CID), the project has registered some achievements:

In Tanzania, The Africa Parliamentary Strengthening Programme (APSP) was one of the many initiatives started in order to boost parliamentary strengthening in the country. The APSP is a five-year (2011 – 2015) capacity strengthening programme for seven partner parliaments including Benin, Ghana, Kenya, Senegal, Tanzania, Uganda and Zambia. The programme supported partner parliaments to develop and implement strategies to strengthen their overall role and engagement in the national budget process (Parliamentary Centre, 2014).

It is evident therefore, that efforts have been made in Kenya, Tanzania and Uganda to strengthen parliament visa-a-viz institutional developm-ent, capacity building of MPs and staff; and infrastructure. These developments have enabled visible outputs, which are pre-requisites to legislative oversight.

Data for the analysis of this chapter was primarily generated through documentary analysis. However, limited interviews were conducted with key senior staff of parliament and other government departments in the study area. The research therefore relied on data from interviews, written and printed sources. Documents were obtained from libraries in Kenya, Tanzania, and Uganda and from the Parliaments of East African websites. Data analysis was done thematically. Themes were developed at the beginning of the study while considering the need to strengthen parliament as a prerequisite for oversight, the budget process and the challenges the legislatures face as basis of assessment. The integration of the information generated took the form of arguments, deductions and conclusions in relation to the research issues under study. The comparative analysis clearly delineates the key factors that explain why there is much more to be done in budget oversight in EA to enhance democratic governance, peace and stability.

The Budget Process

This section analyses the significance of parliament's role in a budget process. World over, it is believed that the State budget is in fact a tool to implement the State's duty to promote and protect human rights of the people living within its territory. It does so by setting public spending priorities, including to those who are most in need of protection. The importance of ensuring due scrutiny so that people's needs are met to the best of the state's ability is paramount. With rapidly growing state budgets, growing public debt, the National Assembly is facing tremendous capacity challenges in budget scrutiny, decision-making and oversight. This challenge requires the National Assembly to assert its budget oversight function more strongly by being involved from the early stages in budget estimates planning, assessing priorities for resource allocation and systematically analysing the impact of budget decisions on people's lives. It is through such effectiveness that the citizens will gain confidence in the governance of their institutions to guarantee equitable distribution of resources, peace and stability

Stages of the process

The Inter-Parliamentary Union (2004) identifies four stages through which the budget passes that can be conventionally discerned in more or less all public budgeting systems in the world. First, is the drafting stage that is mostly done by the executive and second is the legislative stage where parliament comes in for the first time – i.e. when the budget has been drafted and tabled in parliament by the Minister of Finance. Experiences in East Africa however, show how other stakeholders outside the executive (e.g. the Budget committee, Parliamentary Budget Office officials) are involved at the stage of formulation to generate consensus on key policy issues and vote ceilings. Parliament can review, perhaps amend or even reject the budget. Third is the implementation stage after parliament has approved the budget. The fourth stage is the evaluation and audit stage where a supreme audit institution assesses whether the budget as approved was actually implemented and whether it was done efficiently and effectively. How have the East African countries under study fulfilled the above conditions? I now turn to the existing legal and institutional framework, the budget cycle and how the actors have executed their roles particularly the Public Accounts Committees and other accountability committees of parliament.

The Legal and Institutional Framework in Uganda

The Parliament of Uganda derives its mandate and functions from the 1995 Constitution, the Laws of Uganda (such as the Local Government Act CAP 243, the Budget Act 2001 and the Public Finance and Accountability Act 2003) and its own Rules of Procedure. Chapter Six of the Constitution Article 77 establishes Parliament, Article 78 details its composition while Article 79 spells out its functions (Uganda constitution, 1995). The Local Government Act, Cap 243 provides the legal basis for local government budget process. This is supported by the Local Government Financial and Accounting Regulations 2007. The Public Finance and Accountability Act 2003 provides for the development of fiscal policy framework, regulation of public financial management, prescribes the responsibilities of persons entrusted with financial management and provides for public borrowing, audit of Government accounts, state enterprises and other authorities of state.

Furthermore, the Budget Act was put in place to provide for and regulate the budgetary procedure for a systematic and efficient budgetary process (Republic of Uganda, 2001). The Act in Section 19 (1) establishes a Parliamentary Budget Committee. And Section 20 further establishes a Parliamentary Budget Office (PBO) The Parliamentary Budget Office therefore plays an important role in supporting parliamentarians to scrutinize the national budget and provides technical support to Parliament in its legislative and oversight functions.

The Legal and Institutional Framework in Kenya

Chapter Eight of the Constitution of Kenya establishes the Legislature. Article 93 of the Constitution states that: 'there is established a Parliament of Kenya,' 'which shall consist of the National Assembly and the Senate.' The two Houses of Parliament shall perform their respective functions in accordance with the Constitution as stated in Article 93 (2) of the Constitution.

The Kenyan Constitution mandates openness, transparency and public involvement in the budget process. However, the achievement of this depends on effective implementing legislation; proper administrative structures; nature, number, powers and capacities of committees, and leadership and technical capabilities of parliamentary committees (AFRICOG, 2012).

Furthermore, there are other mechanisms that facilitate the budgeting process. In particular, the Parliamentary Budget Office (PBO) is created by an Act of Parliament; while the Fiscal Management Act, 2009 comes in to regulate the process. Established in May 2007 as a result of the need to enhance the oversight role of parliament by creating the necessary capacity for scrutiny of the national budget and the economy, its primary function is to provide timely and objective information and analysis concerning the national budget and economy. The Office therefore provides technical support on matters relating to Public Financial Management and financial oversight to all Members of Parliament,

Departmental Committees and Select Committees in addition to being a secretariat to the Budget Committee of Parliament.

In February 2014, the PBO published a report entitled: Keeping the Promise: Budget Options for 2014/2015 and the Medium Term. The key themes in the report namely; An Economy in Transition: Outlooks, Prospects and Opportunities; Fiscal Performance and Outlook; Strategic Interventions for long term, pro-poor growth; Devolution and Economy; provide the legislators an opportunity to debate the budget from an informed position. Kenya therefore enjoys a rich legal and institutional framework concerning legislative oversight of the budget.

The Legal and Institutional Framework in Tanzania

The Tanzania Parliament derives its mandate and functions from the Constitution of the United Republic of Tanzania of 1977, the laws of Tanzania and its own rules of procedure. Chapter 3 of the Constitution contains Articles that provide for the establishment, composition and functions of Parliament. Article 62 (1) states that 'there shall be a Parliament of the Untied Republic which shall consist of two parts, that is to say, the President and the National Assembly' while 62 (2) states that 'the National Assembly shall consist of all categories of members specified in Article 66 of this Constitution, who shall all be designated as Members of Parliament.' Parliament is also accorded legislative powers in Article 64 (1): 'Legislative power in relation to all Union Matters and also in relation to all other matters concerning Mainland Tanzania is hereby vested in Parliament.'

Tanzania's Parliament, known as the Bunge, is unicameral i.e. it has only one legislative or parliamentary chamber. Of its 357 members, 239 are elected by direct popular vote from single-member constituencies, 102 are reserved for women representing their political parties on the basis of proportional representation, five are elected by the Zanzibar House of Representatives, and up to 10 members may be appointed by the President. One seat is reserved for the Attorney General. Members serve for five-year terms. However, Zanzibar has its own House of Representatives, composed of 50 members elected by universal suffrage for five-year terms Tanganyika and Zanzibar merged on 26 April 1964 to form the United Republic Tanzania. However, Zanzibar enjoys semi-autonomous status, with its own government made up of the Revolutionary Council and House of Representatives.

The budget process is backed by a strong legal framework, including the Public Finance Act 2001, the Appropriation Act, the Annual Finance Act, Planning Commission Act 1989 and the Presidential Instrument 2000. Together the above acts outline the roles and responsibilities of the various actors involved at the different stages of the budget cycle. As is general practice, responsibility for the planning, formulation and implementation stages lies largely within the Executive. Parliament's role comes in with the approval of the budget and oversight of budgetary processes.

It must however be noted that unlike Uganda and Kenya, Tanzania does not yet have in place a Parliamentary Budget Office. The debate for the establishment of a PBO has been going on in Tanzania. One member of parliament is quoted to have observed that 'the proposed independent Parliamentary Budget Office would have technical capacity to analyse the budget and to help parliamentarians and other stakeholders to better understand what are otherwise complex technical documents, once established. This would help increase credibility, promote transparent, provide elaborate options for spending cuts and promote accountability' (Luhaga Joelson Mpina 2013, pers. Comm., July, Dar es salaam).

The Budget cycle in the three East African countries combined

In the three East African countries, the budget cycle is a very participatory process and runs through the entire financial year. It begins with the public expenditure review (PER), consultations on the macroeconomic framework and a review and update of the Medium Term Expenditure Framework (MTEF). Theoretically this review forms the basis of the budge guidelines.

The budget cycle also involves other major activities namely; budget formulation, adoption, execution, oversight and control. Apart from the policy makers (parliamentarians), policy implementers in government ministries and departments also play key roles. In particular is the centrality of the ministries of finance, office of the Controller and Auditor General and the accountability committees. Table 1 high lights the sequence of activities in the three countries of East Africa and brings out similarities and harmonization that have been made in the spirit of East African integration.

Table 7.3: The Budget Cycle: Major activities involved in Selected East African Countries

STAGE	KENYA	UGANDA	TANZANIA
Budget formulation	Nov-May: Public expenditure review, consultations on the macroeconomic framework. Review and update of the MTEF. Issue of Budget guidelines (budget strategy, key spending priorities and programmes, proposed allocation of resources – ceilings etc.)	Nov-May: Public expenditure review, consultations on the macroeconomic framework. Review and update of the MTEF. Issue of Budget guidelines (budget strategy, key spending priorities and programmes, proposed allocation of resources – ceilings etc.)	Nov-May: Formulation of Budget policy and resource projections. Issuance of planning and Budget guidelines. Estimating revenues and expenditure. Scrutiny of estimates by Parliamentary sub-committee &inter-Ministerial Technical committee. Cabinet approval of Budget estimates.
Adoption of the budget	JUNE- AUGUST: Tabling in Legislature. Budget speeches presented (Budget day). National Assembly Committees review budgets and budget performance of Ministries under their jurisdiction. Review of Bills and Budget voted into law	JUNE- AUGUST: Tabling in Legislature. Budget speeches presented (Budget day). Sector Committees review budgets and budget performance of Ministries under their jurisdiction. Review of Bills and Budget voted into law	JUNE-AUGUST: Tabling in Legislature. Budget speeches presented (Budget day). Budget voted into law
Budget Execution	JULY-JUNE: Funds allocated to accounting officers of various spending agencies by MoF. The Executive through the National Audit Office audits public expenditures. The office monitors the budget by ensuring that	JULY-JUNE: Ministry of Finance allocates money consistent with approved budget. Monitoring expenditures through IFMS mechanism by the Accountant General.	JULY-JUNE: Ministries, Departments, Agencies (MDAs) prepare action plans (Work plans). Budget executed by cash budget system. Central Government

	all withdrawals from the consolidated Fund are within the Appropriation Act. Spending agencies are expected to periodically submit their vote book balance to MoF which publishes the quarterly monitoring reports.	Public sector performance management systems track the implementation of Departmental strategic plans. MoF publish Execution Reports to maintain transparency on actual use of public funds.	releases money to Districts. Services delivered.
Oversight and Control	Within – year monitoring State Departments put their Books in order, share with the Controller and General (CAG). CAG compile reports and forward to Parliament. PAC, Public Investments Committee analyses reports, make summons, conduct hearings and make recommendations for action including censure for Government Departments that fail to account for money or found to have misused the money. National Assembly has three months (Jan-March) to debate and dispose-off reports. Follow –up on action expected to be taken.	Within –year monitoring. External Audit conducted by the Auditor General. Audit reports tabled in parliament PAC, analyses them, summons accounting officers, conduct public hearings and make recommendations for action. Parliament (plenary) debates and disposes-off reports. Follow-up on action expected to be taken	Within – year monitoring. External Audit conducted by Controller and Auditor General. Audit reports tabled in Parliament PAC, Local Authorities Accounts Committee, and the Parastatal Organisation Committee analyses the reports, make summons, conduct hearings and makes recommendations Follow-up on action expected to be taken.

Source: Compiled by the Author from various parliamentary Reports and fieldwork interviews with officials from the Offices of the Clerk of the three Parliaments.

Public Accounts Committees (PAC) and parliamentary budget oversight in East Africa

This section examines the role of PAC in three East African countries in comparative terms and responds to the proposition made earlier that government accountability becomes successful when public officials are answerable for their actions and their unbecoming behavior is corrected well in advance. The committee examines the government's use of resources and the financial operations of state agencies. The committee also looks at both financial probity and regularity and focuses on whether agency programmes are achieving their objectives. Similarly, the committee looks at reports from Auditor General (AG) to ensure that agencies respond appropriately to the AG's recommendations.

Uganda: The Parliament of Uganda's Rules of Procedure provide for The Public Accounts Committee (PAC). Under Rule No.148 of the Rules, PAC is mandated to examine the audited accounts showing the appropriation of the sums granted by Parliament to meet the public expenditure of government. The law also provides that the Committee be chaired and deputized by members designated by the Official Opposition Party in parliament. PAC comprises of 20 members designated by Party Whips on basis of proportional Party Membership in the House taking into consideration the interests of Independent Members.

   In its line of work, PAC scrutinizes the accounts of different government departments, and if any inconsistencies are found, they summon the accounting officers of these departments to provide an explanation. Accounting officers are required to present valid documents like statutory instruments that authorize transactions, receipts, and account books, among others. The committee also relies on information it gets from public complaints sent through a subcommittee instituted by it. It specifically deals directly with the public through scrutinizing their complaints and investigating them (Yemima, 2008). PAC then exposes those government officials who have been implicated in abuse of office by making recommendations in a report, which is then forwarded to Parliament for debate. By doing this, the committee in effect ensures that public officials are identified, cautioned and where appropriate exposed for other relevant state organs to take action – particularly those responsible for prosecution. To most Ugandans, PAC is one of the most outstanding committees (Yemima, 2008). This is because the committee is well known for grilling public officials to account for funds. Whether PAC has succeeded in effectively executing this oversight role remains a matter of debate. While sections of Ugandans believe that PAC has done its best in ensuring proper accountability in government, others are concerned that the committee's work has not been fully appreciated since not much has been returned from allegedly corrupt officials to the public purse. The Chairperson of PAC (2014 -2016) has been quoted in the media for lamenting on little output from this committee in terms of producing reports by her predecessors. 'The previous leadership held public hearings but with no recommendations. In 2009-10, they listened to everybody and wrote no report. In 2011 to 2012, they listened to everybody and made no report…'. One other commentator observed that 'PAC is a merely barking but toothless dog'. In addition to PAC, the Uganda parliament has another Standing committee that has been instrumental in the budget oversight function. The Government Assurances Committee tracks the promises of government and alerts the House to bring the executive to explain the delays or inconsistencies in implementation. This process enables government officials to correct their shortcomings in order to improve service delivery.

Kenya: The Kenyan Parliament's Public Accounts Committee (PAC) is established pursuant to the provisions of Standing Order No. 205. The committee is mandated to examine accounts showing the appropriations of the sum voted by the House to meet the public expenditure and of such other accounts. It consists of 27 members, including the chairperson.

Since independence, the Public Accounts Committee (PAC), traditionally chaired by the leader of the official opposition in the House, has been the key watchdog tool of budgetary oversight of Government ministries and departments. However, the Committee has had its share of challenges in terms of its effectiveness. For example, over these years the accounting officers in government delay to submit their papers to the Controller and Auditor General and this delay the subsequent submissions to PAC. Public Accounts Committee Chairperson Ababu

Namwamba in, October, 2014, expressed disappointment over this in the media."Many officials often rush to provide critical documents only after they have been adversely mentioned in reports by the Auditor-General...We wonder why people don't provide the required documents in good time to the auditing officials. From now on, we will be very strict on such individuals and will take them to have misused public money... "We need to see government officials demonstrate enthusiasm for accountability just as they often display enthusiasm when they appeal for more funds from Parliament.. But how can the PAC effectively follow-up on the implementation of recommendations? Makumure John a Kenyan scholar observes and proposes constructively on this matter and I quote him extensively:

> First and foremost, the PAC reports should be prepared as soon as possible after the committee concludes an inquiry, while the proceedings are still fresh in everyone's mind. Reporting on completion of each inquiry has the advantage of getting implementation started sooner and facilitates easier monitoring by the committee. The same applies to the Auditor-General reports themselves that must be produced on time. Implementation of recommendations becomes challenging if audit reports are produced several years later when the culprits might have left government. He further suggests that: 'Enforcing Section 11 of the Audit Office Act can assist in the implementation of recommendations. This provision says if at any time it appears desirable to the PAC that any matter relating to public monies or State property should be reported upon by the Comptroller and Auditor-General, the committee shall direct the Comptroller and Auditor-General to prepare a special report thereon for transmission to the committee and to the Minister of Finance and to an appropriate minister if it relates to a public entity, designated corporate body or statutory fund.

On legislative reform Makumure submits that:

> Parliament should review the Audit Office Act and Public Finance Management Act to determine if the provisions are adequate to ensure implementation of PAC recommendations and corrective action for Auditor-General findings. These statutes must be aligned to reflect the letter and spirit of the constitutional provisions on principles of sound

public finance management. There must be penalties for non-compliance with financial reporting requirements. The PAC should establish a follow-up schedule, for example three or six months after the report is tabled. If the committee is unable to hold hearings on all the reports of the Auditor-General, it may send a follow-up letter to the rest of the departments and entities audited asking for a progress report on the reports and recommendations the committee has not reviewed. The PAC should insist on the preparation of action plans by ministries and departments to be used to monitor and report on implementation. The action plans must include targeted dates for implementing the actions

The other committees that deal with oversight functions in Kenya are the Public Investments Committee and the Budget and Appropriations Committee. The Public Investments Committee examines the reports and accounts of the public investments. Similarly, the Budget and Appropriations Committee investigates, inquire into and report on all matters related to coordination, control and Monitoring of the national budget.

Tanzania: The Parliament of Tanzania has three Parliamentary oversight committees each specialized in the oversight of a particular section of the public sector. These include The Public Accounts Committee, The Local Government Accounts Committee and The Parastatal Organization Accounts. The Public Accounts Committee consists of not less than eight and not more than twelve Members appointed by the Speaker.

In addition of the overall general responsibilities of the Parliamentary Oversight Committees, the Public Accounts Committee has two unique responsibilities in accordance with Sections 44 and 46 of the Public Audit Act (2008). Section 44 charges the Public Accounts Committee with the responsibility of discussing the Office budget and recommend such budget for the appropriation of Parliament, while Sect 46 on the other hand gives the Committee the mandate to appoint an external auditor to audit the accounts of the office whose report ultimately finds its way to the National Assembly.

For this paper the question that arises is in relation to the effectiveness of PAC. Does PAC in the Bunge execute its role effectively? With regard to accounts and operations, commentators indicate that the Tanzanian PAC has a fairly wide range of powers. It has the power to examine accounts and financial affairs, the efficiency, economy and effectiveness of government policy, the efficiency and economy of policy implementation (value for money), and the effectiveness of policy implementation (delivery of outcomes). PAC also enjoys on a conditional basis the power to undertake self-initiated inquiries and to consider the budget estimates. In addition, with regard to the relationship with the Audit office, its budget is discussed in a consultative meeting between the PAC members, the Minister of Finance and the Controller and Auditor General (CAG) under the leadership of the Chairperson of PAC. Once the budget had been discussed and agreed by the consultative meeting, it is tabled before the National Assembly for approval. The National Audit Office of Tanzania (NAOT) is audited by an auditor appointed by PAC through a competitive process under the office of parliament. Although the two organs operate independently, they complement each other. It was established that the NAOT carries out studies and subjects the reports to the critical reviews of experts in the relevant fields.

In regard to its effectiveness in the execution of its budgetary oversight role, Pelizzo and Kinyondo (2014) observe that the Bunge's PAC is above regional averages with respect to several organizational features and is the most active in the number of hearings held. In 2012, the 'Tanzania PAC began championing a change of the Budget year so that they could receive the budget in April and complete its review by the end of June. The PAC proposal was accepted and since 2013 the budget year has been amended...In May the same year, the President dismissed the ministers of finance, energy, tourism, trade, transport and health amid allegations of government corruption under pressure following reports tabled in the National Assembly by the PAC, Parastatal Organisations Accounts and Local Authorities Accounts Committees. Actions taken by PAC members based on the Controller and Auditor General's annual report tackled big corruption that is believed to hamper economic growth' (World Bank, 2013) and undermine peace and stability of the state.

However, like most other PACs in Sub-Saharan Africa, the committee faces undue influence from the executive in the execution of its duties. The committee also faces among other challenges inadequate finances for its operations. In the end, some sections of the population believe that 'the committee barks more and bites less'.

In comparative terms, PAC and other accountability committees play key roles in the budget oversight. The above analysis shows that there have been positive attempts in examining the governments' use of resources, financial operations of the state agencies and scrutinizing the AG's reports. Although there are cases where political leaders and public officers have been fired, there is no evidence that the implicated individuals have returned the misappropriated funds to the public purse after dismissal or convictions in courts of law. The general perception of the people is that PAC as a central committee of accountability in the legislature and promotion of democratic governance is negative; and that it barks more and bites less.

The Challenges Legislatures face in East Africa

This section focuses on major challenges facing the legislature in Uganda, Kenya and Tanzania during the execution of their budget oversight role: namely the interference by other arms of government and corruption; Capacity building of human resource; and inadequate time and information.

Uganda: Interference by other Branches of Government and Corruption.

Parliaments do not operate in a vacuum; their functioning and effectiveness are shaped very much by the context – and particularly the political context – of which they are part (Tsekpo and Hudson, 2009). While Uganda opted for multi-party democracy in 2005 and held elections under the new multi-party system in 2006, 2011 and 2016, some commentators have argued that 'Parliament remains overwhelmingly influenced by the legacy of the Movement system and the continued dominance of President Museveni, and is taken as incapable of being no more than provide "a mere rubber stamp" to the budget' (Kiraso, 2008).

Although the quality and effectiveness of parliamentary oversight depends very much on the ability of Parliament to engage in the budget making process, the Executive sometimes tends to regard Parliament as a merely advisory body whose recommendations can be brushed aside.

Quite often the ruling party's parliamentary caucus takes decisions which are endorsed by Parliament since the ruling party commands more than two thirds of the composition of Parliament. In terms of corruption, Uganda is a country that is fairly riddled with the vice which also comes in at a high cost for service delivery. This is despite the fact that even President Museveni has time and again advocated for zero-tolerance to corruption (NRM Manifestos, 2011-2016; 2016-2021). This is also despite the fact that Uganda has a variety of legislations and government bodies focused on eradicating corruption, which in some limited instances have ably prosecuted implicated individuals. However, these bodies have been largely slow in curbing grand-scale corruption.

Parliament has nevertheless tried to play its role in various scandals exposed. In 1998, Parliament impeached ministers for abuse of office, although the president reappointed them later. In the Common Wealth Heads of Government Meeting (CHOGM) scandal, accused former Vice President was briefly incarcerated in Luzira Prison, although the case was later dropped. These and many more examples show that parliament has fairly played its part in exposing corrupt leaders. What remains to be done is to have more public officers prosecuted and their loot returned to the public purse.

Kenya: Interference by other Branches of Government and corruption.
The true test of a democracy is the extent to which Parliament can exercise oversight of the Government by holding it answerable to the people for its policies and actions (Kerrow, 2014). Indeed, as one of the three core democratic roles of Parliament, oversight requires parliamentarians in performance of this function to summon anyone before its committees to provide information or documents. However, in Kenya, there have been instances in which other arms of government have interfered with this role. For instance, in November 2008, a Justice of the High Court issued orders to restrain Parliament from passing a bill to disband the defunct Electoral Commission of Kenya. Although this was rendered inconsequential by the House Speaker, who ruled it as unconstitutional, this was being seen as an attempt by another arm of government to interfere in parliament's work.

Similarly, in another case where MPs wanted to impeach the Embu Governor over allegations of corruption and abuse of office, court stopped the process. Equally, court also stopped parliament from summoning Governors to answer queries in the reports that were submitted to the Senate by the Controller of Budget. These actions have been interpreted by some commentators to be a growing trend in judicial activism and interference, arguing that courts can only determine the constitutionality of a piece of legislation by Parliament after it is assented to, or determine whether the Constitution was followed in the process of its deliberation (Kerrow, 2014).

It is also suggested by some commentators that the review of the constitution after the 2007 post-election unrest and various other pieces of legislation have continued to strengthen the Executive at the expense of Parliament and this has weakened over the years the role of parliament in the scrutiny of the budget, being constrained on one side by the lack of resources and on the other by the erecting of powers by the Executive through the presidency (Institute of Economic Affairs, 2009). Developments after the new constitution have however increased trust in Parliament since the separation of powers are well spelt; only requiring strict observance and practice.

Tanzania: In Tanzania, like many developing countries, the parliament's budgetary oversight function is seen as almost ineffective and a rubber stamping occasion (Inter-Parliamentary Union, 2003). It has been observed that government ranking in respect of its performance in budget transparency and parliamentary oversight is low. Parliament is therefore not seen as playing the important role that it should play in the budget cycle. It does not provide input into the planning phase of the budget as much as it should, it does not demand regular financial reporting from government, and all too often independent audits are late and parliamentary oversight committees do not have adequate resources to scrutinize public accounts (Inter-Parliamentary Union, 2009). But what has transpired since 2009? Is it still 'businesses as usual?

On interference by other branches of Government and on corruption in Tanzania; some commentators observe that the Executive, operating through the President and a small group of Ministers, was highly dominant in the national policy-making process (Lawson and Rakner, 2005). Although it is agreed that Parliament has clearly defined powers of scrutiny, practice shows that the Legislature is more often than not unable to hold the Executive to account. This is mainly because Chama Cha Mapinduzi (CCM), the party holding the reins of power in the country, has such a large majority in Parliament that with the exercise of internal party discipline very well established, members have to tow the party line, thus resulting into control by the executive.

Like in most of the developing world, Tanzania has had its share of corruption scandals that have led the country to lose millions of shillings. Such cases have involved bigwigs in government and have therefore generated difficulty in handling them due to executive's interference or deliberate keeping quiet. As I pointed out earlier, there is progress. The new leadership in Tanzania under President Magufuli has shown zero tolerance to corruption. The accountability committees have been able to prompt the executive to act on alleged cases of corruption. What remains like in Uganda is for the appropriate organs of the state to prosecute the suspects and return their lot to the public purse.

Other challenges in comparative perspective

Lack of a Parliamentary Budget Office in Tanzania

Whereas Uganda and Kenya's parliaments have a budget office in their respective houses, Tanzania does not have this rather important office. Parliamentary Budget Offices (PBOs) are designed to prepare economic forecasts that are independent of the executive, analyse budget proposals submitted by the executive, develop budget projections and prepare spending-cut options for legislative consideration. Establishment of an independent, non-partisan Parliamentary Budget Office would therefore strengthen the legislature's oversight role in the budget process. In many countries, PBOs are usually independent, non-partisan entities within the legislature that examine the draft annual budget proposed by the executive and provide analytical support to parliamentarians so as to enhance their ability to question the tabled proposal and enable them to propose alternative budget proposals. Their professional approach to issues in the budget process is believed to facilitate in the equitable allocation of scarce resources. In East Africa some scholars have argued that a fair distribution of the 'national cake' is a deterrent to political violence and a significant intervention to instability and ethnicity driven politics.

Lack of Capacity

The Inter-Parliamentary Union (2009) further observes that the Tanzanian Bunge also lacks resources to carry out its functions. In addition, the parliamentary staff lacks the skills necessary to support committees, conduct requested research, and analyze legislation and budget and audit documents. Similarly, there is a shortage of offices for staff and MPs both at the Bunge and in the constituencies. Proposed bills and gazetted legislations are usually only available in English, even though Kiswahili is the country's national and official language. Publishing bills in both languages would require additional resources which parliament does not seem to have.

Furthermore, the Open Budget Survey 2010 unveils that Tanzania's budget process lacks adequate transparency, leaving citizens in the dark about how tax and donor monies are used (Uwazi 2010). In addition, audit reports from the Controller and Auditor General (CAG) show how the Government has failed to manage public resources well and taken little action to respond to audit queries.

Lack of technical expertise

Parliamentarians in the three East African countries lack the technical know-how when it comes to budget matters. This is due to the fact that they lack knowledge in Accounts as a subject. Indeed, MPs walk into parliament from all walks of life and academic spheres professional backgrounds such as engineering, medicine, education, social sciences and entertainment. There has also been high turnover of MPs after general elections. The apparent lack of general knowledge of Accounts hence cripples their ability to effectively engage the executive on budgetary matters and in most cases they submit to some policies, not because they agree, but due to ignorance.

Inadequate time and information

Inadequate information for proper analysis also hinders the effective participation of parliamentarians in the budget process. Parliamentarians are handicapped in this regard unless the policy area happens to be one of their own expertise. Even with the information they get, there is never enough time for them to digest and develop credible arguments for debate. The practice is for government to overwhelm parliamentarians with information at the last minute such that they are made to submit to policies not because they agree with them but because of ignorance.

Conclusion

In theory, parliaments play a key role in the budget process. However, in practice, there exists a tremendous gap in many countries around the world between the potential for action by parliaments and the actual role they play. Yet the budget cycle is the key political vehicle which allows parliamentary participation in the shaping of national policy priorities. Parliaments can debate the issues of development policies and priorities, but it is the budget that allocates resources to those priorities, and parliament can play a key role if it is committed to do so and I add if the political actors submit to democratic principles and are committed to peace and stability of the country.

Greater parliamentary involvement results in greater transparency and better government accountability. Instead of budgets being prepared behind the locked doors of the ministry of finance, there can be wider public participation, better economic performance and greater focus on poverty reduction and gender issues. Here, once again, it is the parliamentary committees that can take the lead, with finance, budget and public accounts committees or their equivalents being particularly important. The analysis in this chapter brings out the fact that the legislature in the three East African countries has made positive efforts in its budget oversight role and especially, demanding executives to account for the monies they spend and exposing corrupt leaders and public officers. The National Audit offices are doing a tremendous work while accountability committees have over time improved their methods of work and action oriented recommendations. However, despite these recognizable efforts, the need for better budget oversight and implementation for better service delivery is still needed. A lot of ground work needs to be done especially to allow Parliament exercise independence without losing the principle of cooperating with other branches of government – the executive and judiciary. The legislature in East Africa must focus on areas that enhance capacity and competences of MPs and staff for more effective service delivery within their mandate.

It has been established that one of the weaknesses in the Westminster system is that although there is public and parliamentary input to the budget formulation, if the executive does not actually do what parliament authorized, parliaments often lack the ability to check out what public officers do and what they have been directed to do at service delivery units. Parliaments approve the budget, monitor the budget, audit the budget, but if the executives and their technical staff do not spend as authorized in the first place, then the legislature is frustrated in the oversight function. Nevertheless, Parliament through its established committees, Budget Committee, Parliamentary Budget Office, PAC and other accountability committees can keep the citizens informed about the Budget process. An informed citizenry is likely to develop a demand conscience that ultimately puts pressure on government for value for money. Similarly, the PAC together with the Auditor General can also follow-up on actions taken by the relevant Ministries/Departments/Accounting Officers in relation to recommend-ations/resolutions made. This ultimately affects service delivery and overall development of the country. The legislature and all the institutions established under parliament as alluded to can't work alone; therefore cooperation between different actors of the state is a necessity.

Last but not least this chapter has ably demonstrated that East African countries are grappling with the management and use of scarce resources in order to practice democratic governance. This is important for peace and stability of the states. However, the principles of separation of powers and checks and balances are still developing. It is therefore important to strengthen the legislature through institutional and infrastructure development; and training in order to enable MPs and technical staff to carry out oversight function better. This is critical for democracy, service delivery and overall socio-economic transformation urgently needed if we are to have peace and stability.

Chapter Eight | Elijah Dickens Mushemeza

References

AFRICOG (2012) *Public Participation and Parliamentary Oversight: Legal Reforms and Policy Options.* Nairobi: African Centre for Open Governance.

Bainomugisha, A. and Mushemeza, E. D. (2006) 'No TitleDeepening Democracy and Enhancing Sustainable Livelihoods in Uganda: An Independent Review of the Performance of Special Interest Groups in Parliament', *Policy Research Series.* Kampala: ACODE, No. 13.

Institute of Economic Affairs (2009) 'Parliamentary Budget Oversight in Kenya: Analysis of the Framework and Practices since 1963 to Date', *IEA Research Paper.* Nairobi: Institute of Economic Affairs, (19).

Inter-Parliamentary Union (2003) 'Parliament and the Budgetary Process: Including from a Gender Perspective', in *A Regional Seminar for Parliaments of South-West Asia.* Colombo, New York: Inter-Parliamentary Union.

Inter-Parliamentary Union (2004) 'Parliament and the Budgetary Process, Including from a Gender Perspective', in *A Regional Seminar for Parliaments of South-West Asia.* Colombo, Sri Lanka: Inter-Parliamentary Union.

Inter-Parliamentary Union (2009) 'Parliament's Role in the Development Agenda: Two Case Studies', in. New York: Inter-Parliamentary Union.

Kenya Constitution (2010).

Kerrow, B. (2014) *Courts cannot interfere with internal process of Parliament.* Nairobi: Standard Media. Available at: http://www.standardmedia.co.ke/?articleID=2000105305.

Kiraso, B. (2008) 'Establishment of Uganda's Parliamentary Budget Office and the Parliamentary Budget Committee', in Stapenhurst, R., Pelizzo, R., Olson, D., and von Trapp, L. (eds) *Legislative Oversight and Budgeting.* Washington D. C: World Bank Institute.

Lawson, A. and Rakner, L. (2005) *Understanding patterns of accountability in Tanzania. Component 3, Analysis of values, incentives and power relations in the budget allocation process.* Oxford: Oxford Policy Management.

Madhidha, E. (2011) 'Parliamentary budget office vital to improve budget process'. Available at: http://pambazuka.org/en/category/features/74438.

Parliamentary Centre (2014) 'Project Steering Committee in Ghana reviews governance structure of five-year African program'. Accra: Parliamentary Centre. Available at: http://www.parlcent.org/en/2014/01/29/meeting-in-ghana-wraps-up-final-phase-of-five-year-african-program/ (Accessed: 27 May 2014).

Pelizzo, R. and Kinyondo, A. (2014) 'Public Accounts Committees in Eastern Africa: A Comparative Analysis with a Focus on Tanzania', *REPOA Brief.* Dar es Salaam: REPOA, 44.

Republic of Uganda (2001) 'The Budget Act, 2001'. UPPC.

SUNY/CID (2003) *Uganda Parliamentary Technical Assistance Project (2001 - 2002): Legislative Strengthening, SUN/CID Project.* Kampala. Available at:http://www.cid.suny.edu/our_work/legislative_strengthening/our _work_projects_Legislative_strengthening46.cfm (Accessed: 27 May 2014).*Tanzania Contitution* (1977).

Tsekpo, A. and Hudson, A. (2009) *Parliamentary Strengthening and the Paris Principles: Uganda case study.* London: Overseas Development Institute. 'Uganda constitution' (1995).

World Bank (2013) *Strengthening Parliamentary Oversight of National Budgets in Africa.* Washington D.C.: The World Bank Institute.

Yemima, O. E. (2008) *The Public Accounts Committee - PAC: A barking dog without teeth?* Kampala. Available at: http://www.ugpulse.com/government/the-public-accounts-committee-pac-a-barking-dog-without-teeth/1021/ug.aspx. (Accessed: 8 August 2014).

CHAPTER NINE

East African Customs Union Protocol: Stakeholders' Participation in the Negotiation Process

Onesmus Mugyenyi, Flavian Zeija and Sabastiano Rwengabo

Introduction

One of the peace-building and development-initiating processes in contemporary regionalism is the negotiation of regional-international agreements and other cooperation frameworks that inform organised cooperation in almost all regions of the world (except perhaps in northwest Asia, well known as the Middle East) (Mansfield and Milner, 1999). Regional integration is inherently a peace building process in three ways: first, it facilitates regular, peaceful, interstate interactions, hence the opportunity to resolve nascent interstate as well as open conflicts between and within cooperating states. The European experience reveals this relatonship (Stefanova, 2006). Second, regional integration engenders socioeconomic and political interdependence between states. This precludes temptations for war recurrence in a post-World War II world. Here, regionalism becomes a lower level of global governance (Young, 1999). Finally, regional economic ties are believed to promote the development of regional economies, hence the creation of conditions conducive to domestic peace, security, and stability (EAC, 2006). It is in these lenses that the regional-integration initiatives under East African Community (EAC) ought to be viewed.

During the 1990s, the three East African states–Uganda, Kenya, and Tanzania–strove to revive the organisation following the EAC's unwelcome collapse in 1977. A lengthy negotiation process was undertaken. In 1999, the Treaty re-establishing the EAC was signed (EAC, 1999), and came into force in July 2000. Burundi and Rwanda, formerly members of the Communauté Économique des États de l'Afrique Centrale (CEEAC or Economic Community of Central African States, ECCAS), were allowed observer status in 2004, and officially admitted to the EAC in 2007 through an amendment to the Treaty. The Treaty constitutes a consensus document between the partner states. It guides the process of regional integration (EAC, 2001). Under the treaty, states undertook to establish a customs union, common market, a monetary union and ultimately a political federation.

This chapter assesses the participation of stakeholders in the negotiations leading to the EAC customs union and underlines its peace-building and development implications thus far. The chapter starts by highlighting the theoretical basis of stakeholder participation in customs union negotiations before briefly outlining the historical background to the EAC whose Treaty envisages strong partnerships between state governments, the private sector, and civil society in working toward the Treaty's goal of sustainable socio-economic and political development. Such development, we maintain, contributes to peace building by erasing the objective conditions that disrupt regional peace. This is because the EAC is grounded on a number of operational principles, including: people-centered and market driven co-operation, and subsidiarity which emphasizes multi-level participation and involvement of a wide range of stakeholders in the integration process. The treaty also stresses sustainable and equitable economic development. The chapter examines participation of stakeholders during these customs union negotiations and draws implications for peaceable development in the EAC. The conclusion sums up the main arguments and draws theoretical and practical implications for understanding and managing regional-integration processes in East Africa.

Stakeholder Participation, Customs Unions, and Peaceable Development

> "If we are to remain free, if we are to enjoy full benefits of Africa`s rich resources, we must unite to plan for our total defence and full exploitation of our material and human means in the full interest of our people. To go to it alone, will limit our horizon, curtail our expectations and threaten our liberty". Kwame Nkrumah

Stakeholder participation in regional integration initiatives builds the legitimacy and ownership necessary to consolidate the gains of integration and use these gains to build lasting bonds of friendship and shared destinies that are necessary for peaceable development within the region. Proponents of regionalism are aware of the "need to marshal our initiatives, efforts, resources, and capabilities to collectively address the various defence and security challenges facing the Community, and [to] achieve a common goal of collective regional peace and stability that is the bedrock of economic progress" (EAC, 2009, page 4). To say regional-economic progress depends upon peace and security, as summed up by a Rwandan general-turned-politician, James Kabareebe, during one of the above-quoted EAC meetings, is to reveal one side of the story without denying the other. The other side is this: socioeconomic progress has direct bearing on peace and security. Working toward such progress directly meets the region's peace and security needs. The relationship is cyclic; a kind of double reaction where peace and security facilitates socioeconomic development and develop-ent in turn builds peace, stability and democracy. Peaceable development in a regional context is a consequence of participatory regional-integration initiatives aimed at the socioeconomic transformation of the region. This perhaps explains why socioeconomic, welfarist, functional, cooperation was at the heart of initial regional integration attempts in post-War Europe (Mitrany, 1965).

The world over, the importance of stakeholders' participation in the development process is not only desirable but is essential to the success of development policy formulation and implementation. Throughout this policy process, "participation" usually crops up. The EAC treaty highlights the principle of participation: Article 7 provides for multilevel participation and involvement of wide range of stakeholders. What does it mean?

Participation is the process by which stakeholders influence decisions and processes, share control over development initiatives, and jointly manage resources that affect these processes (Veit, 1998). For many, participation involves stakeholder empowerment, mobilization and involvement. Empowerment is rooted in unequal power. It entails provision of opportunities to hitherto less powerful actors to challenge, change, the institutional status-quo and vested interests (Veit, 1998). Empowerment involves helping citizens to participate in decisions that affect them. The empowered develop confidence in their own capacities. Therefore, participation is both a goal and a means to achieve sustainable development. Participation requires both organizational initiatives that entail consciousness raising.

Participation by mobilization is possibly the major means of linking stakeholders with ongoing development initiatives. This is based on the assumption that there is great inertia in society to change possibly due to collective action problems. Even when society may want to change, it may not know what is in its best interest. Ordinarily, government decides what is to be done, then rallies its people and lets them do it themselves (Veit, 1998). In this sense government, provides the leadership vision, but shares responsibility for clarifying and implementing that vision with citizens. At the regional level, inter-governmental structures may serve this purpose: develop visions, share them with other stakeholders, and act jointly with the latter.

The notion of stakeholder involvement is rooted in the view that people must participate in decisions affecting them. People should be involved in decisions and actions arising from those decisions. Proponents of involvement view stakeholders as people who understand their problems and can contribute to solving them. Accordingly, unless the concerns of interested stakeholders are taken care of while formulating policies and development strategies, implementation will be unsuccessful. At regional level, it is assumed that non-involvement may stall regional progress by slowing down, even preventing, implementation at national and sub-national level, hence failure to achieve the objectives of regional integration. This approach dismisses elitism. It believes in ordinary citizens' capacity to influence decisions, make rational/good choices, and prioritize their known development goals. The challenge, of course, is whether citizens scattered in multiple existential spaces can and do come together to identify problems, articulate and agree on possible solutions, and take centre-stage in applying these solutions. Although the EAC treaty envisaged stakeholder involvement, negotiations for the Customs Union largely negated the principle of participation. There was limited empowerment and mobilisation of relevant non-state stakeholders.

Relevance of Participation

Stakeholders who are affected by, or who benefit from, any development endeavor, need to take active part in its planning, decision-making, and implementation. Development is, after all, most people's concern. It is a condition that most people strive to attain. Thus, everybody aspiring to develop does, theoretically stating, take responsibility, gets involved, in pursuing such development. Individual actions, however, are best coordinated and taken together to attain synergy and optimum results. This is the basis of the notion of collective action (Olson, 1971, 1982). Operationally, therefore, development must be pursued in a way that involves and benefits from complementary actions of three key stakeholder groups: state institutions (government), private enterprises (business), and civil society.

Civil Society is presently a critical actor in development. More often than previously was the case, governments have relied on civil society to handle areas where their reach and services are limited. Civil society can work for and with local communities, is flexible and adaptive to various situations, tries innovative approaches in pursuing set development goals, serves as the voice of its beneficiaries, and connects government and other stakeholders. Organised civil society has the advantage of being able to organize and work at different levels, from grassroots to the global arena, to address wide areas of concerns, to adopt a wide variety of constituents, and to execute its work with greater flexibility. These attributes allow civil society to work more effectively with the people and better influence their thinking (Dicklitch, 1998). Notwithstanding, however, civil society cannot pursue development alone. Its limitations, in capacity, mandate, and regulation and enforcement, call for state authority structures within which policies are defined and appropriate rules of behaviour enforced.

Actions by civil society and business are governed and influenced by government policies and regulations. Government has greater access and better capacity to generate resources, to provide access to and share these resources, to provide legal and regulatory frameworks that give order and direction to development. Government takes the lead in crafting the future and setting development directions, can bank on its mandate and capability to generate and allocate resources necessary to foster development. Where a government ably extracts resources from and beyond its citizenry, and uses these resources to provide political goods that constitute and contribute to development, the necessary and oft-coveted state capacity to exercise control, legitimacy, and authority, is observable (Tilly, 1990). Africa's experience of government effectiveness, and hence of state capacity, remains limited and is still evolving (Herbst, 2000). So, African governments should avoid other stakeholders. Even in western societies with relatively strong states, the imperative of democracy allows other stakeholders' participation.

The state is not a lone agent of development solely responsible for solving problems like poverty. Development concerns are created by the people and affect them directly. A failing government ruling over poor people will fail more miserably. Engaging the people in finding solutions for their problems, therefore, is crucial for development. In recognition for this complementary role, negotiators of the EAC Treaty provided for multi-stakeholder participation in regional integration processes. Consequently, the failure of governments to create the necessary structures and disseminate relevant information to ignite effective stakeholder participation undermines the spirit of the Treaty.

Development also requires the business/private sector working with government and civil society in various geographic and sectoral areas. The business sector is always versatile at identifying and appropriating opportunities through investments, partnerships, and innovation. It dominates the production sector where jobs, goods and incomes are generated. It determines the sustainability of production, and influences the public's consumption behaviour through the goods and services produced, and the manner in which they are promoted and packaged. The sector has the capability and resources to promote and influence sustainable development. If unutilized and unregulated it can rip the economy apart and impoverish the society as extractive experiences have revealed in some countries (Gamu et al., 2015). Yet the sector's participation in development remains critical. As part of the development problem, they are part of the solution through planning and execution of development solutions.

Measuring Participation

The EAC is ambiguous on how the private sector and civil society should participate in the integration process, and how to measure such participation. But Article 127(3) of the Treaty compels partner states to provide an enabling environment for the participation of civil society and private sector in the development activities. Under sub-section (2) the Secretary General is required to provide the forum for consultation between the private sector and civil society organizations, other interest groups and appropriate institutions of the Community. While the treaty does not specify the mode that participation might take, participation can be measured using three parameters:

- who to participates
- the nature of participation (how you tell people's participation), and
- where to participate.

The first parameter is partly answered by the Treaty. The participants are: (i) governments, (ii) private sector, (iii) civil society, (iv) the people, and (v) other interest groups (not defined). The second parameter is not answered: the nature of participation is not defined.

The third parameter, where participation occurs, is perhaps the most pertinent. Participation can take place in policy formulation process, planning and implementation of EAC protocols at regional and national levels, and monitoring compliance. At Community level, the Treaty does not provide for private sector and civil society participation among EAC institutions, but reduces participation to state representatives. The Customs Union protocol does not provide for these non-state actors among the EAC institutional structures. Article 9, which establishes the institutions and organs of the community mentions the Summit (partner states' heads of states or governments), ministerial Council (ministers from partner state executives/cabinets), Coordination Committee (permanent secretaries of responsible ministries in partner states), East African Court of Justice (EACJ), East African Legislative Assembly (EALA), the Secretariat, "and such other organs as may be established by the summit."EAC organs constitute the Community's central governance structures. The EAC organs, therefore, are mainly state-centric (EAC, 1999), despite the awareness that sustainable socioeconomic and political development requires the private sector and civil society.

One of the EAC's operational principles is a people-centered and market-driven integration (EAC, 1999). This gives mandate to private sector, civil society, and "other interest groups" to participate in the integration process. The relationship between EAC organs and participation is this: the organs are decision-making avenues. Within these avenues, stakeholder participation beyond partner states' representatives would contribute to the integration agenda. The integration process, then, becomes people-centered and market-driven only when it provides opportunity for civil society groups and market actors to share in the decision-making process. According to objective 5 of the EAC (also reflected in articles 74-75 of the treaty), partner states agreed to conclude the protocol on the establishment of a Customs Union, one of whose details shall include security and other restrictions to trade [as per Art. 75(1)(h)].

Note that the EAC defies conventional regional integration trajectories. The Customs Union is, according to the Treaty, the first stage in the integration process. This is unique to East Africa because Preferential Trade Areas (PTAs) and Free Trade Areas (FTAs) theoretically precede customs unions (Laursen, 2008). The EAC common market, which creates a single East African economic space, is the second stage in the integration process in East Africa instead of the FTA that would follow. Thus, the EAC jumped two stages of regional integration: the PTA and the FTA. This is possibly explained by the legacy of pre-existing integration ethos that had been entrenched in pre-1977 East Africa. Schiff and Winters reveal that a Customs Union has a common external tariff as well as internal free trade (Schiff and Winters, 2003). The EAC Customs Union being the first stage of regional integration, in compliance with Article 5 of the treaty Uganda, Kenya and Tanzania signed its Protocol on 2nd March 2004. Rwanda and Burundi, then holding observer status, witnessed the signing and joined the EAC in 2007.

The EAC Customs Union: A Historical Background

The EAC Customs Union cannot be analysed in isolation from the historical trajectory of regional integration in East Africa. The EAC dates back to 1897 when construction of a railway linking Uganda and Kenya commenced. It progressed with the Customs Collection Centre in1900, the East African Currency Board in 1905, the Postal Union in 1905, and the Court of Appeal for East Africa in 1909. The Customs Union was established in 1919, an East African Governors Conference convened in 1926, and the East African Income Tax Board and the Joint Economic Council formed in 1945. Through an Order in Council in the 1940s the East African High Commission was established. The East African Common Services Organisation (EACSO) agreement of 1961-66 and the Treaty of East African Co-operation 1967 were later concluded, giving rise to the EAC in 1967 (EAC, 1999).

The EAC arose from colonial Britain's desire to establish effective control over Uganda, Kenya and Tanganyika for it seemed economically unviable to retain three East African countries under separate Governors yet under one imperial control–Britain (Serunkuma, 1987). Therefore, the process of integration was never a people-centered project nor was it private-sector driven. Decisions were made by colonial governors and the British government with little, if any, involvement of East Africans. In 1926, there was an attempt to federate the three East African territories through a Governors' Conference, which became a policy-making organ relying on unanimity for decision making with the Secretary of State for the Colonies as the final judge in case of disagreement (Serunkuma, 1987). The main weakness of the Conference was that over-centralization of decision making. East Africans had no say in the affairs affecting them. In 1932, the Conference was mandated to have a permanent secretariat for developing inter-territorial co-operation and coordination of matters of common interest.

In 1948, the English Queen established a paramount executive authority, the East African High Commission (EAHC), through Orders in Council of 1947. The EAHC, which was intended to administer common services, consisted of the three Governors with a secretariat in Nairobi. This development precipitated the formation of the East African Railways and Harbours and the East African Posts and Telegraphs. The Orders in Council also created a central legislative assembly consisting of mainly of governors' appointees (Mpumbani, 1999). Buganda kingdom, in central-southern Uganda, reasoned that the East African federation threatened the special position it enjoyed during colonial rule. The Kabaka (King) of Buganda, Sir Edward Muteesa II, demanded independence from not only the East African Federation but the rest of the Uganda protectorate. The Lukiiko (Buganda's Parliament) remained opposed to regional integration. Consequently, the colonial government finally abandoned the idea of a federation toward independence.

Growing nationalism among indigenous East Africans supported by the American open door policy increased the demand for self-determination. The idea of East African federation went in limbo. Soon after independence, the three heads of East African states mooted the idea of federation. In 1965, the Phillip Commission was set up to consider the problems of economic and institutional cooperation, and reported in May 1966. A treaty for The East African Co-operation was drafted out of this report and signed on 6thJune 1967. Thus was born the EAC in post-colonial East Africa. The contradictions that had created difficulties in previous integration process could not allow the EAC to survive. In 1977, the organisation was dissolved, and an agreement for sharing assets and liabilities signed in 1984 following the 1981-1983 mediation process led by Victor Umbricht (EAC, 1984; Umbricht, 1989).

The reasons for the dissolution of the EAC vary. Some commentators argue that the unresolved question of benefit sharing threatened the operationalization of the EAC Customs Union as the more industrialised and strategically better located Kenya reaped bigger than other partner states in continuation of a trend had started under the EACSO. As a result, Tanzania and Uganda viewed the EAC project as a project by Kenya to "employ" Uganda and Tanzania as her trade "agents" for a small "commission". Other observers believe that poor governance and political differences reflected in lack of political will to hold the community together and transcend differences and disagreements between Tanzania's Julius Nyerere and Kenya's Jomo Kenyatta on one hand, and Uganda's Idi Amin (who came to power through a coup d'état in 1971) and other leaders on the other. In consequence, the East African Authority could no longer meet, even as some organs continued to function, due to leaderships disagreements that culminated in the final nail to the coffin: Kenya grounded the East African Airways by starting a domestic Airline in 1977, prompting retaliations and counter-retaliations that led to stalemates. Other arguments point to ideological differences, in the context of the Cold War, between socialism in Tanzania, a mixed ideology of socialism and capitalism in Uganda, and capitalism in Kenya mainly influenced (Caucasian settlers and European entrepreneurial class. Un-cordial verbal exchanges took place between state leaders, leading to breakdown of engagements.

Yet, some reasoners blame the paucity of stakeholders' participation. The EAC of the 1990s, they argue, was built on the whims of individual politicians. Like its predecessor during colonial geopolitical machinations, EACSO, the EAC lacked anchorage in the East African society and was bereft of the necessary legitimacy. The population did not participate in the integration process. Popular will throughout the process was naught.

Citizen ownership only existed as long as politicians agreed. This eroded the foundations of continuity.

Efforts to revive the EAC started during the 1990s. On 30th November 1993, an agreement establishing a Permanent Tripartite Commission for East African Corporation was signed. The agreement set up a Council of Ministers mandated to work out key areas of co-operation and to put in place arrangements for regional integration. This was followed by the launching of a Secretariat in March 1996. The secretariat crafted a development strategy document covering the period 1997-2000, which was launched in April 1997. It became the roadmap for the EAC treaty, which was signed on the 30th November 1999 as the apex of extensive negotiations (Muthaura, no date). The treaty, which came into force by the end of the year 2000 when all partner state parliaments had ratified it, spells out the process of integration as follows: Partner states undertake to establish among themselves and in accordance with the provisions of the treaty, a Customs Union, a Common Market, a Monetary Union and ultimately a Political Federation in order to strengthen and regulate the industrial, and commercial infrastructures, cultural, social and other relations of the partners. One of its operational principles is multi-level participation and involvement of a wide range of stakeholders. The extent to which this principle of multi-stakeholder participation was operationalised during the establishment of the EAC Customs Union, is worth analysis.

Negotiating the EAC Customs Union Protocol: Stakeholder Participation

The Customs Union Protocol, like other EAC protocols, is an appendage to the Treaty. As part of the treaty, once ratified, it acquired legal force in partner states. The protocol was greeted with optimism from governments, the business community, and civil society. Yet the participation of stakeholders—especially the business community (private sector), civil society, parliamentarians and the citizenry—in the process of negotiating the Protocol was limited contrary to the Treaty's fundamental and operational principles and some level of consensus that the success of the EAC will largely depend on the involvement and active participation of the population. Ownership is crucial because it gives one a say in the methods and means by which he/she is governed, confers a sense of belonging, and fosters inclusiveness. On this basis, the Community adopted two major principles: (i) people centeredness and (ii) multi-stakeholder participation. Therefore, stakeholders' participation and ownership of the processes leading to the Customs Union informs subsequent processes.

This analysis is largely based on Uganda's experience where the principle of multi-level and multi-stakeholder participation ought to have been operationalized by broadening the scope of consultations and improving information dissemination. The private sector and civil society were not deeply involved. Space for their participation was not open. The accreditation rules were prohibitive. The procedure was a little cumbersome and disenabled a range of stakeholders from obtaining observer status. Future participation of these stakeholders requires easing these restrictions, institutionalizing national consultative structures, allowing predictability of participation, and facilitating feedback mechanisms.

The Protocol, among others, provides for the principle of asymmetry; elimination of internal tariffs and other charges of equivalent effect; elimination of non-tariff barriers; establishment of a common external tariff, rules of origin, ant-dumping measures, subsidies and counter veiling duties; and security and other restrictions to trade. Other provisions relate to competition, duty drawback, refund and remission of duties and taxes, customs co-operation, re-exportation of goods, simplification and harmonisation of trade. Others include documentation and procedures, exemption regimes, harmonised commodity description and coding system. The main goals of the Customs Union include: liberalization of intra-regional trade on the basis of mutually beneficial trade arrangements among states; promoting efficiency in production, economic development, diversification, and industrialization; and enhancing domestic and cross-border trade and foreign investment.

Specifically, the Customs Union creates a Common External Tariff (CET) regime for goods originating from outside East Africa, common customs laws and regulations applying uniformly in partner states, and harmonization and simplification of customs procedures and documentation (EAC, 2004a). The protocol details how these elements will be treated or applied. Details on operationalisation are contained in the annexes that form an integral part of the protocol. The protocol is therefore incomplete without annexes, and must thus be read. Beyond annexes, other basic principles are contained in enacted laws by the EAL Alike the Customs Management Act, 2004, and other policies and laws such as Competition Policy and Law.

Stakeholder participation was important as the customs union promises a lot. It is expected to widen the regional market, despite general poverty in our population; attract investments in the EAC because of wider market; reduce consumer prices and increased supply of goods and services through elimination of tariffs and non-tariff barriers; reduce localised scarcity of foodstuffs via free movement of agricultural produce from areas of plenty to areas with shortages, hence increased food security; and lead to rapid industrial change as industries adopt efficient production techniques, hence specialisation and mass production in response to competition. Whither the spaces for such participation?

Spaces for Stakeholders' Participation during Negotiations

Spaces can be defined as moments in which interventions or events occur that create new opportunities, reconfiguring relationships between actors within the spaces or bringing in new actors and opening up possibilities of a directional shift (Brook et al., 2002). Spaces provide stakeholders opportunities to express various alternatives to the trend and direction of policy and/or development strategies. Different stakeholders use different spaces to influence policies. The common spaces are invited as opposed to claimed spaces. Invited spaces include public discussions or processes where groups are invited to participate. Examples are World Bank Poverty Reduction Strategy processes where international actors and state institutions control the agenda and rules of engagement. When groups are invited in these spaces, the agendas are often preset or pre-arranged in a manner that legitimises the institution's prior goals. Such spaces do not offer the invited group real opportunity to engage on key policy questions. In contrast, claimed spaces, like public accountability sessions, are created by civic groups. The agenda and participation of the state and other actors are set by the civic groups themselves. Therefore, spaces are not only boardrooms or meeting halls and round tables but moments of intervention where stakeholders negotiate possibilities (Brook et al., 2002). There can also be what we call "shared spaces" wherein state, market, and third-sector stakeholders jointly create rules of engagement through discussions and exchanges of ideas before actual engagements.

Regional spaces for negotiations of the Customs Union protocol were complex. The obvious spaces were invited spaces in meeting halls/conference rooms. But many actors were closed out. There was no specifically-designed regional forum to capture the views of civil society in its wider context. Many actors in Uganda were dissatisfied with their involvement. "It was a closed shop for politicians and government technocrats" observed an officer from a regional non-governmental organisation (NGO) with offices in Uganda. Another added: "We were closed out of the key meetings". The major civil society organisations (CSOs) working on trade issues in Uganda confessed that they did not participate in negotiations nor was the timetable for the process publicized. The structures of negotiations did not take care of the civic groups and other relevant stakeholders. They were, instead, dominated by governments.

Development Network of Indigenous Voluntary Associations (DENIVA), a civil society network consisting about 80 voluntary associations, conceded that the process was closed to civil society. This undermining the intent of Article 127, which requires partner states to provide an enabling environment for the private sector and civil society to participate in improving the policies and activities of EAC institutions. DENIVA has since faced operational difficulties and is difficult to attribute any civil society space for its members.

Under Article 3(6) of treaty, the Council sets up rules of procedure for granting observer status. Admission as an observer provides another space for civil society and other groups to participate. The rules of procedure for granting observer status came into force on 13th January 2002. This procedure, however, constitutes another superfluous burden to CSOs. It makes utilisation of this space difficult. Few CSOs in Uganda received observer status. A number of CSOs saw the requirement that interested CSOs be registered in all three partner states as an unnecessary precondition. This is so because the EAC seeks to de-territorialize East Africa, erase difficulties presented by physical/geographical borders, so as to smoothen regional cooperation. Some CSOs that attempted to obtain observer status were unsuccessful. They had not complied with that requirement: registration in the three partner states. While responding to the application by Advocates Coalition for Development and Environment (ACODE), The EAC Secretary General wrote in part:

> Having studied the objectives of ACODE, Strategic Plan and profile, I am of the view that ACODE could contribute to the achievement of the objectives of the East African Community. However, according to The Rules of Procedure for the Granting of Observer Status, a Civil Society Organisation like ACODE is required, apart from the general broad criteria, to bear a regional dimension with registration in each of the partner states.

This was a correct reading of the rules. One is justified saying that the rejection of ACODE's application was legal. Yet most CSOs view this requirement as an obstacle to civil society participation. ACODE's Executive Director insisted that the requirement undermines the objectives of the community. It subjects stakeholders to unnecessary bureaucratic procedures. It limits their participation to influence issues that affect their constituents. He concluded that it is requires interpretation by the EACJ (G. Tumushabe 2005, personal communication, 1 January). The attempt by civil society, in the then three East African countries, to organise and claim space did not yield positive results. CSOs attempted to form a coalition. It collapsed in the formative stages in the 2002-2005 period. The failure of civil society to participate in the negotiation process, according to one correspondent, was partly due to lack of leadership. Both DENIVA and NGO Forum, umbrella organisations in Uganda, did not participate in the process but there was no pro-active action to claim space. In comparison, "NGO Forum did well in the Poverty Eradication Action Plan (PEAP) revision process in 2004. It was able to provide leadership in the process. There was multi-stakeholder participation. But on regional integration, the forum has let us down" (Key informant 2005, personal communication, 1 January).

At a regional workshop held from 28-29 July 2005, several regional CSOs resolved to form an East African NGO/CSO Steering Committee at national and regional level. They also agreed to constitute a forum, the "East African Community NGO/CSO Forum", as an autonomous, umbrella organ for all CSOs in the region. These attempts were pro-active reactions to gain space for the CSOs to effectively participate in subsequent processes. Members of the EALA were also concerned about the level of stakeholder involvement.

Shiela Kawamara Mishambi, a member of the EALA, argued that the negotiation process was closed to many actors: "Imagine, the East African Community Customs Management bill was provided to us and discussed into law in two days. The process was rushed and did not give sufficient time for stakeholder input. We did not have time to consult. I am on record. I did not support the idea. My fear is that the implementation may meet some obstacles because of less involvement of the population" (Key informant 2005, personal communication, 1 January). How, then, would the public participate where organised civil society had faced such difficulty?

Public participation in the process, if any, was poor. Worse still, many technocrats in partner-state governments did not know the outcome of the process. Irene Ovonji-Odida, another EALA member, commented that the process was top-bottom and not people-driven. After the protocol came into force, Kenyan, Tanzanian and Ugandan customs officials did not know what to do. There were no guidelines on the implementation of new customs procedure (Tralac, 2005). Captain Richard Ddudu, also an EALAa member, regretted that government bureaucrats hijacked the negotiation process. He disclosed that through-out the negotiations, Uganda had the thinnest team and civil society was conspicuously absent (R. Ddudu 2005, personal communication).

Another forum would have provided space for stakeholder participation: the Inter- Institutional Trade Committee (IITC), under the Ministry of Tourism, Trade, and Industry. It is composed of government ministries, departments and agencies (MDAs), NGOs, academia and research institutions, representatives of farmer groups, private sector, members of parliament, and more. The IITC was acclaimed as an innovative forum for trade policy formulation and implementation given the diverse expertise from various stakeholders. It was divided into sub-committees on: WTO issues, Cotonou Agreement, and regional agreements and bilateral initiatives. The first two were operational but the sub-committee that deals with regional agreements and bilateral initiatives has been dormant since its constitution.

The IITC would have brought together different stakeholders to deliberate, table their concerns and influence negotiations on the customs union. An audit of the proceedings of IITC meetings during the time of customs union negotiations reflected scanty issues relating to the

Protocol. The sub-committee on Regional Agreements and Bilateral Initiatives should have actively been involved in the negotiation of the annextures to the protocol to ensure compatibility with the national development strategies. Instead, it was inactive during and after negotiations. We have seen governments involve various stakeholders in developing negotiating positions in respect to both WTO and ACP-EU negotiations. But negotiations of the Customs Union took a completely different trend.

On the principle of participation, Oloka-Onyango, a law professor in Uganda's Makerere University, observed that right from inception, the principle of participation had been undermined in the EAC. "Those who were around will recall that the draft Treaty was put to public debate between May 1998 to April 1999. The response was lackluster and indeed the involvement of broader masses and the populace was marginal... Indeed there are several explanations including non-involvement of civil society and other non-state actors in the concept formulation..., lack of publicity and information surrounding the process..." (Oloka-Onyango, 2005). Interestingly, government officials insist that CSOs and the private sector participated in these negotiations: "They were invited to the meetings but they never took the process seriously" (Official from Min. of Tourism 2005, personal communication). Yet eleven CSOs working on trade and development issues in Kampala give the impression that CSOs were not invited or participated in the negotiation of the Protocol. Consultations with the Makerere-University-based Economic Policy Research Centre (EPRC), a state think tank, reveal similar views: that the process left out important actors.

Participation by the Private Sector

President Mwai Kibaki of Kenya, referring to the Customs Union said

> Lessons learnt from the defunct East African Community which collapsed in 1977 show that apart from political will from governments and political leaders, there is need for strong participation of the private sector, civil society and the people of East Africa in general for the integration to work" (M. Kibaki 2003, personal communication, 5 November).

The negotiation process fundamentally departed from his viewpoint. After launching the EAC, partner states established a High-Level Task Force, which comprised of senior representatives from relevant government departments in each partner state, to negotiate a trade protocol in keeping with the terms of the treaty on the Customs Union (USAID-PSF, 2005). The task force comprised officials from the Ministries of: Tourism, Trade and Industry; Foreign Affairs, Finance, Planning and Economic Development; and Revenue Authorities of partner states. The business community and civil society were not represented on this team–if at all, then ineffectively. Under the East Africa Business Council (EABC), the business community enjoyed observer status. This limited their participation in the Customs Union negotiations. According to James Mulwana, the then EABC chairperson, the EABC lobbied for an affiliate status to enable them participates in negotiating the annexes to the protocol (EAC, 2004b).

At the signing of the Protocol, the business community complained that governments had sidelined them. During a press briefing, James Mulwana, also then chairperson of the Uganda Manufacturers Association (UMA), complained that Uganda sidelined the business community up to the date of signing the protocol. No development since 2004 indicates that this misunderstanding between the business community and governments is unlikely to continue into the implementation of the Customs Union and even the common market. This is inconsistent with Article 7 of the treaty that stresses multi-stakeholder participation and private-sector led integration. During negotiations of the Common External Tariff (CET), the EABC, while explaining why consensus had not been reached on many issues, complained that there had been lack of involvement of the private sector in negotiations leading to the conclusion of the Customs Union Protocol.

The EABC observed:

> The East African Business Council and her members are not accorded the proper opportunity to participate in the negotiations by partner states officials. As detailed in the mode of negotiations, the members of the HLTF are expected to collect information from stakeholders and present it as country positions. Private sector interests are sometimes ignored. Nothing comes into the agenda of the HLTF without being initiated by itself. Our submissions are always referred to it as 'a non

paper'. This means it is not given the due attention it deserves…the manner in which negotiations are chaired cannot give chance to the EABC to air its views. The Chairperson always asks Uganda, Kenya and Tanzania positions on general subjects and this way, strong views of the private sector are ignored. In the Permanent Secretary's and Council of Ministers' meetings which are very important, the private sector is not always given the opportunity to participate or observe (EAC, 2004b).

The EABC Secretariat exemplified that in one of the expert meetings of the Nomenclature Customs and Trade group, which is a subcommittee of the HLTF, the Head of Delegation from Kenya chased away the private sector from their team. It took the frantic efforts of appeal to the Kenyan authorities back in Nairobi to allow the Kenyan private sector into the negotiating room. The EABC consistently argued that the Customs Union Protocol was concluded without in-depth analytic studies on its possible impact especially on the business community. It complained that negotiations on the CET were conducted without serious studies on the CET's possible impact on the business community. Few studies that were carried out only focused on macro-level impacts and ignored micro-level ones (Oloka-Onyango, 2005). Trade imbalance between EAC economies had caused the 1977 breakup. But the same question seems to have been given inadequate attention.

As already observed, the representation of the IITC at the critical stage of protocol negotiations was still narrow, unrepresentative. Much of the processes took place with little involvement of the IITC members. Private Sector Foundation (PSF) claimed it held several consultative meetings and generated proposals. During negotiations of the East African Customs Management Act (EACUMA), PSFUMA, and the Uganda Freight Forwarders Association (UFFA) held a consultative workshop in Kampala, attended by majority of the stakeholders, as one of the series of consultative meetings during the process. In December 2002, the Uganda technical Working Group (UTWG) organised a workshop on regional integration. The workshop highlighted key developments in the negotiation of the Customs Union. In February 2004, UMA held a briefing meeting for its members on the Common External Tariff. At the meeting the chairperson indicated that the EABC was lobbying for an affiliate status to participate in the negotiations, and communicated that the Council had successfully lobbied for a three-band tariff under the CET. In government's judgment on this basis, therefore, it is untrue to say that private sector did not participate.

Further consultations with UMA revealed that the Association has an EAC sub-committee charged with monitoring regional developments and participating in negotiations. The committee was charged with developing strategies for engagement in customs union negotiations. This private-sector participation was further corroborated by a series of other meetings that were attended by its officials within and outside Kampala.

However, the coming into force of the Customs Union protocol produced negative reactions in Kampala. Traders were involved in strikes. Consultations with the majority of the traders revealed ignorance about the outcomes of negotiations. This casts doubt on the effectiveness of the consultations. Amanya-Mushega, then EAC Secretary General, described the UMA's discomfort with the protocol as "fear of the unknown", arguing that the business community failed to take the Customs Union seriously. Why, then, was the reception negative? Oloka-Onyango argues that either the consultants did not take the objections seriously or they did not listen to them. One is hard-pressed, therefore, to conclude that the consultations were effective. Most studies conducted on the issue were largely initiated by government. The private sector did not participate in drawing the Terms of Reference and choosing critical areas of research. Independent inquiries on the issue were either inadequate or almost inexistent. Consultations with an uninformed business community that did not appreciate the impacts of the positions adopted cannot pass as effective participation.

Operationalizing Multi-level and Multi- stakeholder Participation

The EAC Treaty recognizes that the success–and future survival–of the Community depends on active involvement and participation of its people. From the findings on stakeholder involvement in negotiation of the customs union protocol partner states had better consider increasing access to information to stakeholders and establish an efficient feedback mechanism. Negotiating schedules, time frames, smooth flow of information and input into the negotiations are important. Broadening the scope of participation to include a wide range of stakeholders neutralizes the top-bottom approach that had hitherto been used to revive the EAC, giving way to people-centredness. Otherwise, the EAC risks missing the benefits of public participation and associated gains from multi-stakeholder engagement (Bainomugisha and Rwengabo, 2016).

Empowering the citizenry by providing information on negotiation processes, through sensitization of the masses to appreciate the opportunities and challenges associated with regional integration, and seeking their input to such processes, is critical. The population needs to appreciate its role in regional integration processes in order to consolidate the EAC. By deepening the involvement and participation of the private sector and civil society, and supporting and facilitating these stakeholders to be more proactive, the EAC will strengthen its post-customs-union forms of integration, such as the common market whose implications for regional identity and unity has been addressed in recent literature (Rwengabo, 2015). Mass support is important not just for economic reasons but peaceable development.

Implications for Peace and Security in the Region

Stakeholder participation in regional integration initiatives improves peace and security, that are the bedrocks of the region's socio-economic progress, in three ways: prevention of disruptive resistance, legitimation, and conflict management. The first deals with the notion that regionalism touches people's livelihoods and ought to be construed as directly affecting people's wellbeing. Resistance from sections of the regional societies ought to be avoided. The second builds on the first and seeks to legitimate regional decisions and processes to ensure wide acceptance. The third consists in ensuring inbuilt mechanisms for forecasting possible conflicts and preventing or resolving them whenever they crop up.

Preventing Disruptive Resistance

Disruptive resistance arises when regional integration programs are devoid of their base, the people; when these processes are initiated behind closed doors, and suddenly brought to bear on an unprepared society; and when regional cooperation programs initiated by pro-regionalist coalitions face anti-regionalist coalitions. The last condition deserves elaboration: According to Etel Solingen, regionalism is a function of the nature and relative strength of domestic political coalitions within integrating countries. Some countries are ruled by anti-integration, anti-cooperation coalitions—almost akin to ruling groups that prefer isolationist foreign policies. These can be statist-nationalist and confessionalist coalitions. Both kinds of coalitions are opposed to regional integration. Internationalist coalitions, however, tend to support regional cooperation than the former two: where they are relatively stronger, regional integration/cooperationarises. This is because, Solingen argues, the ruling coalition's grand strategy becomes that state's raison d'être at a given time (Solingen, 1998).

During the 1970s, it appears, there were competing coalitions and, subsequently, statist-nationalist [and possibly confessionalist] coalitions, especially in Kenya, prevailed over internationalist ones. This becomes so if the blame not just the political and ideological imperatives for the collapse of the EAC but the deliberate workings of some influential East Africans who led to the EAC's dissolution (Ogot, 2006). As this study has revealed, there had been limited people's participation in the integration plans and processes. Instead, there had been participation of twofaced but influential East Africans. Disruption did take place since there was no citizen pressure to maintain the Community.

When a ruling coalition is pro-regionalism and its opposition is anti-integration two scenarios can arise. First, the ruling coalition determines whether or not regional integration takes place. But if the nation is riddled with antithetical views and opposing coalitions, the opposition may ignite disruptions against regional integration. Sometimes regionalism, such as entails trade non-restrictions and open markets, can be costly and cause domestic unease among local investors facing competition from regional peers. After-all, unequal sharing of benefits in part led to the collapse of the EAC in 1977, and this same question needs to be addressed if the customs union (and common market) is to last. Such disruptions can affect movement of means of production, sometimes causing trade and economic crises. One recalls the disruptions Uganda suffered during the 2007-2008 post-election crisis in Kenya, when Kenyan rioting mobs uprooted the Kenya-Uganda railway (VOA, 2009). To avoid disruptions engendered by feelings of unequal benefits, or suspected transnational political meddling, stakeholder participation prepares the country for the challenge of regional integration.

The second scenario is the possible disruption against an anti-integration coalition (in this case a statist-nationalist and/or confessionalist ruling coalition) by a pro-integration coalition in opposition. This arises when demands and expressions of interest in regional integration arise—a scenario that is unimportant here. What needs emphasis is that with an unprepared citizenry, regional integration may be disrupted when reason for discontent arises. Disruptions have serious socioeconomic and politico-security implications.

Legitimisation of Regional Integration Efforts

For whom is regional integration/cooperation taking place? Stakeholder participation legitimizes the process. Legitimacy implies that people have blessed the integration process. The customs union, for instance, depends on people accepting goods and services from across borders and purchasing these supplies for their own use. It also means preferential treatment for regional goods and services as against external supplies. The customs union [and the common market] entails such practices and initiatives as: simplification, standardisation and harmonisation of trade information and documentation; prevention, investigation and suppression of customs offences; anti-dumping, countervailing, and safeguard measures; elimination of barriers to trade; measures to address imbalances arising from the establishment of the customs union (EAC, 2004a); freedoms; and free movement of means of production. Some of these measures touch the core of state legitimacy. It is important that the whole process is legitimate at regional level.

The state may sacrifice its legitimacy at the altar of the customs union when citizens are subjected to standards, procedures, demands, and expectations they are unprepared for. Once domestic investors and ordinary citizens are thrust into an unexpected avalanche of demands they may question the legitimacy of their government, leading to political and economic conflicts with serious security ramifications. Either the state is prepared, and prepares its citizens for the sovereignty bargains that are attendant to regionalism or it risks losing its domestic legitimacy (Mattli, 2000).

Finally, the customs union is a means of legitimizing strategic economic plans for both the country and the region–at a point of interest convergence. Stakeholders are important in these strategic plans and decisions. EAC partner states "resolved to abolish tariff and non-tariff barriers to create the most favourable environment for the development of regional trade." This would, they hoped, "enhance economic growth and the development of the Community", consistent with broader international commitments to contribute to world trade under the World Trade Organisation (WTO) regime (EAC, 2004a). There are also individual obligations and commitments under other regional economic partnerships, such as Southern African Development Community (SADC) and the Inter-Governmental Authority on Development (IGAD). Investment stakeholders are necessary to implement these commitments. In case of failure or noncompliance the country loses regional and domestic legitimacy with costly political implications. This awareness makes it imperative that stakeholders are involved in these processes in order to avoid conflicts within the country, the region, and between regional powers and the rest of the global economic and political community.

Conflicts Management

Conflict management consists in ensuring inbuilt mechanisms, within the instrument, for forecasting possible conflicts and preventing or resolving them when they arise. This preventative approach is preferable to reactive conflict management for it is rooted in the awareness that human interactions have inherent conflict potentialities organised societies need to be aware of. Measures to detect, avoid, prevent, and (where needed) resolve, conflicts are helpful. But since conflicts arise from interactions between multiple stakeholders, few elites are not positioned enough, given limitations of time, knowledge, experience, and idiosyncrasies, to forecast and prepare for all possible conflicts. Engagement of multiple stakeholders in the negotiation process assures broad and deep inbuilt mechanisms for conflicts management because of the multiple voices and concerns that may be raised during negotiations. This gives rise to what Galtung calls "institutionalized conflict resolution" (Galtung, 1965).

The customs union protocol envisages investigations in the behaviours of regional companies to ensure such measures as anti-dumping, countervailing measures to counteract the effect of injurious subsidies, developing and enforcing standards, and preventing serious injuries to partner state economies. Such measures can generate conflicts in which customers, ordinary citizens, companies, involved in regional trade and exchange of goods and services are enmeshed. To maintain that state bureaucrats alone are equipped to anticipate and cushion the Community against possible conflicts arising from these multifarious engagements is to demand too much from state officials. The involvement and participation of relevant non-state stakeholders widens and deepens appreciation of the possible sources of conflicts and thus the institutionalisation of possible conflict-management measures.

During the 1971-77 conflicts, the Tanzania-Kenya border was closed. Kenya recalled its officials working in Arusha. Tanzanian citizens were chased from Uganda. This lack of ownership meant the integration process had been reduced to the whims of top political leaderships. Disagreements between top leaders affected the whole Community. Instituting measures for handling negative consequences of increased intra-EAC economic and political dealings is consistent with the objective of people-centered regional integration (Rwengabo, 2015). It cushions the community against overdependence on the whims and interests of few elites. This has important implications for the kinds of institutional establishments that are crafted for future conflicts management. It follows, therefore, that stakeholder participation and involvement in the negotiations of the protocol would have augmented institutional measures for conflicts management during the implementation of the protocol.

Conclusion

Negotiations of regional-international agreements and other cooperation frameworks is central to peace-building and development initiatives even when these processes appear to be more welfarist and economic. The nation-state presently faces many transnational and regional phenomena. No state can sufficiently control today's transnational pressures. States are shifting toward functional activities: interdependence and integration among hitherto sovereign states are replacing national self-sufficiency.

Not unlike in other world regions, the EAC customs union is indicative of integration processes in East Africa that appear as though more economic, but as Stefanova argues, are inherently peace building measures. These initiatives opens doors for peaceful interstate interactions, resolution of nascent conflicts, consolidation of interstate socioeconomic interdependence in order to preclude conflict escalation, and creation of conditions conducive to domestic peace, security, and stability (Stefanova, 2006).

This chapter has also assessed stakeholder participation, mainly by business entities, civil society groups, and other actors provided for under the Treaty, in negotiations leading to the EAC customs union protocol. The chapter has unearthed limitations on participation in these negotiations, with direct bearing on compliance with the protocol. Where participation would contribute to peace building by erasing the objective conditions that cause conflicts and disrupt regional peace, limited participation is inconsistent with the provisions of the treaty on people-centered and market driven co-operation. The implications for understanding regionalism in East Africa are: (i) the need to further assess the learning processes and experiences between the customs union and other latter process like the common market and monetary union;(ii) examining the relationship between stakeholder participation in these negotiations and implementation of resulting protocols; and (iii) comparatively analyzing the nexus between stakeholder engagement and peaceable development initiatives in which prevention of disruptions, legitimacy, and conflict management measures are inbuilt in the negotiations and resulting protocols. In a word, to what extent is the EAC customs union a form of conflicts management measure like European integration endeavors were?

In terms of policy and practice, there are few possible considerations to make. First, the need to deepen the involvement/participation of the private sector in future negotiations comes out strongly. The paradox of people-centered, private-sector-driven integration as specified in the Treaty, and limited private-sector participation in customs union negotiations requires settlement. Second, reviewing of the accreditation rules is necessary if stakeholders are to acquire the necessary space and legal opening to access and participate in decision-making spaces of the EAC. Third, national consultative structures, such as Uganda's Inter-Institutional Trade Committee, seem to lack institutionalization and coordination that are necessary to avoid an ad hoc operations unrecognized by government and the EAC. Fourth, non-state actors, such as civil society and private sector, have yet to position themselves to demand what belongs to East Africans. Proactive engagement is necessary for these stakeholders to acquire claimed space instead of invited space. Equally needed are Joint Spaces. These observations have vital implications for implementing and consolidating the EAC customs union in manner and to a degree that it leads to peace development and change.

References

Bainomugisha, A. and Rwengabo, S. (2016) 'The Promise and Efficacy of the East African Community', *Policy Research Series*. Kampala: ACODE, No. 41.

Brook, K., Rosemary, M. and Richard, S. (2002) *Poverty Knowledge and Policy Processes: A case Study of Ugandan National Poverty Reduction Policy.* Brighton: Institute of Development studies.

Dicklitch, S. (1998) *The Elusive Promise of NGOs in Africa. Lessons from Uganda.* Basingstoke, New York: Macmillan Press, St Martin's Press.

EAC (1984) 'The East African Community Mediation Agreement', in. Arusha: EAC.

EAC (1999) 'Treaty for the Establishment of the East African Community'. Arusha: EAC.

EAC (2001) 'Protocol on Decision Making by the Council of the East African Community', in. Arusha: EAC.

EAC (2004a) 'Protocol for the Establishment of the East African Customs Union', in. Arusha: EAC.

EAC (2004b) 'The East African Proposed Common External Tariff (CET): Brief on the Negotiations', in. Dar es Salaam: EAC.

EAC (2006) 'Strategy for Regional Peace and Security in the East African Community'. Arusha: EAC.

EAC (2009) *Minutes of the Meeting of the Consultative Committee on Cooperation in Defence Affairs: Report of the Meeting.* Arusha: AEC.

Galtung, J. (1965) 'Institutionalized Conflict Resolution: A Theoretical Paradigm', *Journal of Peace Research*, 2(4), pp. 348–397.

Gamu, J., Billon, P. Le and Spiegel, S. (2015) 'Extractive industries and poverty: A review of recent findings and linkage mechanisms', *The Extractive Industries and Society*, 2(1), pp. 162–176.

Herbst, J. (2000) *States and Power in Africa: Comparative Lessons in Authority and Control*. Princeton NJ: Princeton University Press.

Laursen, F. (2008) 'Theory and Practice of Regional Integration', *Jean Monnet/Robert Schuman Paper Series*, 8(3). Available at: http://aei.pitt.edu/8219/1/LaursenLongSympos08RegIntegedi.pdf.

Mansfield, D. E. and Milner, H. V. (1999) 'The New Wave of Regionalism', *International Organization*, 53(3), pp. 589–627.

Mattli, W. (2000) 'Sovereignty Bargains in Regional Integration', *International Studies Review*, 2(2).

Mitrany, D. (1965) 'The Prospect of European Integration. Federal or Functional', *Journal of Common Market Studies*, 4(2), pp. 119–149.

Mpumbani, G. (1999) 'In Search of Closer Cooperation: A Critique of the Revival of the East African Community'. Nairobi.

Muthaura, F. K. (no date) 'The Process for the East African Integration: A Seminar paper on Regional Integration'. Dar es Salaam.

Ogot, B. (2006) *My Footprints on the Sands of Time: An Autobiography*. Kisumu: Anyange Press Limited.

Oloka-Onyango, J. (2005) *Who Owns the East African Community?* Kampala: Presentation a DEVIVA Public Dialogue on the East African Community, Hotel Equatoria.

Olson, M. (1971) *The Logic of Collective Action: Public Goods and the Theory of Groups*. Cambridge Mas: Harvard University Press.

Olson, M. (1982) *The Rise and Decline of Nations: Economic Growth, Stagflation, and Social Rigidities*. New Haven and London: Yale University Press.

Rwengabo, S. (2015) 'From Migration Regime to Regional Citizenry: Migration and Identity Implications of the East African Common Market', *Eastern Africa Social Science Research Review*, 31(2), pp. 35–61.

Schiff, M. and Winters, A. L. (2003) *Regional Integration and Development*. Washington D.C.: World Bank and Oxford University Press.

Serunkuma, K. (1987) *Regional Corporation and Economic Integration in East Africa: Viability of the Economic Community*. Kampala: Makerere University.

Solingen, E. L. (1998) *Regionalism at Century's Dawn: Global and Domestic Influences on Grand Strategy*. Princeton, NJ: Princeton University Press.

Stefanova, B. (2006) 'Regional Integration as a System of Conflict Resolution: The European Experience', *World Affairs*, 169(2), pp. 81–93.

Tilly, C. (1990) *Coercion, Capital, and European States, A.D. 990–1990.* Cambridge, MA: Cambridge University Press.

Tralac (2005) *Start of the EAC Customs Union causes widespread confusion, Tralac.*

Umbricht, V. H. (1989) *Multilateral Mediation: Practical Experiences and Lessons.* The Hague: Martinus Nijhoff.

USAID-PSF (2005) *Trade Policy brief. Regional Trade arrangements EAC, COMESA, SADC and Cotonou Agreement.* Kampala: Private Sector Foundation.

Veit, P. (ed.) (1998) *Africa's Valuable Assets: A Reader in Natural Resource Management.* Washington D.C.: World Resources institute.

VOA (2009) *Opposition Leader's Hometown Suspicious of Ugandan Support for Kenyan President.* Washington D.C. Available at: https://www.voanews.com/a/a-13-2008-01-21-voa33/404489.html (Accessed: 1 November 2009).

Young, O. R. (1999) *Governance in World Affairs.* New York: Cornell University Press.

CHAPTER TEN

From Concept to Action: The Protection and Promotion of Farmers' Rights in East Africa

Ronald Naluwairo

Introduction

The adoption of the International Treaty on Plant Genetic Resources for Food and Agriculture (hereinafter referred to as "the Treaty") represents an important milestone in the protection of farmers' rights (United Nations, 2001). It represents international consensus on the need to recognize, protect and promote farmers' rights. The concept of farmers' right derives legitimacy from the important role farmers in all regions of the world have played over the millennia and continue to play in conserving, improving and making available plant genetic resources for food and agriculture which are the foundation of agricultural systems and food security in the world (United Nations, 2001).

Despite the international recognition of farmers' rights, many stakeholders in East Africa including policy and decision-makers who are charged with the responsibility of realizing these rights at the national level do not appreciate the nature and extent of these rights and the different options available for their realization. Often times, the debate on farmers' rights has always narrowed down to the farmers 'right to seed. Though one of the most important rights, the concept of farmers' rights includes other rights beyond the right to seed. This diffused and inadequate understanding of the concept of farmers' rights is hampering the design and development of effective mechanisms of effectively realizes these rights and their full benefits at the different levels.

This Chapter explores and analyses the concept of farmers' rights and makes a case for countries in East Africa to recognise and adequately protect farmers' rights. The Chapter also explores the different policy options or the protection and promotion of farmers' rights in East Africa.

The Chapter is comprised of 5 sections. Section 1 is the introduction. Section 2 explores the origins of farmers' rights. In detail, Section 3 analyses the concept of farmers' rights and highlights the differences between framers' rights and plant breeders' rights. In Section 4, a case is made why countries in East Africa should recognise and adequately protect farmers' rights. Section 5 discusses the farmers' rights provided for in the Treaty and discusses the different options for their protection and realization in East Africa.

The origins of farmers' rights: a historical exposition

It is difficult to understand the importance of farmers' rights without first understanding their origins. For this reason, as the foundation for the next section, this section explores the origins of farmers' rights. The concept of farmers' rights resulted from debates in the Food and Agriculture Organisation (FAO) that started in the early 1980s concerning the development of privately held intellectual property rights over plant genetic resources (Anderson, 2005). It resulted from the initiatives taken by FAO in promoting adherence to the International Undertaking on Plant Genetic Resources (hereinafter referred to as the Undertaking). FAO was concerned that a number of countries had expressed reservations to the Undertaking and that adherence to its provisions was generally poor.

Through its Commission on Plant Genetic Resources, FA Orecommended that the secretariat prepares a paper, for consideration by the Commission at its next session, analyzing the countries' reservations to the Undertaking and delineating possible courses of action, including suggestions for possible interpretations of the text to increase acceptance of the Undertaking. The Commission established two major reasons for the reservations and poor adherence to the treaty. The first reason related to the Undertaking's approach to plant genetic resources for food and agriculture as a common heritage of mankind which should be generally available without restriction and the second concerned the need to recognize plant breeders' rights (Anderson, 2005).

Recognition of plant breeders' rights therefore emerged as one of the ways of increasing adherence to the Undertaking. Debate about the need to recognize farmers' rights then started in response to the push for recognition of plant breeders'rights.

These debates were protracted and characterized by a lot of controversy, suspicion and uncompromising spirit between the developed world and the developing countries. The concern especially from the developing countries was the inequity of continuing the historical review of low germplasm from their countries to the developed industrialized countries which were seen as the major beneficiaries of plant breeders' rights. The developing countries also argued that extension of intellectual property rights over plant genetic resources was unjustified and unfair unless the farmers were rewarded first for their role in nurturing and making available these resources which are the foundation of modern plant breeding. They considered the formal breeders' role as mere "minor improvements" on varieties already developed by farmers and their local and indigenous communities. There was also concern that plant breeders 'rights would disrupt and destroy the customary practices of farmers to save, reuse, share and develop plant varieties; practices which were seen as a basis for their continued contribution to conservation and innovation in plant genetic resources (Anderson, 2005).

The developed countries on the other hand sought to justify the need for recognition of plant breeders' rights on the basis that their scientists invest a lot of time and money in research into techniques that enable them make genetic improvements. For that matter they needed to recoup their investment and be rewarded for their effort. They also argued that there was no concept either in national or international jurisprudence that would provide a sufficient basis for recognition of farmers' rights (FAO, 1986). In other respects, they argued that it was a fantasy to believe that the world's first farmers knew they were improving the value of species for mankind so as to justify the need to recognize their effort in nurturing and availing plant genetic resources.

In an effort to have a negotiated and acceptable solution, it was agreed that an interpretation to the Undertaking be provided that would recognize both plant breeders' rights and farmers' rights.Thus, by Resolution 4/89, the FAO Conference at its 25th Session in Rome provided an agreed interpretation to the

> **Five Key Things to Know about the Concept of Farmer's Rights**
>
> - It emerged as counterbalance to Plant Breeders' Rights
> - It is a political concept aimed at motivating farmers.
> - It is based on equity considerations and conservation concerns
> - It is intrinsically linked to Human Rights.
> - Farmers' rights are collective rights as opposed to individual rights.

Undertaking that recognized that plant breeders' rights as provided for by the International Convention for the Protection of New Varieties of Plants were not incompatible with the Undertaking (UPOV, 1961). The resolution simultaneously recognized farmers' rights which were subsequently defined in Conference Resolution 5/89. The concept of farmers' rights was thus introduced in the Undertaking as a response to the developed countries' pressure to recognize plant breeders' rights.

Resolution 5/89 defined the concept of Farmers' Rights in terms of the substantive grounds for the concept, the entities in which the rights are vested and the objectives for which they should be recognized (Moore and Witold, 2005). It defined farmers' rights as "rights arising from the past, present and future contribution of farmers in conserving, improving, and making available plant genetic resources, particularly those in centres of origin/diversity". It also provided that these rights were vested in the international community, as trustee for the present and future generation of farmers, for the purpose of ensuring full benefits to all farmers, and continuation of their contributions, as well as attainment of the overall purpose of the Undertaking.

FAO Conference Resolutions 4 and 5 were therefore landmark decisions in the history and struggle for recognition and protection of farmers' rights. These resolutions were however not binding nor did they provide any measures for realization of farmers' rights. Thus, in 1991, while adopting a new annex to the Undertaking, the FAO Conference in its Resolution 3/91 also provided that farmers' rights were to be implemented through an international fund on plant genetic resources. This Fund was supposed to support plant genetic conservation and utilization programmes. For reasons difficult to discern from available literature, this Fund never materialized. Within the Convention on Biological Diversity (CBD) negotiation and post negotiation processes, aspects of farmer's rights had been considered at different fora and in different contexts. There was however no major conclusion reached on the concept except Article 8(j) of the CBD which is an expression of agreement by the Parties to respect, preserve, maintain and promote traditional knowledge, innovations and practices of indigenous and local communities relevant to the conservation and sustainable use of biological diversity.

In May 1992, while adopting the agreed text of the Convention on Biological Diversity (CBD), countries also adopted Resolution 3 of the Nairobi Final Act. This Resolution recognized that access to existing collections not acquired in accordance with the Convention, and farmers' rights, were outstanding matters which the CBD had not addressed. It therefore called for solutions to be sought within FAO's Global System on the Conservation and Sustainable Use of Plant Genetic Resources for Food and Agriculture. It also urged for ways and means to be explored to develop complementarity and cooperation between the CBD and the FAO Global System on the Conservation and Sustainable Use of Plant Genetic Resources for Food and Agriculture.

In June 1992, the United Nations Conference on Environment and Development (UNCED) held in Rio-de-Janeiro called for the strengthening of the FAO Global System on the Conservation and Sustainable Use of Plant Genetic Resources for Food and Agriculture and its adjustment in line with the CBD, as well as taking further steps to realize farmers' rights (Meakin, 1992).

Accordingly, the FAO Conference requested the Director General of FAO to provide a forum for negotiations on revision of the Undertaking and adapting it in harmony with the CBD as well as considering the issue of realization of farmers' rights. Negotiations to the above effect commenced in November 1994 and in April 1999, the Commission on Plant Genetic Resources for Food and Agriculture at its 8th Regular Session agreed to establish a Contact Group to continue the process. Within the Contact Group, countries negotiated and agreed on three major Articles of the Undertaking including Article 15 which was later adopted into Article 9 of the Treaty which provides for recognition, protection and promotion of farmers' rights.

Understanding the concept of farmers' rights

The concept of farmers' rights generally emerged as a counter balance to the increased demand for plant breeders' rights in international negotiations. It is premised on the fact that all modern plant breeding is in one way or another based on plant genetic resources developed, nurtured and made available by farmers over the generations. The concept therefore came into view to draw international attention to the unremunerated innovations of farmers that were seen as the foundation of all modern plant breeding (Anderson, 2005).

The plant genetic resources and associated knowledge that farmers and their local and indigenous communities have nurtured, developed and conserved are not the product of any single farmer or farming community but are collective products of many farming communities developed through many generations worldover Farmers' rights are thus collective rights as opposed to individual rights.

The rationale for farmers' rights is to provide farmers and farming communities rewards for their contribution to agro-biodiversity and give them incentives to continue improving and making available plant genetic resources for food and agriculture which are the foundation of modern plant breeding and sustainable agriculture. The concept of farmers' rights is therefore based on equity considerations and conservation concerns. It is an acknowledgement that farmers and their local and indigenous communities are innovators too and as such deserve recognition and rewards just as the formal plant breeders do.

The concept of farmers' rights thus emerged as part of the international political effort to correct the inequity created by the growing use and expansion of intellectual property rights to plant genetic resources than as a legal or property right (Bragdon et al., 2005). It does not therefore necessarily create any legal obligations per-se on state parties to the Treaty or any one unless and until the individual national Governments decide so within the meaning of Article 9.2 of the Treaty. It is a political motivation to farmers and farming communities to continue nurturing, conserving and making available plant genetic resources for food and agriculture.

Farmers' rights differ significantly from plant breeder's rights. Plant breeders' rights are a form of intellectual property rights created to provide incentives especially to the private sector actors to engage in plant breeding. They are defined by the International Convention for the Protection of New Varieties of Plants as exclusive rights granted to a person over the commercial production and marketing of reproductive or vegetative propagating material of the protected variety.

Farmers' rights on the other hand are rights arising from the past, present and future contribution of farmers in conserving, improving and making available plant genetic resources which are the basis of modern plant breeding and the foundation of agriculture systems and food security in the world. Farmers' rights are thus collective rights as opposed to individual rights.

The demand for protection of plant breeders' rights particularly in developing countries arose from the conclusion of the General Agreement on Tariffs and Trade (GATT) Uruguay Round and its agreement on Trade Related Aspects of Intellectual Property Rights (TRIPS) at Marrakech in 1994. The TRIPS Agreement obliged the members of GATT (now World Trade Organisation) to provide some form of intellectual property protection on plant varieties either through patents or some "effective sui-generis system or by any combination thereof". Since then, countries party to the TRIPs Agreement that had no protection for new plant varieties started on the process of fulfilling their newly incurred international obligation to provide such protection. This has mainly been by way of recognizing plant breeders' rights. Thus, whereas the origins of protection of plant breeders' rights in most developing countries are to be found in TRIPs and are therefore trade related, farmers' rights are recognized and provided for in the Treaty and other instruments dealing with the conservation and sustainable use of biodiversity. They are largely based on the need to reward farmers and provide them with incentives to continue nurturing, improving, conserving and making available plant genetic resources for food and agriculture.

Distinguishing Farmers' Rights from Plant Breeders' Rights

	Plant Breeders Rights	Farmers Rights
Type of Rights	They are a form of intellectual property rights that are exclusive in nature	They are collective rights
Ownership of Rights	Rights awarded to Individuals	Vested in communities to be held in trust for the present and future
Extent of the Rights	Rights limited to a particular plant variety	A bundle of rights that extend to plant genetic resources for food and agriculture
Scope of the Such Rights	Rights recognize a single step as long as the variety is "new" and clearly distinguishable from any other variety whose existence is a matter of common knowledge	Rights recognize the Cumulative intellectual contributions of many Preceding and successive generations of farmers
Duration	Unlimited	Unlimited

Why countries in East Africa should protect farmers' rights?

Agro-biodiversity considerations

One of the major reasons why countries in East Africa should protect farmers' rights is in the very reason for their international recognition. The basis for the international recognition of farmers' rights lies in the enormous contribution that the local and indigenous communities and farmers of all regions of the world have made and will continue to make in the conservation, sustainable use and development of plant genetic resources which constitute the foundation of agriculture production and development throughout the world (United Nations, 2001). Smallholder farmers in East Africa and their farming communities are undoubtedly part of those world farmers that have enormously contributed and are still contributing to nurturing, enhancing and making available plant genetic resources which are the foundation of modern plant breeding and agricultural development. Over the years, through their various farming techniques, innovations and practices, they have developed and continue to develop many plant varieties and adopt existing ones to suit different environments and climatic conditions. In this way, the farmers enrich and contribute to the sustainable management of agricultural biodiversity which is key for agricultural production. As Andersen put it,

> …the realization of farmers' rights is a precondition for the maintenance of crop genetic diversity which is the basis of all food and agricultural production in the world (Anderson, 2009).

Through protection of their traditional knowledge relevant to plant genetic resources and ensuring that farmers and their communities benefit from the utilization of plant genetic resources, farmers' and community rights therefore represent a strategic instrument for ensuring the continuation of the farmers' practices of nurturing, maintaining and enriching agro-biodiversity (Anderson, 2009). This is very important for ensuring the future availability of diversity of plant genetic resources which are the foundation of agriculture development and food production. Future availability of diversity of plant genetic resources is critical given that the region's biological resources are getting lost and eroded at very alarming levels, moreover at a time when the region's population growth is raising very fast.

Food security and sood sovereignty considerations

Perhaps the most important justification why countries in East Africa should protect farmers' rights lies in the need to ensure food security and food sovereignty. Since majority of farmers in East Africa and their communities are very poor people who cannot afford to buy commercial seeds every planting season, they rely on their traditional system of seed saving, reusing and exchange as the most important source of seed supply for agricultural production. This system, backward as it may be branded, has been very instrumental in contributing to household and national food security for centuries (Republic of Uganda, 2003). In particular, the farmers' system of seed saving, reusing and exchange has helped to ensure that farmers and their communities maintain sovereignty and control over their systems of food production, distribution and supply.

With the advent of genetic engineering techniques, which are monopolistically controlled by the big multinational companies based in the industrialized countries (Ekpere, 2000), the protection of plant breeders' rights without the effective protecti-on of the farmers' rights to save, reuse, exchange and sell their farm-saved seed and propagating material threatens to remove local and national control over seed and food production and place it into the hands of multinational corporations. This spells doom in terms of ensuring household, national and regional food security.

National security considerations

Closely linked with the need to ensure food security is the question of national security. Food sovereignty/security is one of the most important guarantees for ensuring national security. A nation that does not produce its own seed and food cannot be considered a secure country. Ensuring that farmers and their local communities maintain control over their systems of seed and food production, distribution and supply should therefore be considered a very important strategy for ensuring national and regional security.

Poverty reduction strategy

Poverty eradication remains one of the biggest development challenges for countries in East Africa. Over 80% of East Africa's poor live in rural areas and depend on farming to meet their every day needs and survival. Despite their enormous contribution to national GDPs, East Africa's farmers and their rural communities remain undoubtedly some of the poorest and most vulnerable group in society. One of the major objectives of farmers' rights is to ensure that farmers and their communities fairly and equitably share in the benefits derived from the utilization of plant genetic resources. These benefits can be monetary or non-monetary. The benefits range from access to and transfer of technology to exchange of information, capacity building and sharing of monetary and other benefits arising from commercialization. The protection and effective realization of farmers' rights to the fair and equitable sharing of benefits arising from the utilization of plant genetic resources can therefore immensely contribute to the fight against poverty in the region. Also, the protection and effective realization of the farmers' right to save, use, exchange and sell their farm produce and other propagating materials means that the farmers can save a lot in terms of not having to buy commercial seeds and the necessary inputs from the market each planting season. This can therefore also be one important way in which the protection of farmers' rights can help in the fight against poverty which remains one of East Africa's major development challenge.

Farmers' rights under the treaty and the possible options for their realization

The Treaty affirms that the basis of farmers' rights is their past, present and future contributions to the conservation, improvement and sustainable use of plant genetic resources for food and agriculture. It recognizes in particular the enormous contribution that the local and indigenous communities and farmers of all regions of the world, particularly those in the centers of origin and crop diversity, have made

> **Elements of Farmers' Rights under the Treaty**
>
> - Protection of traditional knowledge relevant to plant genetic resources for food and agriculture
> - Equitable sharing of benefits arising from use of plant genetic resources for food and agriculture
> - Participation in decision making processes touching on the conservation and sustainable use of plant genetic resources for food and agriculture
> - The right to save, use, exchange and sell farm saved seed/propagating material of farmers' varieties

and will continue to make in the conservation and development of plant genetic resources which constitute the basis of food and agriculture production throughout the world. The Treaty therefore recognizes the effective realization of farmers' rights as key in ensuring food security and sustainable agriculture.

It enumerates the possible elements of farmers' rights and vests the responsibility for their realization at national level in individual Governments. National Governments are encouraged to take appropriate measures to protect and promote farmers' rights in accordance with their needs and priorities. Strictly interpreted, Article 9.2 of the Treaty shows that implementing and realizing farmers' rights is not an international legal obligation on the member States per se (United Nations, 2001). It is a mere moral obligation which member States may or may not take on as they so wish "in accordance with their national needs and priorities and subject to their national legislation". National Governments are however encouraged to take measures to protect and promote these rights in accordance with their needs and priorities. Such measures could include development of national policies, legal and institutional frameworks for realization of these rights and their benefits. The measures could also include support and assistance to farmers and their local and indigenous communities.

Although the Treaty provision on protection of farmers' rights may not amount to an international obligation on member states, countries in East Africa have everything to gain out of their realization. These rights if effectively implemented and realized have great potential to address some of East Africa's chronic problems including poverty, disease and food insecurity among others. These countries should therefore embrace these rights and incorporate them in national policy, legislation and development planning processes.

The elements enumerated by the Treaty for the realization of farmers' rights include: the protection of farmers' traditional knowledge relevant to plant genetic resources for food and agriculture, participating in decision making processes regarding plant genetic resources for food and agriculture, the right to save, use exchange and sell farm saved seeds and the equitable sharing of benefits arising from utilization of plant genetic resources for food and agriculture.

Protection of traditional knowledge

The need to protect traditional knowledge as it relates to plant genetic resources for food and agriculture arose from the recognition that current intellectual property rights regimes, in particular plant breeders' rights do not recognize and reward the local communities of farmers whose knowledge, innovations and practices play an important role in nurturing and making available plant genetic resources which are the basis of modern plant breeding. Concern over the rapid loss of traditional knowledge and the need to promote such knowledge in ensuring conservation and sustainable use of plant genetic resources were also big issues that informed and shaped the debates leading to the recognition and protection of the farmers' right to their traditional knowledge in the Treaty.

What amounts to "traditional knowledge" has been a subject of considerable discussion and although the debate is not yet completely resolved, there is now a generally acceptable agreement of what it entails. Traditional knowledge comprises knowledge which has been developed by local communities over generations, but which still continues to be developed. The debate regarding protection of traditional knowledge has also revolved around the difference (if any) and relevancy of the distinction between traditional knowledge and local & indigenous knowledge (Crucible Group, 2002). Whatever the difference, many international instruments, organizations and processes have recognized the need to recognize, protect and promote traditional knowledge of farmers and their local and indigenous communities. The CBD for instance recognizes and asserts that the knowledge, innovations and practices of indigenous and local communities are essential for the conservation and sustainable use of biodiversity and that they must be recognized and protected.

The protection of traditional knowledge has also been a subject of discussion in other international organizations such as World Intellectual Property Organization (WIPO), World Trade Organization (WTO), World Health Organization (WHO), United Nations Educational Social Cultural Organisation (UNESCO) to mention but a few (Commission of Intellectual Property Rights, 2002). The discussions in these bodies are considering promoting and protecting traditional knowledge in different contexts but th e common thread in all these efforts is to enable the local and indigenous communities and their people benefit from their knowledge and have a say on how, by whom and when it should be used.

The obligation to protect and promote traditional knowledge by the Treaty is intended among other things to enable the indigenous and traditional people benefit from their knowledge. It is also intended to compensate indigenous and traditional communities for their role in nurturing, conservation and sustainable use of plant genetic resources. The protection of traditional knowledge is therefore a critical element in the equitable sharing of benefits arising from use of plant genetic resources for food and agriculture. National Governments are therefore encouraged to put in place mechanisms for the recognition, protection and compensation of knowledge and innovations of traditional communities.

Although the debate on how to recognize and protect traditional knowledge has been on-going for over two decades now, final universally acceptable solution to achieve such objective has not emerged. But what is generally acceptable is that, because of its nature, the best way of protecting and promo-ting traditional knowledge is through development of a sui generis system of protection and rewards that takes into account the peculiarities of traditional knowledge as it relates to plant geneticresour-ces for food and agriculture. Such system should among other things define what traditional knowledge relevant to plant genetic resources for food and agriculture is and should stipulate the conditions for the grant of the protection/ rights. The sui-generis system should also specify the rights to be conferred and those entitled to such rights. In order to be effective, the system should also have criminal and civil sanctions for the violators of the rights conferred (Crucible Group, 2002).

> **Nature of Traditional Knowledge**
> Traditional knowledge comprises knowledge which has been developed by local communities over generations, but which still continues to be developed. It is not static; it evolves and generates new information as a result of improvements and adaptation to changing circumstances

Effective protection of traditional knowledge would also require national Gover-nments to enact mandatory Requirements of disclosure of the source of germplasm used, in the application procedures for plant breeders' and other suigeneris rights touching on plant genetic resources for fo od and agriculture. Where such germplasm belongs to a local community or group of

> **Challenges in Developing a Sui-Generis System for Protection of TK**
> - Defining Traditional Knowledge
> - Requirements for protection
> - Rights to be conferred
> - Entitlement to rights
> - Modes of acquisition
> - Duration
> - Enforcement measures

farmers, evidence of Prior Informed Consent (PIC) for its use and arrangements for the equitable sharing of benefits should also be required. The customary laws and practices and the knowledge governance systems of traditional communities should also be recognized and reinforced (Crucible Group, 2002). Documentation of traditional knowledge relating to plant genetic resources for food and agriculture would also go a long way in addressing its rapid loss and promoting its wider use.

The Right to Equitable Sharing in the Benefits of PGRFA

The right to equitable sharing of benefits arising from use of plant genetic resources for food and agriculture is one of the main cornerstones of farmers' rights. Farmers' rights were adopted to allow farmers, their communities, and countries in all regions, to participate fully in the benefits derived, at present and in the future, from the improved use of plant genetic resources, through plant breeding and other scientific methods. This aspect of farmers' rights directly flows from the major objectives of the Treaty and the CBD (United Nations, 2001).

There is increasing evidence that economic returns of trade in genetic resources and particularly plant genetic resources for food and agriculture has been steadily rising over the last decades yet the local communities and farmers who nurture and supply these resources have received insignificant or no benefit at all (Chishakwe and Young, no date). The farmers' right to equitably participate in the benefits arising from the utilization of plant genetic resources for food and agriculture is therefore intended to enable farmers to share in the productivity and profitability of these resources. This right to equitable sharing of benefits applies in relation to the results of research and development and the benefits arising from the commercial and other utilization of plant genetic resources for food and agriculture (Correa, 2000). These benefits can generally be classified as monetary and non-monetary and could range from sharing financial benefit to exchange of information, access to and transfer of technology and capacity building (United Nations, 2001).

Benefit sharing may also be implemented through farmers' access to funds arising from taxes or levies associated with trade in seeds, or through other charges imposed on breeders that benefit from farmers' contributions (Correa, 2000). The success of this option would however require mechanisms to ensure that the seed industry does not shift the burden of such taxes and levies to the farming communities through charging high price for the seed. The regulatory authorities would therefore be expected to monitor and control the pricing system. For this option to work well also, national patents, plant breeders' rights and other seed laws should establish the obligation to reveal the source of genetic material used for creation of the new variety and where it belongs to farmers and or their local and indigenous communities evidence of PIC and benefit sharing arrangements.

The other option for ensuring equitable sharing of benefits is for farmers and their local and indigenous communities to negotiate for joint ownership of intellectual property related rights over new plant varieties. This mechanism will ensure that farmers and their communities share in the royalties of the commercial exploitation of the particular variety. For this option to be successful however, farmers and their communities should have the capacity to monitor the sales and other means of exploitation of such varieties. They should also have capacity to enforce their rights under the joint ownership arrangement in case of violation.

Equitable sharing of benefits could also entail supporting and assisting farmers' programmes, projects and other initiatives aimed at encouraging innovations, conservation and sustainable use of plant genetic resources for food and agriculture. For this purpose, it may be necessary for the farmers and their local and indigenous communities to establish funds where national Governments, the international community and other entities could make their contribution towards such programmes and initiatives.

The Right to Participate in Decision Making Processes

The right to participate in decision making processes extends to taking part in decision making at the national level, on matters related to the conservation and sustainable use of plant genetic resources for food and agriculture. This right is premised on the fact that in many countries particularly in the developing world, farmers generally but in particular the vulnerable group of farmers which comprise the women, youth and the old are marginalized and discriminated against in critical decision making processes regarding plant genetic resources for food and agriculture. As such, their efforts and innovations in plant genetic resources management are hardly recognized and their specific needs and priorities are often not adequately provided for in national policy (Moore and Witold, 2005).

The farmers' right to participate in decision making processes therefore calls for mechanisms and strategies to be put in place that will ensure the effective and equitable participation of farmers in the development and implementation of plans, policies, programmes and processes concerning plant genetic resources for food and agriculture. Taking part in decision making processes is part and parcel of the farmers' democratic rights. However, for farmers to be able to effectively enjoy this right, there are a number of things that have to be guaranteed. These include: access to information, capacity building, strong and well organized farmer groups and ability to read and write among others. Unless Governments in the region address these issues, the farmers' right to participate in decision making processes would largely remain a myth. Appointing farmers and/or their representatives to critical policy decision making organs is also one practical way of having farmers participate in making decisions related to the conservation and sustainable use of plant genetic resources for food and agriculture at the national level.

The Right to Save, Use, Exchange and Sell Farm Saved Seed/Propagating Material

Seeds are the first and most essential input into any agricultural based production system in the world. They are the foundation of agriculture and food security. In East Africa where over 80% of the region's population live on agriculture, the right to save, use, exchange and sell farm saved seed becomes a very critical economic issue to the population's welfare and livelihood security.

Seed saving is not just an activity of keeping seeds for the next planting but is intimately linked to a whole gamut of cultural traditions, social relationships and economic support systems that characterize and allow farmers and farming communities to survive and adapt through generations (Borja, 2005). Thus other than their importance to food security and agriculture production system, seeds constitute a strong social and cultural bond among farmers and between communities. It has helped define and reinforce kinship, friendship and solidarity among farmers through sharing and exchange of seeds (Borja, 2005). Seed saving is also a very important economic resource for farmers. It translates into economic savings for farmers who do not have to purchase from other farmers or from the market.

Despite its importance to the social, economic, cultural and political wellbeing of farmers and their communities, the right to seed in the Treaty is limited to matters pertaining to plant genetic resources for food and agriculture. The right is recognized and protected within the context of securing the farmers' customary practices of saving, reusing and exchanging seed as a basis of ensuring their continued contribution to the conservation and innovation in plant genetic resources. The importance that the Treaty accords the farmers' right to seed cannot be overemphasized. It provides that "Nothing in this Article shall be interpreted to limit any rights that farmers have to save, use, exchange and sell farm-saved seed/propagating material" (United Nations, 2001, article 9.3). The Treaty however subjects the farmers' right to seed to "national law and as appropriate" meaning that Governments have the absolute discretion to determine whether or not to recognize and protect the right, the extent of protection if any and the means of protection.

Given the importance of this right as highlighted above, countries in East Africa should not lose any opportunity to put in place mechanisms and strategies that ensure that their farmers' right to seed is guaranteed. Such measures could include securing the farmers' right to seed in plant breeders' legislation, seed legislation and other sui generis plant variety legislation. In such legislation it would also be important depending on the extent of protection accorded to the right, to render null and void any transaction that would require farmers to give up their right. The biggest challenge that national Governments face in implementing this component of farmers' rights is how to reconcile this right with plant breeders' rights when it comes to protected plant varieties.

There is a strong belief among a cross section of stakeholders that the unrestricted use of intellectual property rights protected material by farmers will erode the incentives to commercial breeding and create a threat to future world food security (Correa, 2000). One solution to this challenge could be to provide for varying exceptions in plant breeders' legislation that allow different categories of farmers reuse protected seeds in varying proportions (Correa, 2000). This would however require careful analysis before determining the categories of farmers, the nature of exceptions and how the entire arrangement would be monitored and enforced.

It is important to note that the elements of farmers' rights enumerated in the Treaty are not exclusive. The language used indicates that farmers' rights under the Treaty are inclusive. This therefore gives room to national governments to provide for more rights as they deem appropriate according to their national needs and priorities. In addition to the rights provided for under the Treaty, the African Model Law on the Protection of the Rights of Local Communities, Farmers and Breeders, and for Regulations of Access to Biological Resources (hereinafter referred to as the Model Law) provides for more rights to be protected under the framework of farmers' rights. These include: the farmers' right to; use a new breeders' variety protect-ted to develop farmers' varieties, including material obtained from gene banks or plant genetic resource centers; and collectively save, use, multiply and process farm-saved seed of protected varieties. In addition, the model law recognizes farmers' varieties and breeds and accords them protection under the rules of practice as found in, and recognized by the customary practices and laws of the concerned local farming communities, whether such laws are written or not. In this regard, the model law provides further that a variety with specific attributes identified by a community shall be granted intellectual protection through a variety certificate which does not have to meet the criteria of distinction, uniformity and stability.

Major Challenges in Realization of Farmers' Rights at National Level

- Inadequate awareness and lack of sufficient knowledge pertaining to farmers' rights
- Economic and political obstacles
- Inadequate legislation and policies
- Weak implementation capacity
- External pressure and influence of multi-national seed companies
- Inadequate advocacy and lobbying by CSOs
- Threats from Genetically Modified Organisms.

Source: Anderson R (2005)

Conclusion

The international recognition of farmers' rights presents enormous opportunities to countries in East Africa in particular and Africa in general. The struggle for realization of these rights and their benefits in national and regional development is however just beginning. Given the controversial history of the negotiations for these rights and the manner in which they are provided for in the Treaty, it is likely that countries and

---

corporate entities that were opposed to their recognition will continue to fight their effective protection.

The most important thing however, is that the Treaty has given national Governments the opportunity and responsibility to implement these rights in accordance with their needs, priorities and national law. The challenge is therefore for the countries in East Africa to seize this opportunity and devise effective mechanisms for the protection and promotion of these rights. This Chapter has

Key Issues to Consider in Realizing the Farmers' Rights
▪ Supporting & Facilitating the Formation of Farmer Group ▪ Guaranteeing the right of access to information ▪ Capacity building ▪ Working towards creation of a literate Class of Farmers ▪ Appointing farmers and their epresentatives to key decision-making bodies.

explored some of the options available to these countries in the above regard. Given that farmers and farming communities in East Africa share a lot in common, taking a regional approach along the lines of the African Model Law is highly recommended.

References

Anderson, R. (2005) *The History of Farmers' Rights: A Guide to Central Documents and Literature.* Lysaker: The Fridtjof Nansen Institute.

Anderson, R. (2009) *Information paper on Farmers' Rights submitted by the Fridtjof Nansen Institute, Norway, based on the Farmers' Rights Project".* *Third Session of the Governing Body of the International Treaty on Plant Genetic Resources for Food and Agriculture.* Tunis. Available at: http://www.farmersrights.org/pdf/FNI-infopaper-on-FR-GB3.pdf (Accessed: 14 September 2017).

Borja, P. (2005) 'Terminator Seeds: Terminating Farmers Rights?"', in *IS GURTS (Terminator) the Answer to Transgene Contamination?* Montreal: ETC Group.

Bragdon, S., Fowler, Z., Franca and Goldberg, E. (2005) *Law and Policy of Relevancy to the Management of Plant Genetic Resources.* Rome: International Plant Genetic Institute and the International Food Policy Research Institute.

Chishakwe, N. and Young, T. R. (no date) 'Access to Genetic Resources, and Sharing the Benefits of their Use: International and Sub-regional Issues', pp. 1–18.

Commission of Intellectual Property Rights (2002) *Integrating Intellectual Property Rights and Development Policy*. London: CIPR.

Correa, C. (2000) *Options for the Implementation of Farmers' Rights at the National Level.*

Crucible Group (2002) *Seeding Solutions: Options for National Laws Governing Access and Control Over Genetic Resources and Biological Innovations.*

Ekpere, J. A. (2000) *The Protection of the Rights of Local Communities. Farmers and Breeders, and for the Regulation of Access to Biological Resources: An Explanatory Booklet*. Lagos: Organization of African Unity.

FAO (1986) *Progress Report on the International Undertaking on Plant Genetic Resources. CPGR/87/4*. Rome: FAO.

Meakin, S. (1992) 'Agenda 21, the Rio Declaration and the Convention on Biological Diversity', in. Available at:
http://publications.gc.ca/collections/Collection-R/LoPBdP/BP/bp317-e.htm.

Moore, G. and Witold, T. (2005) 'Explanatory Guide to the International Treaty on Plant Genetic Resources for Food and Agriculture', *IUNC Environmental Policy and Law Paper*. Gland VD, (57).

Republic of Uganda (2003) 'The Uganda Food and Nutrition Policy, Ministry of Agriculture, Animal Industry and Fisheries and Ministry of Health, Section 1.3'.

United Nations (2001) *The International Treaty on Plant Genetic Resources for Food and Agriculture*. New York: UN.

UPOV (1961) *International Convention for Protection of New Varieties of Plants*. Geneva: UPOV.

CHAPTER ELEVEN

Community-Based Property Rights in East Africa

Godber W. Tumushabe and Sabastiano Rwengabo

Introduction

The world over, indigenous, mobile, and local communities have, for millennia, played a critical role in conserving the earth's patrimony: protecting forests, wetlands, rangelands, marshlands, hunting grounds, watersheds, rivers and other ecological systems. These resources are the basis of prosperity for today's nations. "Community" husbandry of these resources has been done for wide-ranging reasons: economic, cultural, spiritual, aesthetic and so on. Near consensus now obtains amongst analysts that conservation and sustainable use of these resources is much older and perhaps more effective than contemporary government practices of "exclusion", "participation" and other "jargons" being used in modern-day conservation literature. Despite the acknowledged and recognized contribution of indigenous communities to the science and practice of natural-resource conservation, the growth of governmental institutions as the dominant authority in conservation seriously threatens these long-held notions. In this context, the concept of Community-Based Property Rights (CBPR) has attracted interest in scholarship and advocacy as a means of articulating, clarifying, and securing the livelihoods of these communities.

In spite of this attention, national policies and laws either pay "lip service" to CPBR or entirely undermine and violate the right of such communities to access, control, and own these resources. The meaning and practice of conservation is manipulated in favour of powerful actors, such as states, multinational investment companies, and powerful local and regional elites. This chapter develops a theoretical understanding of CBPRs grounded in traditional principles of modern property rights theory and conservation practice. The study also explores implications of CBPRs for sustainable development in East Africa, as well as for conducting policy-relevant empirical research on the applications of CBPR. At present, there is lack of clarity on the meaning of CBPR among policymakers and practitioners. The resulting policy distortion, with respect to the usage and application of CBPR, undermines the recognition, protection, and promotion of these rights. This marginalization and disenfranchisement, which keep affected communities in perpetual poverty, threatens regional peace and stability.

The starting point for this theoretical analysis is the specification of the concept of property as it relates to other putative concepts and CBR. Then the legal basis of CBPR is outlined, before examining the relevance of CBPR for peaceful development in East Africa. The conclusion summarises these ideas and outlines a possible research agenda.

The Concept of Property

The mention of "property" intuitively evokes ideas of wealth, entitlement, possession, and resource ownership. The debate on the nature and meaning of property, and the rights that accrue to those entitled to property, has been with us since time immemorial. In property rights theory, it is important to ask and perhaps answer at least four inter-related questions with a strong bearing on CBPR: (i) What are the sources of property rights?, (ii) What happens in cases of competing property rights?, (iii) What is the historic origin of property law? and (iv) Does distributive justice apply to property?

Let us start with Talmudic and Biblical times. The author(s) of the book of Genesis mentions that God gave the earth to man for his support, comfort, and wellbeing. Accordingly, property in the world, call it "world wealth", was originally granted by God to man. In theosophical and moral terms, the presumed mysteries of life and nature are to be grasped by referring to God's relationship with man: as grantor, provider; and man as receiver, caretaker, and subduer. This divine grant forms the basis for property relations. Man is, theosophically speaking, entitled to nature because God grants man such entitlement. Discrimination, denial, and exclusion defy divine and natural laws: they negate, violate, the laws of God. Thus, post-Genesis developments related to man's relationship with nature and fellow man, and which entail discriminatory ownership and control over nature's generosity to humanity, are rooted in selfishness that is anti-nature (though possibly not unnatural to man) and rooted in evil. The writings of thinkers like Aristotle, Hugo Grotius, and John Locke, show an evolving rigorous and intellectually dynamic debate on the issue of property in general and property rights in particular (Grotius, 2001).

Grotius bases his conception of property on the "social contract", a relational form of existence in which human beings exchange their consent and some of their freedoms to a more powerful body of human beings, Hobbes calls it the Leviathan (Hobbes, 1999), in exchange for the protection of their remaining human rights. This implies that some rights have been threatened in a natural human world: the social contract and the resulting Leviathan are indicative of human selfishness which engenders Hobbesian threats, a war of man against man. For Grotius, entry into a social contract has the effect of intensifying the freedom and rights of citizens; one of these rights affects property ownership. He suggests that originally all things were in a class of *res nullius*, a situation of non-ownership in which everyone may lay claim to, and possess, a property yet no one owns it before such possession. With the coming in force of the social contract there is introduced a general agreement for the division of material goods among individuals. The processes by which property is defined appear, and are refined, at a relatively later stage in man's social development. They include: division by individual participation in the agreement by which specific acquisitions are made; discovery or acquisition; and/or lawful acquisition from persons who have exercised their natural rights of disposition (Grotius, 2001).

John Locke justifies property rights by arguing that individuals who take action, who mix their labor [and intelligence] with natural resources, become entitled to the property and are protected in controlling the fruits of their labours–akin to the biblical reaping where one sowed. Hebases this entitlement on the moral imperative of rights, and the utilitarian ground that legal protection for property justly produced or possessed through labor promotes useful work and increases social welfare (Locke, 1690). This assertion apparently found support in an 1805 case of Pierson v. Post. In this case, Post was chasing a fox. Suddenly Pierson popped out of nowhere, killed the fox, and took it away. Post sued Pierson, claiming right ownership of the fox: he had been chasing it. The trial court ruled in favor of Post. Pierson appealed. On appeal, the question was whether ownership is established by active pursuit, physical capture, or mortal wounding. In the case, both parties agree that possession or labor, in some form, establishes ownership rights. But Locke and other utilitarian philosophers also recognize the essence of collective rights. They advocate appropriation of one's labor through guarantees of property rights, but argue that labor creates rights "at least where there is enough and as good left in common for others" (Locke, 1690, page 17). This tended to subject private property interests to the interests of the common good. So, beyond principles of labour and possession, Lockean theory believes in protection of the "common good" where questions of individual property rights are at issue.

Related to "common good" is John Rawls' concept of "primary social goods". Rawls argues that participants in the social contract intend to evolve their charter on the basis of rationality. The communal structure which evolves as a result of the "reflective equilibrium" of the group is concerned with the rational distribution of "primary social goods"–those goods which a rational person is presumed to want more of; which have a use whatever may be a person's rational life-plan; whose distribution is always a matter of concern. Rawls' primary social goods include: rights and liberties, opportunities and powers, income and wealth. Later Rawls added self-respect, covering a person's sense of his own value, his secure conviction that his good, his plan, or life, is worth carrying out (Rawls, 1971). This discourse suggests that property rights can be derived from formal and informal sources, natural and man-made processes.

Appropriation, through labor, possession, or government grants, is possibly the commonest formal source of property rights. On the other hand, informal sources may include "adverse possession" and acquisition of property rights through social arrangements such as family relationships. The principle of adverse possession holds that if an owner visibly occupies property for long enough a period of time, that person becomes the owner, taking away the title from the "true owner." Whatever the form of acquisition, property has two fundamental attributes: possession, that is, control over a resource based on the practical inability of another to contradict the ends of the possessor of that property; and title, the expectation that others will recognize one's right to control a resource, even when it is not in one's possession. Once established, full property ownership entitles the property-holder to four basic entitlements or a bundle of rights: (i) the right to use or benefit from the property (a right common among advocates of private or individual property rights).Scholars like Adam Smith argue that the expectation of profit from "improving one's stock of capital" rests on private property rights–rights which encourage property holders to develop their property, generate wealth, and efficiently allocate resources based on market operations; (ii) exclusion rights, the entitlement to exclude others from the enjoyment of that property; (iii) immunity from loss without one's consent; and (iv) the power to transfer the property to others.

The literature tends to emphasize private property rights as opposed to other rights. Therefore, current notions of property put much emphasis on protecting individual property owners. This approach addresses the conditions under which citizens may get property but does not include the premise that certain structural conditions are needed to offer everyone the right to get property. This view focuses on individuals and the actions they must take to acquire property rights that will then be defended by the state (Singer, 1997). Property theory also suggests that one can lose property in different ways. Since the state is vested with power to regulate property relations, state authority includes the power to take away property from an individual in one way or the other. This may take the form of confiscation, exercise of the power of eminent domain, fines, regulatory fees or costs and zoning restrictions.

However, history is replete with examples of successful resistance to state attempts to deprive owners of their property unless full, fair, adequate and timely compensation has been paid and/or state acquisition is intended for public purposes (Republic of Uganda, 1995). Contrarily, compulsory takings of lands that historically belonged to indigenous and minority communities, including through forceful evictions and "enclosures", especially in Africa, has been common. During colonial occupation, indigenous communities were forced off their lands and these lands given to the colonial state and Caucasian settlers in countries like Kenya, Zimbabwe, South Africa. The post-colonial state in Africa joined in: indigenous and minority communities, such as the Bennet, Batwa and the Basongora in Uganda, and the Mungiki and Saboat in Kenya, have lost their ancestral lands through state takings in the bid to create protected areas and other programs. In this regard, a re-thinking of the theory and practice of CBPRs provides a useful vehicle to initiate a fresh dialogue in policy and practice to address the injustice and human rights violations that have been inflicted on these communities.

Putative Concepts Linked to CBPR

The concept of CBPR remains elusive mainly because it is often confused or used interchangeably with related concepts, such as Common Property or Common Pool Resources (CPR), Community-

Based Natural Resources Management (CBNRM), Collaborative Forest Management (CFM) in forestry or Community Conservation in wildlife. These concepts themselves differ. They have been at the centre of the discourse on the merits and demerits of state or private property regimes in the management of the environment and natural resources. Tenkir Bonger observes that the dichotomy between state and private property regimes is colored and mystified by broader ideological and geo-political controversies. Proponents of privatization of natural resources management suggest that market dynamics, coupled with long-term security of tenure, provide the best incentive for their sustainable use and efficient management. On the other hand, proponents of state management regimes counter by laying emphasis on equity considerations or collective societal interests in CPR (Bonger, 1999). What Bonger and others do not explain is how each of these two regimes relates to the long-held African traditional conceptions of property which were largely premised on collective self-assertion and protection of the common good for all–the fundamental basis of CBPR.

The concept of CPR itself dominated public policy discourse since Garrett Hardin published "The Tragedy of the Commons." Hardin's rationality thesis is used to explain overexploitation of key shared resources, including deforestation, over-fishing, overgrazing, and abuse of public lands and generally misallocation of resources. The "tragedy of the commons" is this: when property rights to natural resources are absent or un-enforced, what Hardin called "open access", no individual bears the full costs of resource degradation. Individuals lack incentives to act in a socially-efficient and perhaps responsible way (Hardin, 1968; Stevenson, 1991). This makes a CPR regime inherently inefficient as it suffers collective action problems.

Other concepts related to CBPR recently emerged during the 1980s and the 1990s, when major conservation organizations, such as the International Union for the Conservation of Nature (IUCN), World Wildlife Foundation (WWF), Conservation International (CI), started designing programs aimed at working with communities living around protected areas. The initiatives were "baptized" with selling names: "community-based natural resources management"; "community-based conservation"; "decentralization of natural resources management;" "sustainable utilization projects"; etc. This cocktail of conservation initiatives became collectively known as Integrated Conservation and Development Projects (ICDPs) during the 1990s. The philosophy of ICDPs was this: to achieve sustainable development, conservation projects had to integrate communities adjacent to protected areas in the overall conservation agenda to ensure community support. By whatever name called, ICDPs were similar in both design and execution. Most striking, though not surprising, all these terms or concepts were crafted by conservation NGOs–and none of them by, nor in consultation with, indigenous peoples. And all conservation programs that fitted within the Integrated Conservation and Development Project (ICDP) concept were designed and executed by conservation NGOs and none by the communities.

The implications of these concepts were far reaching. First, the initiatives constituted the most "strategic" way of communicating the intentions of these conservation agencies, to work with local communities, with the outside world. It was fashionable to coin conservation projects as "community conservation" in wildlife, or "collaborative management" in forestry or "co-management" in fisheries. In many ways, ICDP initiatives kept donor funds flowing to these conservation organizations especially since the declared objectives of these initiatives fitted in well with the philanthropic rhetoric of many donors (Chapin, 2004).

Second, governments followed these conceptual entrepreneurs for two major reasons. First, the ICDP advocates brought much-needed funds into states' conservation programs. Agencies which hitherto suffered cutbacks in public spending being pursued under the World Bank-sponsored Structural Adjustment Programs became funded. Second, perpetuating the deprivation of community-based property rights initiated during the colonial era, ICDP initiatives facilitated, consolidated, state control over natural resources. Community Based Natural Resources Management CBNRM became the dominant conservation program of the 1990s: Communal Areas Management Programme for Indigenous Resources (CAMPFIRE) Program in Zimbabwe exemplified this alliance between governments and propon-ents of ICDP initiatives.

Finally, the full meaning and utility of conservation initiatives dubbed ICDP was never clear from the beginning and perhaps has never been. It remains unclear whether "community-based conservation" is the same as "community conservation"; whether "collaborative forest management (CFM)" was the same as "community forestry." Given this ambiguity regarding the meaning and implications of these concepts, conservation remained a beehive of activity as scholars sought to out-do one other in expounding the concepts. Scholars and practitioners alike–both with vested interests, not communities as victims of disenfranchisement and deprivation–arrogated to themselves the responsibility of defining the legal and political content of all conservation initiatives into these programs. Consequently, concepts such as restitution and compensation were only alluded to in passing in these initiatives.

From the foregoing, these concepts are not and should not be equated to CBPR, which is both a legal and conservation concept that connotes rights of ownership over land and all the attendant property rights. As a legal concept, it implies the legal foundation upon which the property and human rights of indigenous and minority communities must be premised, recognized and protected. As a conservation concept, it establishes the scientific foundations for tapping on the important knowledge base of these communities, which is essential for the conservation and sustainable use of biological and other environmental resources. On the contrary, the above-examined putative concepts are mere conservation concepts and do not confer any legal rights to the intended target beneficiaries of these conservation programs. Unfortunately, these putative concepts continue to be incorporated in national policy and legislation without full recognition of the property or human rights of the victims of the global conservation agenda. Therefore, the conservation legislation agenda of the last four decades represents one of the most enduring conspiracies of our time executed against indigenous and minority communities by the state and globalized conservation practitioners.

CBPR as a Distinct Property Regime

The origin of CBPR is not particularly clear. However, the earliest form of what could be considered CBPR may be traced to Aristotle and Theophrastus. As early as 200BC, Theophrastus inherited The Lyceum, an Aristotelian school specializing in cooperative research. Before his death, Theophrastus acquired property for The Lyceum in Athens where the school library and work place were housed. He later bequeathed this estate to his scholarly colleagues in his will where he stated: "I give the garden, the peripatos, and all the houses along the garden to those of my friends, named herein, who wish continually to practice education and philosophy together in them...; my condition is that no one alienate the property or devote it to private use but that all should hold it in common as if it were a sanctuary" (Lindberg, 1992). Since the bequest of the

Lyceum, the concept of "common interest" in property has remained a key feature of property relations even in the face of the growing dominance of the classical property theories that emphasize private ownership.

Especially in traditional African societies, common interests and joint ownership of property were deeply embedded in cultures and traditions of many communities. Fishing, agricultural and pastoralist communities practiced common property interests, which were embedded in the notion that human beings are mere parts of a large "organism" often referred to as "humanity". In the intellectual discourse of our time, people make reference to humanity–as when they talk about sacrificing oneself or one's self interests or materialistic goals for humanity.

In terms of CBPR, this collectivism is expressed by making reference to community or ethnic groups that are bound together by common traditions of property relations. But the practice of CBPR can be distinguishable from other forms of collective rights. CBPRs are a kind of property rights usually vested in a community or group of individuals. To qualify as CBPR, the rights need three basic characteristics: common or collective ownership of a given natural resource–often a common pool resource; sharing rights to access and use of the resource in accordance with established traditions or regulations; and a right to regulate access to the resource by outsiders or non-members of the community. In CBPR, land upon which the property rights are premised is collectively owned. Improvements may be individually owned but those improvements may not be transferred outside of the community. CBPRs are essentially derived from historical relations of long use and dependence on natural resources for the survival and well-being of the community concerned. Today, these relations and rights claims have also been legislated and legalized.

The Legal Basis of Community-Based Property Rights

CBPRS have acquired legal recognition. This recognition may not cover and/or reflect the entirety of property relations as traditionally understood and practiced, but contain some of the elements that reflect traditional and classical CBPRs. The legal basis of CBPRS is traceable from three arenas: international law, constitutional basis, and judicial recognition.

CBPRs in International Law

This section therefore explores the main sources of international law relevant to the international acceptability and recognition of CBPRs. The extant large body of international law sets out rights of all human beings, and advances obligations of the international community and individual states to recognize, protect and promote these rights. Through a series of legally binding agreements, soft law instruments and declaratory principles, common principles of international law have emerged and gained general acceptance as establishing minimum standards for state conduct on human rights. International human rights law has expanded significantly, over the last five decades, to the extent that widespread or state-inspired abuse of human rights is now a basis for foreign intervention against the state or legitimate use of force under the United Nations Charter (Report of the International Commission on Intervention and State Sovereignty, 2001). The African Union has also regionalized these legalities through a shift from non-intervention to non-indifference (Williams, 2007) in cases of war crimes, crimes against humanity, what are considered "just-cause thresholds" for intervening against affected states under the Responsibility to Protect (R2P) (Zamaris and Prat, 2015).

There are at least twelve major international instruments that reflect international recognition and protection of human rights. These instruments cover such areas as economic, social and cultural rights, civil and political rights (United Nations, 1966), elimination of all forms of racial discrimination (United Nations, 1963), discrimination against women (United Nations, 1963), prohibition of torture and other cruel and inhuman or degrading treatment or punishment (United Nations, 1984) and protection of children (Machel, 1996). Although not specifically mentioning the rights of indigenous communities in general and CBPR in particular, these instruments suggest widespread international acceptance of the need to protect human rights and the rights of special groups.

Examples are not hard to show. Article 1 of the International Covenant on Economic, Social and Cultural Rights (CESCRs) enjoins States to desist from depriving any people of its means of subsistence. Article 2 guarantees non-discrimination in the exercise of these rights. The International Covenant on Civil and Political Rights (ICCPR), adopted by the UN General Assembly simultaneously with the CESCR, also contains provisions related to CBPR. The ICCPR also provides that "in those States in which ethnic, religious or linguistic minorities exist, persons belonging to such minorities shall not be denied the right, in community with the other members of the group, to enjoy their own culture, to profess and practice their own religion, or to use their own language.

The concept of CBPRs is closely associated with the term "indigenous communities", "indigenous peoples" as used in the UN system. Some reasoners despise CBPR as an old fashioned property rights regime. They argue that indigenous communities/peoples are not a legally-defined term or corporate entity in whom property can vest. A rigorous debate has taken place within the International Labor Organization (ILO) during the process of revising its Indigenous and Tribal Convention (Convention 107) as early as 1959.

From 1972 to 1986, the UN Special Rapporteur to the Sub-Commission on Prevention of Discrimination and Protection of Minorities conducted a study discrimination against indigenous populations that provides the intellectual framework for using and applying the term "indigenous peoples". Martinez's report recognizes the right of indigenous peoples themselves to define what and who is "indigenous". He described indigenous peoples as those who have historical continuity with pre-invasion and pre-colonial societies that developed on their territories; consider themselves distinct from other sectors of the societies now prevailing on their territories; constitute non-dominant sectors of society; desire to reserve, develop and transmit their ancestral territories and ethnic identity, cultural patterns, social institutions, and legal systems to future generations as the basis of their continued existence.

The essential elements of this continuity include: occupation of, or at least part of, ancestral lands; common ancestry with original occupants of these lands; common culture; etc. International processes and practice tends to emphasize that indigenous peoples identify and define themselves as opposed to adopting a structured and exclusive definition. On27 July 1996, representatives of indigenous communities adopted a resolution "endorsing the Martinez Cobo Report" and "categorically reject any attempts that Governments define indigenous peoples" (United Nations, 1996). The 15th Session of the Working Group on Indigenous Populations in 1997concluded that an international-level definition of "indigenous peoples" was impossible then, and not necessary for adopting the Draft Declaration on the Rights of Indigenous Peoples. Unsurprisingly, then, the ILO Convention (No. 169) on Indigenous and Tribal Peoples in Independent Countries does not define these terms. Instead, a statement in article 1 of the Convention covers the scope of its application. CBPRS of indigenous communities also find support in the African Charter on Human and Peoples Rights. The OAU Charter binds the Member States of the Organization of African Unity (OAU; predecessor to African Union, AU) to protect and promote human rights of African peoples. It proclaims that the right to equality and human dignity belongs to all individuals, including the individual members of indigenous communities. It recognizes collective rights of "peoples", a concept with direct reference to the rights of indigenous peoples.

The debate over the rights of indigenous communities transcends ILO and the UNCHR, and featured in global discourse on environment and development. As early as 1987, the World Commission on Environment and Development (WCED) or the Brudtland Commission, sought to put the rights of indigenous communities on the global environment and development agenda. The Commission observed that "the standard for a just and humane policy for such groups is the recognition and protection of their traditional rights to land and the other resources that sustain their way of life – rights that they may define in terms that do not fit into standard legal systems" (United Nations, 1987). Its recommendations are reflected in global environment and development discourses. Several of the outcomes of the UN Conference on Environment and Development (UNCED), particularly Agenda 2 (the outcome of the Conference, the Rio Declaration); the political statement of the Conference; and the Convention on Biological Diversity, either alluded to or contained specific recognition of indigenous peoples as being critical in the conservation and sustainable use of global environmental resources.

By signing and/or ratifying international human rights instruments, states impose accept obligations to respect, promote, human rights. These obligations extend to marginal populations like indigenous communities and minority groups. Widespread signature, ratification or accession to these instruments suggest that these covenants occupy a major place in international human rights law. In East Africa for example, Kenya, Tanzania, and Uganda have signed most of the covenants and additional protocols where applicable. This indicates that EAC countries are committed to respecting international human rights law and practice related to CBPRs. In jurisprudential terms, it may be unclear whether signature and ratification of these instruments is necessary and sufficient for the recognition and promotion of CBPR within the EAC for three reasons: first, nowhere in EAC instruments, including the Treaty, is the CBPR or human rights of indigenous communities mentioned. Second, although EAC partner states ratified or acceded to instruments and incorporated some of the provisions in national constitutions, indigenous communities in these countries remain marginalised. Those that still occupy ancestral lands, such as the Mungiki of Kenya, have been involved in protracted legal battles for the recognition of their land rights (Kenya Constitution, 2010) and face extinction.

The foregoing discussion reveals that CBPRs has gained increasing acceptance in international law and practice. The variety of international instruments that directly or indirectly allude to the existence and importance of these rights represent sufficient opinio juris—an essential precondition for the existence of an acceptable norm in international law. This growing recognition provides compelling evidence that the existence of these rights is no longer a subject of much legal contestation.

The Constitutional and Legal Basis for CBPR in East Africa

The preceding section reveals that CBPRs have widespread expression in international treaty law and state practice. Like all fundamental human rights, CBPRs are not granted by the state but it is essential that the state recognizes, protects, and promotes them to facilitate their enjoyment. This section examines the constitutional foundations of CBPR in three East African countries: Uganda, Kenya, and Tanzania. Save for the 2005 draft and 2010 Kenya constitutions (Kenya Constitution, 2010), the current constitutional instruments do not provide adequate provisions for CBPR. The constitutionality of these rights is only reflected in general principles embedded in Bills of Rights, and, to a large extent, land laws. States include certain declaratory statements as national objectives and guiding principles of state policy in national constitutions.

In this regard, Uganda's Constitution contains general provisions that guarantee the protection and promotion of CBPR. Principle XI provides guiding principles on the state's role in the development process, stating, inter alia, that:

> The State shall give the highest priority to the enactment of legislation establishing measures that protect and enhance the right of the people to equal opportunities in development.

Other principles also enjoin the state to ensure balanced development, protection and promotion social and cultural wellbeing of Ugandans (Ug andaconstitution, 1995). The 1997 Tanzanian Constitution makes similar provisions. Article 9 states:

> the object of the Constitution is to facilitate the building of a United Republic as a nation of equality and free individuals enjoying freedom, justice, fraternity and concord, through the pursuit of the policy of Socialism …

State programs must ensure/promote respect for human rights, preserve human dignity, and promote the common good. Rawls' essential elements of primary social goods are evident in Tanzanian Constitution (Rawls, 1971).

Two critical issues, however, inhere in constitutional provisions that are characterized as "principles of state policy". First, this part of national constitutions is a new phenomenon. It emerged around the 1980s when a wave of constitutionalism and democratization swept through Eastern Europe and Africa. Principles of state policy are found in constitutions that were either "substantially" revised or promulgated after 1988. The provisions are noticeably missing in the Constitution of Kenya which passed with minor amendments in 1992, in contrasted with the 2005 draft which had specific provisions devoted to such principles. Second, these principles are found in the part of the constitution that is often considered non-justiciable or are generally not considered enforceable. Justifiability of these provisions is an unsettled question of constitutional jurisprudence and has not been settled in constitutional law and practice. Tanzania's constitution specifies that "the provisions of this Part of this Chapter are not enforceable by any court. No court shall be competent to determine the question whether or not any action or omission by any person or any court, or any law or judgment complies with the provisions of this Part of this Chapter" (Constitution of the Republic of

Tanzania, 1997). In some cases courts have held these parts justiciable, hence creating rights and obligations on the part of the state and the citizens. To the extent that this debate continues, the extent of the utility of these constitutional provisions with regard to CBPR remains a matter of juridical inquiry.

The legal uncertainty regarding principles of state policy notwithstanding, provisions in substantive sections of national constitutions render tenable the argument that CBPR is part and parcel of the human rights recognized and guaranteed by these constitutions. The current constitutions guarantee the rights to property and proscribe deprivation of property without the due process (Uganda constitution, 1995). They provide for affirmative action in favor of marginalized communities. In East Africa, however, only the 2010 Constitution of Kenya contains elaborate proposals for the recognition, protection and promotion of CBPR. Chapter 5, on land and environment, stress equity, security of land rights, and settlement of land disputes "through recognised local community initiatives [that are] consistent with this Constitution" (Kenya Constitution, 2010). Article 81(1) of the 2005 draft had provided that "Community land shall vest in and be held by communities identified on the basis of ethnicity, culture or community of interests", but did not pass the test of time.

How are CBPRs recognized and implemented in practice? None of the constitutions in East Africa addresses the issue of restitution or compensation. Policy and programmatic interventions based on affirmative action only target groups that have strong voices in the policy arena such as women, people with disabilities, and the youth. Countries have not developed specific and coherent programs for protecting and promoting CBPR let alone integrate indigenous peoples in national policy and planning. The lack of conceptual clarity at international level is, in part, a major cause of national-level policy distortion. Uganda, for instance, is developing a land acquisition, resettlement, and rehabilitation policy (LARRP) whose spirit seems to be aimed at eroding the provisions or Article 26 of the constitution, on protection of land rights. The recently-proposed amendments to the same article have already caused public anxiety about the fate of land rights protections in a context of land governance failures in the country alongside the pressures for, and interest in, large-scale capitalist land acquisitions.

Non-articulation and non-recognition of CBPRs in key regional and national legal instruments within the EAC highlights one important point: that the articulation of these rights in international law was not accidental but resulted from struggles by representatives of indigenous peoples around the world. Only a similar campaign waged at regional and national level will change constitutional-legal articulations within the EAC. The EAC provides a rare but realistic opportunity to bring issues of indigenous and marginalized communities at the centre of regional policy and legislation, mainly through judicial and political engagement of state and non-state parties reliant on the East African Court of Justice (EACJ) and East African Legislative Assembly (EALA). But reversals in Uganda and difficulties in other countries make the problem protracted. Recall that the EAC common market protocol does provide that land be governed under national laws, hence retaining differential national legal-constitutional provisions and their limitations on CBPRs.

Judicial Recognition of CBPR

There is generally no well-established judicial practice on the enforcement of CBR either by national courts or international tribunals. Most cases that have been brought before such judicial or quasi-judicial bodies are often cases of individual property rights violations. Nevertheless, three judicial decisions may be highlighted here which suggest that CBPRs are recognized in the context of the general provisions on property contained in international and regional human rights instruments.

In 1982, the European Court of Human Rights, in Sporrong and Lönnroth Vs. Sweden, found that interference that affects property rights and which cannot be defined as deprivation, nor as limitation, can still be an unjustifiable interference with property rights. In that case, the Swedish Government granted the City Council expropriation permits pending expropriation taking effect. During this period, construction or alterations of the property were prohibited. This affected the possibility to sell the estates, and diminished the value of the applicants' properties. The court observed that a gradual interference with property rights contravened the provisions of the European Convention guaranteeing the right to property. The case covers property rights of an individual nature. But the principle enunciated by the Court is relevant to CBPRs. In most cases, CBPRs are expropriated through gazzetment of indigenous peoples' lands as conservation or protected areas, and changes in the status of a given protected area (like elevation of game reserve to national park or local forest to central forest reserve). Access to selected resources can be had under collaborative management, community conservation or co-management depending on resources in question. In such cases, indigenous communities can still make a case for gradual interference with their traditional and legal property rights.

In a 1984 case of Ominayak (Lubicon Lake Bank) v. Canada, Chief Bernard Ominayak of the Lubicon Lake Band brought a complaint before the UN Human Rights Committee (Sepúlevda et al., 2004). Chief Ominayak alleged that Canada had denied members of the Lubicon Lake Band their rights to self-determination and to dispose freely of their natural wealth and resources. He claimed that Canada's actions contravened the Indian Act of 1970 and Treaty 8 of 1899 which recognized the Band's right to continue its traditional ways of life. Thus, by expropriating approximately 10,000 km2 of the Band's land, Canada had denied the Lubicon Lake Band its means of subsistence and enjoyment of the right to self-determination, causing irreparable damage to its members. In its views of 26 March 1990, the Committee observed:

While all peoples have the right of self-determination and the right to freely determine their political status, pursue their economic, social and cultural development and dispose of their natural wealth and resources, as stipulated in article 1 of the Covenant, the question whether the Lubicon Lake Band constitutes a "people" is not an issue for the Committee to address under the Optional Protocol to the Covenant. The Optional Protocol provides a procedure under which individuals can claim that their individual rights have been violated. These rights are set out in part III of the Covenant, articles 6-27 inclusive. There is, however, no objection to a group of individuals, who claim to be similarly affected, collectively to submit a communication about alleged breaches of their rights (Sepúlevda et al., 2004, page 421).

In a recent case of Mayagna (Sumo) Awas Tingni Community v. Nicaragua, a petition was filed with the Inter-American Commission on Human Rights (IACHR) on behalf of the Mayagna Awas Tingni Community, which lives in the Atlantic coast region of Nicaragua and is made up of approximately 142 families. The applicants denounced Nicaragua for failing to demarcate the Community's communal land and to take the necessary measures to protect the Community's property rights over its ancestral land. They sought precautionary measures to prevent the proposed awarding of 62,000ha of tropical forest to a private company in communal lands. On June 4, 1998, the Commission submitted the case to the Inter-American Court of Human Rights (IACHR), which, on 31 August 31, 2001, declared that the state had violated the right to judicial protection (article 25 of the American Convention on Human Rights) and the right to property enshrined (article 21 of the Convention), to the detriment of the members of the Mayagna (Sumo) Awas Tingni Community (Inter-American Court of Human Rights, 2006).

In the case of Uganda Land Alliance Ltd v. Uganda Wildlife Authority (UWA) and the Attorney General (The High Court of Uganda at Mbale, 2004), the applicants representing the forest-inhabiting Benet community on the Uganda side of Mount Elgon challenged the decision of UWA to evict the Benet from their domicile. Court's consent judgment recognized the Benet's historical rights to live in the area. The Court observed that the Benet Community "are historical and indigenous inhabitants of the said areas which were declared a Wildlife Protected Area or National Park", and that the Community "is entitled to stay in the said areas and carry out economic and agricultural activities including developing the same undisturbed."The court approvingly highlighted the need for the state to take "affirmative action in favour of the said Community to redress the imbalance which presently exists in the said area in terms of education, infrastructure, health and social services in the spirit of Article 32(1) of the Constitution (Uganda) in lieu of general damages, commencing in the Financial Year2005/06."

This judgment sets an important precedent: (i) recognizing the rights of indigenous minority communities; (ii) ordering payment of damages for the wrongs and marginalization inflicted on them. But the case failed to proceed to full hearing. This denied the Court an opportunity to pronounce itself fully on key principles applicable to situations of this nature beyond the Benet community. This evolving body of judicial precedents suggests growing consensus on the legal validity of CBPRs in national and international law. Yet the numerous cases of deprivation of indigenous peoples' lands and other rights, the limited number of court cases decided, reflects weak judicial protections for CBPR. Most indigenous communities affected by decades of property rights deprivation lack capacity and legal representation to obtain remedy from existing international and national judicial bodies or tribunals.

The Relevance of CBPR in Peaceable Development

The theory and practice of CBPRs is relevant for peace, security, democracy and development. There is constitutional and judicial recognition of CBPRs both in international and constitutional legal practice. Conceptual consensus is also emerging on CBPR sand the indigenous peoples/communities which are entitled to these rights. Beyond legal solutions, CBPRs are founded on strong historical and ancestral relationships between indigenous communities and the lands and resources upon which they depend, and are part of the deep-seated philosophical traditions of humanity predating the modern state system. Thus, CBPR and the livelihoods of indigenous communities are not undermined because of their newness. The lack of their articulation in international law and constitutional practice is not a result of novelty of the issue or lack of human knowingness and experience about CBPRs, but rather because of governments' failure to implement their human obligations, philosophically speaking, as well asstate and non-state complicity in violations of international and national legal obligations.

Since CBPRs are central to indigenous communities' livelihoods, they can no longer be avoided or neglected in development discourses in societies where such communities live. This is because violations of these kinds of rights touched off by capitalist interests in, for instance, natural-resource-rich areas have engendered backlashes and forms of insecurity that have affected the operations and image of multinational companies and governments alike. How, then, is CBPR relevant to contemporary peace and security in East Africa and regional development policy and practice? Three peace-building and security considerations answer this question here: management and de-escalation of grievances; equitable development via integration of indigenous communities' livelihoods; and promotion of rule of law and constitutionalism that are consistent with regional and international commitments.

Management and de-escalation of grievances

Violation of CBPRs generates objective, livelihood-related, grievances, sowing seeds of conflicts. Though recent literature seems to show that greedy conflict entrepreneurs cause conflicts more than objective grievance, it is agreeable that greedy war entrepreneurs tend to exploit and present grievances as justifications for conflict. This is because grievance, in the form of development inequality, human rights violations, livelihood disruptions, creates incentives for starting and/or engaging in a civil conflict (Collier and Anke, 2004). Examples are not hard to find.

Angola and Nigeria were once prime examples of the resource curse. Their histories of conflict and underdevelopment surrounding oil-rich regions had rendered them exemplars of violations of human rights of communities living in oil-rich regions. These violations affected not only the security of petro-extraction businesses but whole countries. After years of violent conflicts, including oil sabotages (Onuoha, 2010), the countries recently embarked on reevaluations of their local content policies and the benefits accruing to communities affected by petro-extraction to build cordial relations with such communities (Ovadia, 2014). For instance, due to marginalization of Nigerian communities living in the oil-rich region, environmental destruction, and exclusion from the benefits of the oil and gas sector–hence the failure to trade violations of indigenous CBPRs with petro-sector benefits–anti-oil sentiments arose in Niger Delta. Royal Dutch/Shell commissioned a study in the mid-2000s, which put the amount of oil stolen each year by "bunkerers" (colloquial name for vandals that siphon oil from perforated pipelines which they sell in black markets) in Nigeria at between 100 million and 250 million barrels. Consider an average of US$60 per barrel: this theft, then, translates to an estimated loss of about US$15 billion per year. This excludes costs to the state. These expressions of oil-driven grievances in which members of local communities are involved of oil bunkering, pipeline vandalism and scooping, and "oil terrorism", negatively impacted oil companies, the Nigerian state, and the community itself (Onuoha, 2010). Initial inattention to indigenous communities' interests boomeranged, laying bare the supposed wisdom of capitalist interests and the state to ignore CBPRs.

East Africa has had its share: During the early 2000s, Kenya sought to allocate land in the Chebyuk Settlement Scheme in the Mt. Elgon district. Government's plan to evict squatters in the area triggered off a conflict that metamorphosed into a rebel group, the Saboat Movement for the Defence of Land (Rwengabo, 2018) with an armed wing, Saboat Land Defence Force (SLDF). This rebel movement reportedly killed hundreds of people and committed atrocities. More than 60,000 people were displaced in less than two years. The rebellion revolved around community land rights violatons. It was dominated by the Saboat, a sub-ethnic component of the Kalenjin (former President Arap Moi's ethnic group consisting less than 11% of Kenya's population). The movement was reportedly led by a mysterious former presidential bodyguard, whose deputy and face of the rebellion was Wycliffe Matakwei Kirui-Komon. By the end of 2007 Kirui-Komon allegedly commanded over 35,000 fighters exploiting the proliferation of small arms and weapons in the region (some of this relates to CBPRs in East Africa's pastoral communities), and imposed taxes upon local residents. After a brutal counterinsurgency operation government forces killed Komon in May 2008 during Operation Okoa Maisha (Operation Save Lives), in which Kenya's state apparatus also violated human rights (Human Rights Watch, 2008; IRIN, 2008 Rwengabo, 2018).

From the foregoing examples–and there are countless such examples in Uganda's oil-rich Albertine Graben (Moore, 2013; Bigiriwenkya, 2016a, 2016b), mineral-rich Karamoja, northern Uganda (Hopwood, 2017), and Tanzania, with potential to generate insecurity–it is clear that neglect of CBPRs is counterproductive. Management and de-escalation of grievances can be achieved by recognising, respecting, and upholding CBPRs of indigenous peoples on their lands and properties. In northern Uganda, for instance, much of the "rural land is occupied and managed communally by kinship groups–clans, sub-clans, and extended families" (Hopwood, 2017, page 2). Here, CBPRs are relevant. Land-holding groups have traditional land-governance customs, and own land as communities. Traditional authority structures, which are rooted in indigenous conflict-resolution infrastructure, would be inevitable in grievance handling. "Supporting the mediation efforts of local actors, both customary and elected, is most likely to reduce conflict while avoiding undermining social cohesion and security" that holds this society together (Hopwood, 2017, page 4). This recognition of CBPRs on communal lands indicates the theoretical and practical relevance of CBPRs. Inadequacies of legalistic solutions to such conflicts are not unbeknownst to policy practitioners. This is consistent with notions of security for developments undertakings and equitable development.

Equitable Development

Unequal development generates feelings of marginalization and inequality. These feelings may, in turn, ignite disruptions against development. We exemplified with oil sabotages in Nigeria. These disruptions need not take the form of violence or terror; they can also be legal contestations, which tend to be less effective in upholding CBPRs given the slow pace at with which international and national legal regimes were crafted Capitalist pressures also render most judicial processes in the developing, pursued by less powerful community members against the more resourced, more influential/connected, and more staffed capitalist groups and rentier states, world ineffective.

Kimberling examines legal contestations in Ecuador, Latin America, where indigenous people's CBPRs have been violated by oil companies for half-a-century. She reveals that judicial struggles have not upheld indigenous people's rights (Kimerling, 2006). Besides, indigenous peoples, such as the Huaorani and the Kichwa in Ecuador's Amazon Rainforest, only begun to contest petro-extraction when the oil interests had caused environmental pollution and lots of other damage. The result: a form of "bi-national injustice" born of these transnational operations (Kimerling, 2007). Ecuador demonstrates violations of CBPRs in the oil and gas sector and the implication of these violations for the conflict-management struggles the country has gone through.

Uganda is aware that the petroleum sector should generate equitable development while protecting local communities' interests. This is envisaged to take place within and across the border in cooperation with neighboring states like Democratic Republic of Congo (DRC), whose CBPRs may be violated by cross-border environmental damage: "The interests of local communities in areas where oil and gas production is undertaken shall be taken into account by, among other things, sharing of royalties in line with the Constitution and any relevant laws passed by Parliament. All efforts shall be made to avoid the development of conflicts and emphasize peaceful resolution of disputes. Where oil and gas activities or their impacts extend to neighbouring countries, this spirit shall be exercised in accordance with the principles grounded in the country's foreign policy" (Republic of Uganda, 2013). This reads more like grievance management and de-escalation. But it has elements of equity and recognition of communities' CBPRs through "sharing of royalties." While royalties may not necessarily imply that CBPRs were respected during the development of the sector, especially through land acquisitions and resettlement (Anyuru et al., 2016), it does indicate the desire to ensure equity by assuaging most-affected communities.

In area like Niger Delta, it was normal for oil companies to extract oil, export it, and ignore local communities. The state generated oil revenues that were not ploughed back to benefit communities whose environment and livelihoods had been destroyed. The resulting community struggles had direct implications for rethinking notions of equity and security in Nigeria (Ikelegbe, 2001). It follows that CBPRs in East Africa would provide grounds for ensuring equity, and local content in extractives sector, in areas where indigenous communities live. This balances developments with local livelihoods (Anyuru et al., 2016), which promotes security in general.

Rule of Law, Constitutionalism and Regional and International Commitments

The international recognition of CBPRs has one direct bearing on states: adoption and reflection of CBPRs constitutions. Rekindling the debate on the recognition and promotion of CBPR, restitution of those rights, is no longer a debate based on "emotions" but a discourse anchored on the relevance of CBPRs to conservation, national development, and rule of law within and between states. East African states are signatories to international conventions on human rights. They are also participants in international processes, such as humanitarian and peacekeeping interventions, aimed at preventing state and non-state excesses in politico-security governance (Inter-American Court of Human Rights, 2006). These commitments on peace, security, democracy, and development imply that violations of CBPR are increasingly becoming intolerable. The EAC Legislative Assembly (EALA) recently raised concerns about human rights violations during disarmament in Karamoja region of northeastern Uganda/northwestern Kenya (EALA, 2011).

The potential internationalization of CBPRs violations indicates that governments suffer potential interventions as transnational networks highlight and showcase concerns about CBPRs violations. Individual human rights violations are being brought to the attention of regional bodies. Clearly, then, contentions over human rights violations against indigenous communities will increase. Kenya's human rights violations during the counterinsurgency operations against the SMDL led to judicial struggles in the East African Court of Justice (Rwengabo, 2017).

Finally, rule of law and constitutionalism is more than a call for legal-constitutional sanity within East African countries. The call is central to democracy, which entails respect for rights of indigenous peoples, minorities and marginalized groups. We need not theorise the tenets of post-modern democracy to convince the reader that respect for CBPRs is a major component of democracy world-over. Democratic development consists in socioeconomic, techno-scientific, infrastructural, institutional, and other undertakings that respect and uphold the rights of indigenous communities. These can either be specifically legislated or reflected in bills of rights of national constitutions. Democracy also entails respecting international instruments that articulate these rights. CBPRs are relevant for democratic development, a development that ensures equity while striking a balance between development and community livelihoods (Anyuru et al., 2016). Excesses would, therefore, provoke international interest which may lead to interventions with serious implications for the affected state's security and legitimacy.

Conclusion

The concept of CBPRs has evolved over time, and now has strong foundations in international human rights jurisprudence and national legal-political reality. It is also relevant for peaceful development in East Africa given the prevalence of indigenous communities claiming land and other property rights throughout the region. Specifically, CBPRs has direct bearing on management of grievances and conflicts; avoidance of disruptions against development, in areas where indigenous communities live; ensuring development equity and continuity; and promotion of peace-enhancing rule of law and constitutionalism. Indigenous peoples play a vital role in the conservation and management of the environment; hence, ecological peace is to be had when we uphold and respect these community contributions (Meakin, 1992). Indigenous communities embody traditional/indigenous knowledge and customs that provide key insights in land governance, sustainable utilisation of natural resources, understanding the functioning of key ecological systems (such as breeding cycles and breeding grounds for fish), and knowledge of behavior and biochemical properties of animal and plant species that could provide a basis for conserving endangered animal species.

Second, constitutions commit the three EAC states to promote equity, social justice, and development for indigenous communities, and respect for their cultural identity and dignity. Fulfillment of these obligations and commitments is, of course, a different question here. Lastly, CBPR provides the legal foundations for building state-community partnerships in the conservation agenda, and for communities to negotiate "meaningful" partnerships with the state and the market on management of common resources: beyond legal ownership of the resources in question, indigenous communities can partner with states and the private-sector, to peacefully and cooperatively exploit such resources for the "common good". Once the rights and obligations are defined and understood by all parties, it forms the basis for meaningful negotiations on development. This is the notion of democratic development.

Yet, despite widespread support for and recognition of CBPR, national-level practices seem to be different. Many communities (Batwa, Basongora and Bennet in Uganda; Mungiki in Kenya; Masaai in Kenya-Tanzania) have been deprived of their CBPR by decades of colonialism, marginalization and privatization. This undermines their human rights and dignity, the credibility of the conservation agenda, and threatens the region's peace, security, and stability as the case of the SMDL demonstrates. Three interventions may be need to enhance CBPRs in the region: legislative representation of indigenous communities, such as Burundi has done; legal representation to promote the democratic principle of access to justice and judicial redress; and involvement of indigenous communities' authority structures and traditional institutional practices in resolving conflicts involving CBPRs.

We propose a new research agenda for testing the theoretical propositions advanced here. First, the conceptual distortion pervading conservation agenda contorts our grasp of CBPR. Re-articulation of these conceptual conflations is necessary for erasing this confusion. Second, conservationists are comfortable using these concepts while comforting indigenous communities with misleading terms like "involve-ement" and "participation" in this agenda. But enfranchisement of these communities and security of their livelihoods is the more important: to what degree are these conservationist innovations recognising and promoting the ancestral land rights claims of indigenous communities? Third, to inform national policy, legislation and development planning and practice, comprehensive, action-based research is needed to enhance our understanding of the social, economic and political status of these communities; the changing basis of claims to CBPR; and how conditions of the different communities can be changed through redesigning development interventions. Finally, the relationship between violations of CBPRs and national and regional security needs deeper inquiry.

The starting point can be the analysis of the evolution of grievances, such as Saboat land grievances, into outright rebellions. The other is to examine spillover effect: identify possible links between ongoing conflicts related to CBPRs and the eruption of new conflicts. Finally, we need to examine the changing livelihood adaptations of indigenous communities faced with massive land-acquisitions driven by oil and gas developments, large-scale agriculture, conservation and similar developments. These studies would not only enrich our understanding of the security dimensions of capitalist developments affecting indigenous communities but the changing imperatives of CBPRs in the face of these developments in East Africa.

References

Anyuru, M. A., Rhoads, R., Mugyeni, O., Manoba, J. A. and Balemesa, T. (2016) 'Balancing Development and Community Livelihoods: A Framework for Land Acquisition and Resettlement in Uganda. Environmental Democracy Programme', *ACODE Policy Research Series*. Kampala, 75. Available at: http://www.acode-u.org/Files/Publications/PRS_75.pdf.

Bigiriwenkya, A. (2016a) 'BUKITAREPA sues Attorney General, Oil Companies for Outrageous oil activities', *GMEPA News*, 24 June. Available at: http://gmepa.com/bukitarepa-sues-attorney-general-oil-companies-for-outrageous-oil-activitiesgmepa-news/.

Bigiriwenkya, A. (2016b) *High Court Permits BUKITAREPA to Sue District Land Boards in Bunyoro*. Masindi. Available at: http://gmepa.com/high-court-permits-bukitarepa-to-sue-district-land-boards-in-bunyorogmepa-news/ (Accessed: 14 August 2017).

Bonger, T. (1999) 'The CAMPFIRE Programme in Zimbabwe: Institutional innovation and implications for environmental governance', in Okoth-Ogendo, H. W. O. and Tumushabe, G. (eds) *Governing the Environment: Political Change and Natural Resources Management in Eastern and Southern Africa*. Nairobi: ACTS Press.

Chapin, M. (2004) 'A Challenge to Conservationists'. Washington DC: Worldwatch Institute.

Collier, P. and Anke, H. (2004) 'Greed and Grievance in Civil War', *Oxford Economics Papers*, 56, pp. 563–595. *Constitution of the Republic of Tanzania* (1997).

EALA (2011) *Report of the Committee on Agriculture, Tourism and Natural Resources on the Tour of Lake Jipe Aquatic Trans-boundary Ecosystem.* Arusha: EALA.

Grotius, H. (2001) *On the Law of War and Peace.* Kitchener: Batoche Books.

Hardin, G. (1968) 'The Tragedy of the Commons', *Science*, 162(3859), pp. 1243–1248.

Hobbes, T. (1999) *Leviathan.* Oregon: The University of Oregon Renascence Editions.

Hopwood, J. (2017) 'Land Conflict and Security in. Acholi, Northern Uganda', *JSRP Policy Brief 7.* London: LSE. Available at: http://www.lse.ac.uk/internationalDevelopment/research/JSRP/do wnloads/JSRP-Brief-7.pdf.

Human Rights Watch (2008) 'Kenya, army and rebel militia commit war crimes in Mt. Elgon - End Murder, Torture, and Rape of Civilians'. HRW. Available at: https,.

Ikelegbe, A. (2001) 'Civil society, oil and conflict in the Niger Delta region of Nigeria: Ramifications of Civil Society for a Regional Resource Struggle', *The Journal of Modern African Studies*, 39(3), pp. 437–469.

Inter-American Court of Human Rights (2006) *Judgment of August 31, 2001 International Conference for the Great Lakes Region (ICGRL).* Dar es Salaam & Bujumbura: ICGLR.

IRIN (2008) 'Guns recovered, militiamen surrender after leader's killing'. online, IRIN. Available at: http, (Accessed: 22 June 2016).

Kenya Constitution (2010).

Kimerling, J. (2006) 'Indigenous Peoples and the Oil Frontier in Amazonia: The Case of Ecuador ChevronTexaco, and Aguinda v. Texaco', *International Law and Politics*, 38(663), pp. 413–664.

Kimerling, J. (2007) 'Transnational Operations, Bi-National Injustice: ChevronTtexaco and Indigenous Huaorani and Kichwa in the Amazon Rainforest in Ecuador', *American Indian Law Review*, 31, pp. 445–508.

Lindberg, D. C. (1992) *The Beginnings of Western Science: The European Scientific Tradition in Philosophical, Religious, and Institutional Context, Prehistory to A.D. 1450.* London: University of Chicago Press.

Locke, J. (1690) *The Second Treatise of Government.* Indianapolis: Bobbs-Merrill.

Machel, G. (1996) *Promotion and protection of the rights of children: impact of armed conflict on children.* Available at: https://www.unicef.org/graca/.

Meakin, S. (1992) 'Agenda 21, the Rio Declaration and the Convention on Biological Diversity', in. Available at: http://publications.gc.ca/collections/Collection-R/LoPBdP/BP/bp317-e.htm.

Moore, A. (2013) *Investigating Causes of Ethnic Identification and Mobilisation in Oil-Rich Regions: Ethnicity, Birthplace, and Revenue Sharing in Bunyoro, Uganda.* Yale: Yale University.

Onuoha, F. C. (2010) 'Oil pipeline sabotage in Nigeria: Dimensions, actors and implications for national security', *African Security Review,* 17(3), pp. 99–115.

Ovadia, J. S. (2014) 'Local Content and Natural Resource Governance: The Cases of Angola and Nigeria', *The Extractive Industries and Society,* pp. 137–146.

Rawls, J. (1971) *A Theory of Justice.* Harvard: The Belknap Press.

Report of the International Commission on Intervention and State Sovereignty (2001). Ottawa: InternationalDevelopmentResearchCentre.

Republic of Uganda (1995) *The constitution of the Republic of Uganda.* Entebbe: UPPC.

Republic of Uganda (2013) *The National Oil and Gas Policy (NOGP) for Uganda.* Kampala: MEMD.

Rwengabo, S. (2017) *Security Cooperation in the East African Community.* Trento NJ: Africa World Press.

Sepúlevda, M., von Banning, T., Gudmundsdóttir, D. G. and Chamoun, C. (2004) *Universal and regional human rights protection: Cases and commentaries.* 3rd edn. Ciudad Colon, Costa Rica: University for Peace.

Singer, W. J. (1997) 'Property', in Kairys, D. (ed.) *The Politics of Law: A Progressive Critique.* 3rd edn. Basic Books.

Stevenson, G. G. (1991) *Common Property Economics: A General Theory and Land Use Application.* Cambridge: Cambridge University Press.

The High Court of Uganda at Mbale (2004) *Miscellaneous Cause No. 0001 of 2004.*

Uganda constitution (1995).

United Nations (1963) 'International Covenant on the Elimination of All Forms of Racial Discrimination', in. New York.

United Nations (1966) *The International Covenant on Civil and Political Rights (CCPR).* New York: UN.

United Nations (1984) 'Convention Against Torture and Other Cruel, Inhuman or Degrading Treatment or Punishment', in. New York, United States of America: UN.

United Nations (1987) *Our Common Future: Report of the World Commission on Environment and Development.* Oxford and New York: Oxford University Press.

United Nations (1996) *Report of the Working Group on Indigenous Populations.* UNDoc.E/CN.4/Sub.2/1996/21).

Williams, P. D. (2007) 'From Non-Intervention to Non-Indifference: The Origins and Development of the African Union's Security Culture', *African Affairs*, 106(423), pp. 253–279.

Zamaris, S. and Prat, L. (2015) 'From Cause to Responsibility: R2P as a Modern Just War', *Australia Law Review*, 17(7), pp. 135–172.

CHAPTER TWELVE

Policy Options and Conclusion

Sabastiano Rwengabo and Arthur Bainomugisha

A frica's quest for peace, democracy and sustainable development remains an urgent policy imperative for the African Union and indeed the African people if the continent is to navigate the 21st century more successfully than it did the 20th, a century that was marked by violent conflicts, widespread poverty, disease and the paucity of democracy and development. The core challenge, however, lies in the paucity of transformational leadership in most countries on the continent. While African leaders face various and difficult challenges— infrastructure underdevelopment, colonial legacies of socio-political and development distortions, and structural problems like ethnic and social tensions that predate the current demand for transformation—many leaders have not risen to the occasion to generate minimum consensus that facilitates meaningful democratisation processes. As a result of leadership deficit, violent conflicts of varying magnitude remain unresolved. Ethnic tensions stifle state building and national cohesion. Socio-economic development suffers under the weight of kleptocratic, personalised, and autocratic rule. Democratic progress, in countries like Uganda, is stymied by constitutional manipulations, autocratic tendencies, endemic corruption, trends toward personalization of power, and a strange fusion between individual rulers, ruling parties, government, and the state. The continent's natural resource endowments are rendered a curse to Africans as they are exploited by foreigners in collusion with corrupt local elites sometimes in destructive ways. Some countries like Uganda, Rwanda, and Ghana are trying to address these challenges but still lag behind their peers like Botswana, Namibia and Mauritius.

This brief chapter concludes the debates captured in the foregoing chapters. Unlike the introductory chapter, however, it draws broader implications for the African continent as a whole. It focuses on three issues: first is the question of whether the theoretical and practical link between peace, democracy, and development is worth our intellectual and policy attention. The second is an outline of the conditions that need to be fulfilled if Africa is to achieve peace, democracy, and development. The third is the concluding observation that these challenges are not insurmountable.

Linking Peace, Democracy, and Development: Worthy of Attention?

If we agree that peace is a state of affairs in which people do not fear for themselves and their socioeconomic undertakings, then we can reasonably suppose that peace is a universal desire and aspiration. In organised polities, the role of political leadership is to promote peace and thereby allow people pursue economic, sociocultural, ideational-intellectual and other interests unhindered by threats to their lives, property, and wellbeing. This is the idea that people need physical and nonphysical security. Thomas Hobbes prescribes that men living in an anarchic society would fear threats from one another and, seek to secure themselves by agreeing to a social contract aimed to establish a sovereign authority ("Leviathan" who will be an absolute monarch) above themselves. This "Leviathan", arises because men naturally love liberty and dominion over others. Its work is to preserve people in a commonwealth. Hence, it is a result of people's "foresight of their own preservation" (Hobbes, 1999). African countries have these Leviathans: state governments.

The role of government is not just to facilitate the state's extraction function; it is to secure society and provide the necessary conditions for the realisation of the common good. A prudent and effective government is a necessary and sufficient condition for peace, democracy, and development in organised polities: "Reputation of prudence in the conduct of peace or war is power; because to prudent men we commit the government of ourselves more willingly than to others" (Hobbes, 1999, page 74). Governments are by their nature concentrations of human power composed of the powers of different peoples, groups, and institutions that operate under some form of united constitutional arrangement under specified leaderships. It is necessary therefore that Africans pay serious attention to the question of peace, whether through policy deliberations, theoretical debates, and practical interventions such as have been demonstrated in the AU's peacekeeping and peace building indicatives.

As revealed in Chapter 1, peace is a result of deliberate human efforts. Governmental effort is but an example. Without government effort, society degenerates into anarchy as we have observed in post-1993 Somalia and presently Central African Republic. Once governments provide peaceful environs private and public actors alike undertake productive activities that engender development. Development in turn leads to the consolidation of existing peace and democracy. This is not a question of what should precede which: while development helps in the consolidation of democracy it can also encourage travesty of democracy depending on the nature of leadership at a given time as Nazi Germany demonstrated to the world during the 20th Century. This is a question of the cyclic link between the three, such that one leads to the other and vice-versa. At the same time, we in no way imply that developed democratic polities are conflict-free and do not face crime-related insecurity; we aver that developed democratic societies tend to have, or have the wherewithal to establish, effective functional mechanisms for preventing the escalation of conflicts to levels that would threaten or erase peace and security.

The foregoing does not also imply that underdeveloped societies cannot democratise; Botswana has done it reasonably. But democratisation and development should happen concurrently for democracy to last. The Huntingtonian perspective is relevant here: democratization processes tend to over-politicize society. A politically conscientised and mobilized society is difficult to govern when there are no minimum institutional restraints upon the people. Political institutions may not function effectively in today's world without reasonable amounts of wealth to keep them running: we have indicated in Chapter 1 that Tanzania's Ujamaa failed not because it was a wrong approach to local democratic development but the country lacked resources to implement the strategy. Thus, African societies are under pressure to democratize, but many lack minimum levels of institutional development underpinned by economic capacity to provide political goods. Without functioning political institutions, the democratization process has, in many respects, created disorder, chaos, generated new conflicts, and disrupted socioeconomic development (Huntington, 1968). The Kenyan experience of 2007-8 is still alive in African memory. For this reason, it behoves us to admit that Africans have all the reasons to pick direct interest in the link between peace, democracy, and development.

Finally, the mutually reinforcing nexus between these conditions is difficult to dispute. The AU has developed a comprehensive strategy, with multiple instruments, for supporting the three aspects of peace, democracy, and development. If the research community in Africa is to be helpful and relevant to the continent it must pay attention to this realisation at continental level. AU member states have embraced peace building initiatives in conflict-affected states and have progressively overcome some of the many obstacles that make it difficult for the continent to achieve the socio-economic and political development aspirations of its people. For one, the intervention in Somalia, one of the most protracted and most expensive in the world, has been anchored on commitment of the AU, IGAD, and member states; shared Pan-African values; and a sense of ownership of the elusive peace in Somalia. These principles created incentives for withstanding inordinate capacity limitations that would otherwise have stifled African interventions; persistence amidst the mounting costs of the mission; integration of hitherto disparate intervention efforts into a single, more effortful, Africa-sanctioned, Mission, and mobilisation of foreign support (Rwengabo, 2015). These developments deserve our attention with the view to amplifying them, consolidating the gains so far made, and drawing useful lessons for understanding and operationalizing the principle of African Solutions to African Problems (Touray, 2005). This begets the question of when, given these initiatives and interests, Africa can achieve peace, democracy, and development.

Achieving Peace, Democracy, and Development: Conditions to be Fulfilled

Certain conditions need to be fulfilled if Africa is to achieve peace, democracy, and development. The question of when societies transform themselves from conditions of underdevelopment, broadly conceived, to development, is addressed in many circles. Some analysts argue that social mobilisation is necessary for political development, including democratic development. For Karl Deutsch, social mobilisation, a continuing aspect and a significant cause of modernisation, involves the erosion or breakdown of major clusters of old social, economic and psychological commitments, so that people are made available for new patterns of socialisation and behaviour. It involves new forms of social recommitment for politics that are associated with each other, reinforce each other's effects, and have thresholds at which their effects may dramatically change. For instance, democratisation and nation-building require new patterns of group membership, organisation, and commitment that transcend previous attachments to ethnic group, region, and other forms of sub-national identity (Deutsch, 1961).

Tanzania's nation-building trajectory demonstrates elements of this Deutschian process, a route that eludes many other African countries (Rwengabo, 2016). Perhaps post-1994 Rwanda is undertaking similar processes intuitively or deliberately. Somalia and South Sudan may need to consider similar initiatives. Socioeconomic development reasonably requires mobilisation of the productive forces of society. If this is accepted, it follows that certain conditions need to be fulfilled for Africa to attain peace, democracy, and development. Consider three conditions: leadership commitment and will; development of human resource capacity; and acquisition and utilisation of post-modern technologies.

Addressing the Leadership Question

It is universally acknowledged that confident, committed, visionary and accountable leadership is necessary for overcoming challenges facing society, for addressing crises afflicting global humanity, such as terrorism, extremism, climate change, and calamities. Here and there transforma-tional leaderships arise and change society. Nyerere and Lee Kuan Yew are examples. Here and there poor leaderships wreak havoc on society: Amin and Hitler exemplify this. There are times when transactional leaders auction their societies in the market place of neoliberal accumulation, consumerism, and unequal development: Zaire's Mobutu and Marcos of the Philippines are examples (Aseka, 2005). It is unclear when and why good leaderships arise in some societies and not others. Perhaps crisis is the begetter of exceptional leadership behaviours as the experience of Singapore, post-1994 Rwanda, and Israel demonstrates. Perhaps experience teaches: apartheid South Africa taught important lessons to the leaders of the African National Congress (ANC). Perhaps personality matters: distinctions between corrupt and incorrupt leaderships, visionary and mediocre leaders, can be drawn between many in Africa. It is not our task here to explain these variations, but to stress that good leadership is necessary for attaining peace, democracy, and development in three ways.

First, leadership engenders political will and bureaucratic commitm-ent to initiate peace building, democratisation, and development strate-gies. These strategies, in turn, create institutional and behavioural legacies that outlive leaders. Where leaderships make counterproductive choices they set apace developments that may get out of control even after these leaders leave office. For instance, in 1964 military mutinies erupted in Uganda, Kenya, and Tanzania. Uganda's leadership chose to appease the mutinying soldiers, involve them in policy decisions, and hence politicised the military. Kenya's leadership chose to professionalize the military. Tanzania de-militarised, disbanded the whole military establishment, and started from scratch. As a result, civilian control over the military failed and Uganda suffered coups, purges, civil wars; Kenya acquired a professional military, and avoided military interference in politics; while Tanzania constructed party-military fusion which ideologically conscientised the military without losing civilian control. This indicates that the strategic choice the country's leadership makes, in the face of a problem at critical junctures, determines the fate and future of the polity in unpredictable ways but historically demonstrable ways (Rwengabo, 2016).

Second, political will to exploit every available opportunity to promote intra-state and inter-state peace, and correspondingly the commitment of major bureaucratic institutions like the civil service, intelligence services, and the military, will engender processes of peace building with lasting consequences for society. Political will and bureaucratic commitment to democratise society, to prepare the people for the unfolding challenges of democracy, will help to initiate minimum institutional benchmarks for democratic development. The constitutional process of the 1990s in Uganda and post-2007 Kenya are demonstrative of this.

Finally, political and development institutions are offsprings of leadership commitment, and in turn influence and determine leadership behaviour. In societies with weak institutions the leadership must prepare to establish not just the rules of the game, such as constitutions, laws, regulations and other paper-based instruments, but the leadership must undertake to organise these rules into structures of authority. These structures and practices, in turn, evolve beyond the leaders, leading to continuity and sustainability.

The challenge, then, is: how do such leaderships arise? This is a difficult question. We mentioned crisis, experience, and personality. The challenge with Africa, one can aver, is that it lacks mechanisms for leadership development, placement, and evaluation. Leaders arise spontaneously, and, unprepared for the insurmountable challenges they are to face, stumble upon unworkable solutions that exacerbate, instead of solve, the continent's peace, democracy, and development challenges.

Perhaps at continental and regional levels the process of leadership grooming and mentorship is necessary for preparing Africans for the challenges of transformational leadership they face. Failure to groom successors perhaps explains the political uncertainty facing countries like Uganda and Zimbabwe. Tanzania has demonstrated that ruling parties need mechanisms for leadership selection, grooming and mentorship, in order to ensure continuity of peaceful governance and power transitions. At the same time consensus between the top contending political elites is necessary for preventing violent conflicts and election crises, such as occurred in Kenya in 2007. Masses hardly erupt into peacelessness and insecurity unless they have been mobilised, ignited, by political elites—many times for selfish interests. Thus, mechanisms for promoting consensus among top leaders will be helpful for ensuring peaceable democratisation processes and institutional constraints upon a highly politicised people as Africa democratises (Huntington, 1968).

Development of Human Capacity

The development of Africa's human resource capacity should be viewed in a broad sense. This is not the traditional human resources development in management sciences but holistic capacity development that entails three main aspects: civic education for promotion of peace and democracy; human capacity development to meaningfully participate in the development process; and preparation for continuity and change.

On civic education for promotion of peace and democracy, the Deutschean notion of social mobilisation comes in handy. According to this view, what Manheim calls "fundamental democratisation" is a two-stage process (Manheim, 1940). First, the stage of uprooting, or breaking away from old settings, habits, and commitments entails embracing the coming or current change. Uganda's experience of the alliance between the conservative, traditionalist, Kabaka Yekka (KY) and the UPC, as addressed in Chapter 1, demonstrates that Buganda's failure to recognise that Uganda was now broader than Buganda, and that a nationalism should transcend sub-nationalism, led to irreconcilable differences between Obote and Mutesa, which led to the 1966-67 crisis with devastating consequences for the country's political future. Tanzania's emphasis on Swahilisation and mobilisation for nation building indicates a realisation that post-independence Tanzania needed to evolve as one nation.

Second, the "induction of the mobilised persons into some relatively stable patterns of group membership, organisation, and commitment" (Deutsch, 1961, page 494) indicates the importance of civic education and conscientisation. Perhaps Tanzania did this better for its reconstituted military and people, while Uganda and Kenya failed to prepare their peoples for new group organisations and memberships, a reason why intra-party and inter-party conflicts always degenerate to national crises. Similarly, civil education is important for generating minimum acceptance of the functioning of political institutions, so that perceptions are not rendered uncontrollable to the chagrin of state institutions: East Africa sometimes witnesses election violence as a result of perceived, not real, misconduct in election processes. Conflict-resolution mechanisms, such as dialogues and court adjudication are ignored and actors resort to violence partly because of limited civic awareness. The building of trust in state institutions is rooted in leadership but creating such legitimacy entails civic education — a component of holistic development of the human capacity to appreciate the importance and role of existing mechanisms for conflicts resolution. Peace and democracy will remain elusive until East Africans are civically awakened.

Human capacity development for meaningful participation in the development process is a skills question and institutional-organisational one. As a skills question it entails developing the capacity of the people to compete in the labour market as employable and productive labour that earns from its skills and contributes to economic processes through consumption and good lifestyles. As an institutional-organisational one it entails development of domestic institutions for human development, such as training, vocational, and research institutions, as well as support for local business enterprises to make them competitive in the global economy. Africa has lagged behind the rest of the world in terms of individual and institutional skills capacity. At independence the skills and training gaps were humongous. These gaps have not been adequately addressed, hence leaving masses of unskilled young people that are easily drawn into resource conflicts as pawns in the exploitation of Africa's natural resource endowments. The local bourgeoisie is only an append-age of foreign capitalist interests, as it depends on such interests for capital and technology and skills (Meredith, 2005). This creates a cycle of dependence. As East Africa embarks on the road to exploitation of its oil and gas sector, these two aspects of capacity development constitute a key element of what has been called "Local Content" (Mushemeza and Okiira, 2016; Mushemeza et al., 2017). This includes strategies like skills development, employment creation, and local industry participation, all of which necessitate minimum capacity to meaningfully participate in the quality-sensitive, high-standards, oil and gas sector.

Finally, preparation for continuity and change is simple: it is about succession and related to the earlier notion of leadership grooming and mentorship. Tanzania has demonstrated that it is possible to craft a mechanism by which leadership succession need not be divisive and violent as Burundi, Kenya, Rwanda, and Uganda have witnessed, as South Sudan seems destined to suffer unless the root causes of the conflict in the young country are quickly addressed mainly through leadership consensus. Political groups, such as parties, are theoretically leadership development platforms. In Uganda and Kenya parties have, in the main, been ethno-political configurations, hardly ideological constructions, that break apart at the earliest convenience as the weaknesses in Uganda's opposition political parties have demonstrated (Khisa and Rwengabo, 2017). The failure by many leaders to prepare their countries for peaceful continuity of governance after their rule, and for adaptive response to rapid changes wrought by techno-scientific developments on global scale, has created new forms of uncertainty that straddle national borders as East Africa has suffered from domestic crises that have afflicted countries in the region.

It follows that development of human capacity also entails psychological preparation of elites, their close cronies and masses alike for the inevitable changes that must arise when leadership changes; new threats, challenges, and opportunities (such as brought by the nascent oil and gas industry in the region) emerge; and technological and demographic changes force a rapturing of pre-existing forms of socio-political organisation and control.

Acquisition and Utilisation of Post-Modern Technologies

Acquisition, adaptation, and utilisation of post-modern technologies is our last condition that needs to be fulfilled for Africa to achieve peace, democracy, and development. First, threats to peace are changing. Agents of insecurity, their creativity, and their interconnectedness transcend and dwarf traditional methods of security governance. The agents of insecurity, their methods and instruments, and security and conflict pattern have been changing (Tavares, 2008), and an understanding of some of these requires technological sophistication in such matters as counterterrorism, counter-piracy, and controls of human and drug trafficking.

At the same time post-modern technologies are necessary if Africa is to leapfrog its current trajectory and rate of development, not necessarily in competition against any other part of the world—though this too is a strategic likelihood—but to save itself from perpetual marginality. According to Lee Kuan Yew, societies facing the challenge of development may decide to leapfrog others, as Israel did to its hostile Arab neighbours, by identifying and focusing on key areas of excellence: security of person and property, skilled human resources, infrastructure, acquisition of high technology in large scale operations, employment creation, linking with the developed world for strategic trading and investment attraction, adopting pragmatic responses to development problems, and creating islands of excellence. Singapore focused on creating "a First World oasis in a Third World region": training the people to create "First World standards in public and personal security, health, education, telecommunication, transportation and services". Any African country can "re-educate" and re-orient" its people using schools, trade unions, community centres and social organisations, in order to attract investor confidence, ensure skills productivity, and ensure that the polity is "more rugged, better organised, and more efficient than others" (Yew, 2000). The civil society can be re-oriented to inculcation of certain productive values in society that enhance self-confidence, self-respect, a culture of saving and investment, and continuous knowledge acquisition amongst people.

Post-modern technologies are necessary, therefore, for Africa to address its huge infrastructure gap that limits intra-Africa trade, attraction of industries in industrial mineral processing, agro-industrialisation, health services provisioning in rural and urban areas alike, monitoring vast geo-social spaces for instances of threats to peace and security, and coordination and monitoring of the operations of public and private-sector entities. This promotes efficiency, timely delivery of services and circulation of useful ideas and values, and building people's confidence in both the public and private sector. For instance, as East Africa embraces the oil and gas sector in a world of climate change concerns, techno-scientific innovativeness is needed to green the petroleum sector, avoid associated gas (AG) flaring, and maximisation of possible ranges of products that can be extracted from this Black Gold. This is a key ingredient of the efficiency, sustainability, and exist strategy necessary for the petroleum sector in the region and the rest of Africa (Rwengabo, 2017). It follows that technology will not only allow Africa to develop faster, to leapfrog the rest of the world; it will also heighten the levels of creativity and innovativeness of the continent's young population.

Conclusion

This book has revealed that for Africa to capture the moment and achieve total socio-economic and political transformation of its people, the leadership must deal with two stark paradoxes: first, despite resource endowment of the continent, Africa still lags behind the world. Its foreign aid dependence has exacerbated its problems (Moyo, 2008). Traumas of fluctuations and vagaries of global market prices and international financial systems threaten economic stability and continuity of positive development. Insecurity, endemic conflicts, and democratic deficits limit Africa's abundant potentials and capacities to lend itself a long term basis for sustainable peace and development (Francis, 2005). Second, leadership in some countries seems to be slow to realise that it is the fulcrum around which measures for ensuring sustainable peace, development and democracy revolve. As a result of these two paradoxes, the African research and intellectual community still retains some pessimism even as the AU and international community have advocated the promotion of peace and democracy that are necessary to transform the continent into a viable and respected player in international affairs (Francis, 2005).

The chapters in this book reveal that the challenges are not insurmountable in many respects. First, first-mover experiences are awash and accessible to Africa from all parts of the world. Second, Africa's own experiences teach sufficient lessons about the cyclic link between peace, democracy, and development, and the need to pursue these ends for Africa's strategic future. Third, pockets of positive change and progressive adaptation to these changes in other countries indicate a positive trend. Fourth, the rapidity with which demographic and techno-scientific changes are taking place in Africa will inevitably force even the most recalcitrant of leaders to succumb to mounting pressures. Finally, opportunities have been availed for Africa to leapfrog both its current conditions and other parts of the world in the transformation of its current conditions leadership foresight, capacity development and local content development, infrastructure development, and adoption and utilisation of technology in almost all realms of life. It remains to be seen whether East Africa, indeed the whole of Africa, consolidates its current peace and security, resolves current conflicts, strengthens state and regional institutions for democracy, and exploits available opportunities for rapid socioeconomic transformation of our economies.

References

Aseka, E. M. (2005) *Transformational Leadership in East Africa: Politics, Ideology and Community*. Kampala: Fountain Publishers.

Deutsch, K. W. (1961) 'Social Mobilization and Political Development', *The American Political Science Review*, p. 55(3), 493-514.

Francis, D. J. (2005) *Uniting Africa, Building Regional Peace and Security Systems*. New Hampshire: Ashgate Plushing Company.

Hobbes, T. (1999) *Leviathan*. Oregon: The University of Oregon Renascence Editions.

Huntington, S. P. (1968) *Political Order in Changing Societies*. New Haven, London: Yale University Press.

Khisa, M. and Rwengabo, S. (2017) 'Beyond Legal Reforms in Understanding Opposition Underperformance', in Oloka-Onyango, J. and Ahikire, J. (eds) *Controlling Consent: Uganda's 2016 Elections*. Trento: NJ: Africa World Press.

Manheim, K. (1940) *Man and Society in an Age of Reconstruction*. New York.

Meredith, M. (2005) *The State of Africa: A History of Fifty Years of Independence*. London: The Free Press.

Moyo, D. (2008) *Dead Aid: Why Aid Makes Things Worse and How there is A Better Way for Africa*. New York: Farrar, Straus and Giroux.

Mushemeza, E. D. and Okiira, J. (2016) *Local Content Frameworks in African Oil and Gas Sector: Lessons from Angola and Chad*. ELLA Programme. Practical Action Latin America, Lima and ACODE.

Mushemeza, E. D., Okiira, J., Morales, M. and Herrera, J. J. (2017) 'Local Content in Latin American and African Oil and Gas Sector: A Comparative Analysis of Selected Countries', *Global Journal of Human-Social Science*, 17(3), pp. 45–59.

Rwengabo, S. (2015) 'AMISOM and African-Centred Solutions to Peace and Security Challenges', *AfSol Journal*, 1(1), pp. 91–138.

Rwengabo, S. (2016) *Nation Building in Africa: Lessons from Tanzania for South Sudan*, MINDS Discussion Paper. Dar es Salaam.

Rwengabo, S. (2017) *Efficiency, Sustainability, and Exit Strategy in the Oil and Gas Sector: Lessons from Ecuador for Uganda*, ACODE Policy Research Series. 81. Kampala.

Tavares, R. (2008) 'Understanding Regional Peace and Security: A Framework for Analysis', *Contemporary Politics*, 14(2), pp. 107–127.

Touray, O. A. (2005) 'The Common African Defence and Security

Policy', *African Affairs*, 104(417), pp. 635–656.

Lee, K.Y (2000) *From Third World to First: The Singapore Story: 1965-2000*. Singapore: Marshall Cavendish Editions.

Index

A

Acholi, 179, 186, 187, 195, 305
ACODE, viii, ix, 38, 118, 145, 148, 167, 168, 173, 175, 227, 243, 255, 304, 320
African National Congress, 313
African research, 19, 319
African Union, 18, 23, 31, 42, 43, 47, 54, 55, 288, 290, 307, 309
Afro-Asian interactions, 31
Agriculture, 80, 123, 144, 259, 260, 263, 277, 278, 305
Al-Qaeda, 38, 47
AMISOM, 24, 34, 45, 320
Auditor General, 204, 214, 215, 216, 219, 224, 226

B

Ban Ki moon, 65
Benedicto Kiwanuka, 26
Bicameral System, 114
Bruce MacKensie, 31
Budget process, 226
Buganda, 25, 26, 27, 44, 114, 124, 155, 163, 237, 315
Bugangaizi, 96
Buyaga, 96

C

Capitalist, 81
Caste system, 21
Cattle rustling, 202
Chaama Cha Mapenduzi (CCM), 35
Charles Mugane Njonjo, 31
Civil society, 168, 201, 233, 305
Civil-military relations, 44
Colonial rule, 72, 74
Commonwealth, 206

Community-Based Property Rights, 41, 279, 287
Conflict management, 252
Conflict Trap, 39
Conservation, 263, 284
Constituent Assembly, 26, 28, 95, 103, 106, 132, 139
Constitutional reform, 135
Constitutional Review Commission, 39, 81, 98, 111
Constitutionalism, 118, 144, 301
Cooperation, vii, 45, 116, 255, 256, 306
Corruption, 27, 33, 37, 43, 80, 85, 90, 207, 220
Counterinsurgency, 33, 42
Courts of Judicature, 119, 204

D

Daniel Arap Moi, 32, 43
Democracy, i, 19, 21, 23, 24, 25, 27, 30, 31, 34, 42, 43, 45, 118, 119, 121, 144, 173, 175, 227, 304, 310, 312
Democratic development, 302
Democratic Party (DP), 26
Democratic societies, 21
Disruptions, 251

E

EAC Treaty, 41, 234, 248
East Africa Community, 95
East Africa Parliament, 204
ECOMOG, 47, 49, 68
Economic mismanagement, 28
Economic performance, 17
ECOWAS, 24, 47, 49, 54, 55, 56, 57, 68, 90
Environment, viii, ix, 129, 147, 148, 150, 159, 173, 174, 243, 263, 290, 304, 307

Environmental governance, 174
Environmental scarcity, 194
Equity, 44
Eriya Kategaya, 29, 106, 135

F

Federal, 256
Forestry, 157, 159, 160, 174
Freddie Mutesa II, 25
Freedom, 43, 106
French military intervention, 38, 47, 51, 55, 56, 57, 58, 60

G

GDP, 17, 67, 68, 123, 151
Godfrey Binaisa, 27
Governance, vii, ix, 23, 62, 76, 123, 173, 227, 257, 306

H

Hopeless Continent, 63, 65
Horn of Africa, 177
Human capacity development, 316
Human Rights Commission, 80, 103, 105, 131

I

ICGLR, 25, 305
Idi Amin, 26, 27, 43, 96, 97, 156, 238
IGAD, 25, 252, 312
Independence, 90, 96, 156, 320
Indigenous, 242, 289, 302, 305, 307
Indigenous peoples, 302
Infrastructure, 28, 34
Innovations, 278
Insecurity, 192, 319
Inspectorate of Government, 103, 204
Integrity, 132
International Criminal Court (ICC), 34
International Monetary Fund (IMF), 28
Islamic radicalization, 33
Islamist Jihadists, 38, 47, 54, 55, 60

J

Jakaya Kikwete, 36

James Gichuru, 31
John Pombe Magufuli, 37
Jomo Kenyatta, 30, 238
Julius K. Nyerere, 35
Justice, 44, 77, 81, 83, 85, 98, 175, 221, 235, 301, 306

K

KabakaYekka (KY–King Only), 25
Kalenjin, 32, 299
KANU, 31
Karamoja, 40, 126, 164, 177, 179, 180, 181, 182, 183, 184, 185, 186, 187, 188, 189, 190, 191, 192, 193, 194, 195, 196, 197, 198, 199, 200, 201, 202, 299, 301
Karimojong, 40, 177, 178, 179, 181, 182, 183, 184, 186, 187, 188, 189, 190, 192, 193, 194, 195, 196, 197, 198, 199, 200, 202
Kikuyu ethnic group, 31

L

Legal Reforms, 43, 227, 320
Legislature, 156, 210, 213, 222
Legitimacy, 251
Liberal peacebuilding, 38, 47, 48, 50, 56, 57, 60, 61
Livelihoods, 121, 173, 227, 304
Loyalty, 30
LRA rebellion, 28
Lukiiko, 26, 155, 237

M

Marginalization, 189, 192
Mau Mau, 30, 42, 43
Middle Income countries, 35
Milton Obote, 25, 193, 195
Mobile penetration, 17
Mobilization, 168, 320
Moiyu Koinange, 31
Mombasa Republican Council, 30, 33
Moshi Conference, 27
Multipartyism, 118
Mungiki, 33, 283, 291, 303
Mwai Kibaki, 33, 245

N

Nandi, 31, 32
Nandi rebellion, 31
Njoroge Mungai, 31
NRA, 27, 94, 155
NRM, 27, 28, 29, 40, 93, 94, 97, 99, 100, 106, 109, 125, 126, 129, 136, 137, 140, 168, 170, 221
NRM/A, 28, 93
Nyerere, 31, 35, 36, 43, 238, 313

O

Oginga Odinga, 31

P

Pastoral communities, 177
Paul Muwanga, 27
Peaceable development, 231
Peace-building, 200
Plant breeders, 264
Plant Genetic Resources, 259, 260, 263, 277, 278
Political institutions, 311
Political parties, 94
Post-Cold War, 65
Post-independence, 96
Poverty Eradication Action Plan, 149, 243
Preservation of Public Security Act, 31
Private Members Bills, 40, 149, 166, 171
Private sector, 246
Public Accounts Committee, 209, 215, 216, 218, 228

R

Reconstruction, 118, 174, 320
Referendum, 134, 166
Regional Economic Communities, 24
Regionalism, 90, 256
Rehabilitation, 168
Resistance Council, 28, 156
Rift Valley, 32

S

SADC, 24, 252, 257
Sahel, 38, 47, 52, 55, 60, 61
Security, vii, ix, 23, 31, 42, 44, 45, 50, 57, 62, 63, 64, 80, 85, 167, 181, 202, 249, 255, 266, 267, 305, 306, 307, 320
Security Council, 23, 57, 64
Settlement, 298
Sierra Leone, 24, 39, 48, 49, 65, 66, 67, 68, 69, 70, 71, 72, 73, 74, 75, 76, 77, 78, 79, 80, 81, 82, 83, 84, 85, 86, 87, 88, 89, 90, 91, 107
Sierra Leone Peoples Party (SLPP), 65
Socialist, 63, 81
Socio-economic, 309
Socioeconomic development, 313
Special Interest Groups, 39, 121, 122, 126, 127, 129, 134, 135, 141, 142, 143, 173, 227
Stability, 45, 117
Stakeholder participation, 230, 241, 249, 251
State Collapse, 78
Sub-Saharan Africa, 107, 108, 219
Supreme Court, 97, 101
Swahilisation, 35, 315

T

TANU, 35
Technology, ix
Ten Point Program, 28
Teso, 177, 178, 180, 181, 184, 185, 186, 187, 190, 191, 192, 193, 195, 196, 198, 201, 202
Tito Okello, 27
Tourism, 161, 244, 245, 246, 305
Traore, Karim, ii
Traumas of fluctuations, 319

U

Uganda People's Congress, 25, 97
Uhuru Kenyatta, 33, 34
Ujamaa, 36, 43, 44, 311

UNCED, 147, 263, 290
UNLF, 27
UPDF, 30, 110, 137, 139, 140

V

Violence, 42, 44
Violent conflicts, 18

W

War, 18, 32, 33, 38, 42, 48, 49, 51, 62, 63, 65, 74, 78, 81, 86, 90, 91, 118, 125, 229, 231, 238, 304, 305, 307

West Africa, 20, 38, 47, 48, 49, 50, 51, 52, 54, 55, 60, 61, 65
William Samurai Ruto, 34
World Bank, 18, 53, 65, 68, 84, 91, 144, 206, 219, 227, 228, 241, 256, 285
World War II, 125, 229

Y

Yoweri Museveni, 27, 97, 156
Yusuf Lule, 27

www.ingramcontent.com/pod-product-compliance
Lightning Source LLC
Chambersburg PA
CBHW020336270326
41926CB00007B/206